Curriculum in Context

Curriculum in Context

Catherine Cornbleth

The Falmer Press

(A member of the Taylor & Francis Group)
London • New York • Philadelphia

UK   The Falmer Press, Rankine Road, Basingstoke, Hants RG24 0PR

USA   The Falmer Press, Taylor & Francis Inc., 1900 Frost Road, Suite 101, Bristol, PA 19007

First published 1990

British Library Cataloguing in Publication Data
Cornbleth, Catherine
    Curriculum in context.
    1. Schools. Curriculum. Theories
    I. Title
    375.0001

    ISBN 1-85000-452-8
    ISBN 1-85000-453-6 pbk

Library of Congress Cataloging in Publication Data available on request

Typeset in 12/14 Bembo by
by Chapterhouse, The Cloisters, Formby, L37 3PX

Printed in Great Britain by Burgess Science Press, Basingstoke on paper which has a specified pH value on final paper manufacture of not less than 7.5 and is therefore 'acid free'.

Contents

Acknowledgments   vii

Part I Curriculum Conceptions and Practice

1   A Point of View   3

2   Curriculum as Contextualized Social Process   12

3   Beyond Hidden Curriculum?   42

4   Curriculum Practice   62

Part II Contexts of Curriculum and Reform

5   Curriculum and Structural Change   99

6   The State and Curriculum Controls   117

Part III Curriculum Action and Inquiry

7   Curriculum Policy and Planning   155

8   Curriculum Knowledge and Knowledge about Curriculum   184

Index   207

Dedication

To my parents, Jack Kornblith and Florence Kohn Kornblith, who encouraged thoughtfulness, questioning, and dialogue.

Acknowledgments

This book grew out of my experience in schools as a student, teacher, and university professor in the US. That experience has been enriched (and occasionally frustrated) by numerous students and colleagues to whom I owe much that cannot be returned directly or cited here. The challenge, support, and constructive critique of ideas and draft chapters provided by Don Adams and Tom Popkewitz have been inestimable and are greatly appreciated. In various ways, Millard Clements, Eleanor Farrar, Esther Gottlieb, Will Korth, Pamela Moss, Susan Noffke, Bob Stevenson, Bob Tabachnick, and the students in my Comparative Curriculum Studies seminar have made important contributions to my thinking and writing about curriculum and schooling. While I am responsible for *Curriculum in Context*, this book would not have been constructed as it is in another interpersonal and socio-structural milieu.

Three chapters (2, 3, 6) are modifications of articles or chapters that have been or will be published elsewhere: 'Curriculum In and Out of Context', *Journal of Curriculum and Supervision* 2, 2 (1988): 85–96; 'Beyond Hidden Curriculum?' *Journal of Curriculum Studies* 16, 1 (1984): 29–36; D. Adams and C. Cornbleth, *Planning Educational Change*, Chapter 6, 'The System and the State' (manuscript in progress).

Part I
Curriculum Conceptions and Practice

Chapter 1

A Point of View

Prelude

My purpose in undertaking this project has been to explore what a critical perspective might mean for curriculum construction and change efforts and for curriculum studies as an area of inquiry and advocacy. My understanding of 'critical' draws on but is not a 'child' of Habermas's conception of critical sciences, critical theory as put forth by the Frankfurt school and C. W. Mills's *The Sociological Imagination*, and interpretations of critical theory in the education literature.

A critical perspective entails questioning appearances and taken-for-granted practices, probing assumptions and implications. Its purposes are enlightenment and empowerment that can foster personal and social emancipation from various forms of domination. It recognizes and values human intention and action in relation to both the limiting and the enabling aspects of people's historical, material, and cultural circumstances. Key features of a critical perspective, then, are its normative stance against forms of domination and its context sensitivity. In order for curriculum to further critical purposes, it must be seen and treated as value laden and contextualized.

Critical perspectives more often have framed accounts of schooling in general than curriculum in particular. And, frequently, these accounts have been presentations of abstract arguments rather than concrete cases or blends of theoretical and empirical forms.[1] This volume can be seen as an effort to consider what a critical approach to curriculum might be, theoretically and experientially. The ideas and cases offered here emerge from and have repercussions for social theory. The emphasis, however, is on curriculum practice. Social theory remains as background to the curriculum foreground.

Curriculum in Context both reflects and contributes to changing views of curriculum. It is both an expression of its time and place and an exposition of an alternative conceptual framework for future curriculum work. It is necessarily bound to my own education and other experience in and around schools over the past forty or so years. At least a few episodes in that personal history seem relevant to the present work, especially those involving curriculum revision or development efforts.

The first episode dates back more than twenty years when, as a new teacher, I was asked to revise the course of study for the World History course required of all tenth graders in my central Texas school district. Flattered and enthusiastic, I eagerly incorporated a conceptual organization and emphasis into what had been a fact-by-fact, follow the (Eurocentric) textbook outline. The new course of study, probably not unlike its predecessor, was distributed to teachers most of whom left it to collect dust on their shelves or in the bottom drawers of their desks.

A year or so later, during the period of federally funded curriculum development projects, I was identified as 'a high school teacher who could write' and invited to work with a Latin American Curriculum Project based at the University of Texas. Here, we researched and compiled 'teaching units' that included subject matter background for teachers, content outlines, supplementary materials (e.g., transparency masters), and teaching guidelines. The units were pilot tested, and many were revised prior to further dissemination. Although favorably received by pilot teachers, the units were neither published commercially or widely used. Another disappointing curriculum change experience.

Nearly a decade later, as a faculty member at the University of Pittsburgh, I was asked to co-ordinate a locally organized and federally funded, science-social studies Urban Environmental Education Curriculum Project that would be field tested in an area school district. This time we involved teachers in planning, drafting, piloting, and revising the teaching units called for by the project proposal. Our assumption was that teachers would be more likely to use curriculum materials that they played a major role in creating. We still were adopting an individualist mode, focusing on teachers, with little attention to setting other than instructional materials and perceived student abilities and interests. While some pilot teachers continued to use the materials after the project ended, they were not widely used by other teachers in the school district or in other districts. Further disappointment.

It was about this time, in the late 1970s and early 1980s when I was becoming increasingly disenchanted with my own and other's research and curriculum efforts, that I began to seek out alternative approaches. Following the conventional guidelines for curriculum change, or slightly more sophisticated RDDA (research, development, dissemination, adoption) models, seemed to have precious little impact on classroom practice. This also was the period in which 'new' ideas about knowledge, curriculum and schooling began to appear in the US education literature. It is in this confluence of events and conversations with a wider circle of colleagues that the themes of *Curriculum in Context* began to be formed.

The intended audience for this volume consists of thoughtful educators who are concerned about realizing the potential of curriculum to contribute to a more meaningful and empowering education of young people. This audience includes teachers and curriculum specialists (co-ordinators, supervisors, developers) who are discontented with current practices and willing to consider alternatives. It also includes curriculum scholars, educational sociologists, and those educators, researchers, and policymakers concerned with school reform and educational change more generally.

Inclusions and Exclusions

Any work necessarily highlights some phenomena and interpretations while it slights or neglects others. In this volume, I offer and illustrate two major themes about curriculum and curriculum change and then consider their implications for both curriculum policy and planning and for curriculum studies. The first theme is that curriculum be conceived as what actually occurs in school classrooms, that is, an ongoing social process comprised of the interactions of students, teachers, knowledge, and milieu. This conception of curriculum stands in contrast and opposition to the prevailing product conception of curriculum as a document or plan. It is similar to what others have characterized as curriculum practice or curriculum-in-use. Curriculum products or plans are seen as one aspect of the context that shapes curriculum practice. A curriculum plan is similar to an architect's blueprint, a more or less detailed outline of a not yet constructed building. The existence of a blueprint does not necessarily mean that the building will be constructed as originally planned or constructed at all — or that, even if constructed as planned, it will well serve its intended functions.

Of particular concern is curriculum knowledge, the selection, organization, treatment and distribution of knowledge made available to students. Curriculum knowledge as the knowledge made available to students refers to opportunities to construct, reconstruct, or critique knowledge as well as the more common offering of knowledge as if it were a product or commodity. It includes social and world knowledge as well as academic knowledge from the recognized disciplines. Knowledge treatment refers both to assumptions about the nature of knowledge, and to pedagogical/instructional practices.

The second, related theme is that curriculum as practice cannot be understood adequately or changed substantially without attention to its setting or context. Curriculum is contextually shaped. The relevant context is both structural and sociocultural. By structure, I mean established roles and relationships, including operating procedures, shared beliefs, and norms. Structural context can be considered at several layers or levels, from the individual classroom to the school organization to the national education system. Sociocultural refers to the environment beyond the education system/structural context. Sociocultural context includes demographic, social, political, and economic conditions, traditions and ideologies, and events that actually or potentially influence curriculum.

The only similar approach to curriculum of which I am aware is Grundy's account of 'curriculum as praxis'.[2] According to Grundy, curriculum as praxis is a social process that

> develops through the dynamic interaction of action and reflection. That is, the curriculum is not simply a set of plans to be implemented, but rather is constituted through an active process in which planning, acting and evaluating are all reciprocally related and integrated into the process.[3]

Among the implications of this position noted by Grundy are that curriculum is constructed within actual learning situations with actual students, learning is a social process, and curriculum knowledge is socially constructed and subject to critique and reconstruction (or interpretation or meaning-making). The latter implication, 'in turn, entails that the curriculum process is inescapably political'[4] because interpretation and critique involve differing and conflicting meanings or constructions of knowledge.

To this point, Grundy's account of curriculum as praxis is compatible with the conception of curriculum advanced here. Differences emerge in my focus on and effort to explicate curriculum context and curriculum in context. I would, for example, argue that curriculum emerges from the dynamic interaction of action, reflection, and setting, not action and reflection alone. Reflection could, of course, be directed toward context as well as action. Grundy, in contrast, acknowledges but does not pursue contextual influences. In presenting action research as a means of fostering critical or emancipatory curriculum praxis, she observes that

> social interaction [e.g., curriculum practice] takes place within a context which impinges upon the situation and often constrains it in unrecognized ways. If a particular set of social interactions is to be improved, then it is often the case that the social and material contexts within which those interactions occur need also to be improved, and it is always the case that these contexts need to be understood.[5]

However, she does not examine more specific questions of what contextual understanding and improvement might involve or how such understanding and improvement might be pursued. Whereas Grundy's approach to curriculum praxis might be characterized as personalized and reflective, individually and collectively, the present approach is contextualized.

This is not to deny person and reflection but to emphasize their biographical, structural, sociocultural and historical contexts. Particular attention is given to structural context because of its seeming importance and relative neglect at least in the US. Sociocultural dynamics such as economic and gender relations do not simply bypass the systemic or structural context of curriculum and enter directly into classroom practice. They are mediated by intervening layers of the education system.

In pursuing a conception of curriculum as a contextualized social process, I contrast it with the prevailing, technocratic conception of curriculum as a product (e.g., plan, course of study). I have chosen not to address what might be seen as an intermediate position, that of a practical, craft, or deliberative approach to curriculum.[6] Proponents of this approach retain a relatively decontextualized, product conception of curriculum. Their curriculum product is to be created by a more representative group than would be the case with a technocratic approach, and by more democratic or consensual means, but curriculum is still a product. Values and local setting are considered, but typically little explicit attention is given to either social critique or broader context. Deliberation is seen as desirable if not necessary, but insufficient, to the position taken here.

In illustrating the major themes of *Curriculum in Context*, I refer to several field studies of curriculum practice and change efforts. I focus on and return to a few studies that are especially relevant and data rich in order to provide continuity. Most but not all of these studies were conducted in public elementary and secondary schools in the US. Readers are invited to recall relevant personal experiences and other studies with which they are familiar to further illustrate or to challenge and modify the arguments offered here. Although my concern is with the curricula of mass public schooling, because that is the educational arena with which I am most familiar and the one that touches most young people today, I suspect that, in broad outline, the themes of *Curriculum in Context* also have relevance to private, parochial and informal schooling. The particulars would vary within and across forms of schooling as well as sociostructural locations.

Overview

This volume consists of eight chapters, organized in three parts. Following this introductory chapter, Part I examines curriculum conceptions and practice. A major assumption is that how we see, think and talk about, study, and act on curriculum matters both reflects and shapes the education made available to students. Discourse matters. Further, curriculum conceptions, modes of reasoning, and practice are not value-free. Implicitly or explicitly, they carry assumptions about valued knowledge, appropriate schooling, the desirable society and relations between individuals and societal institutions. These concerns are not 'merely theoretical'; they emerge from and enter into school practice and its consequences.

In Chapter 2, 'Curriculum as Contextualized Social Process', I juxtapose conventional, technocratic approaches to curriculum with an alternative, critical approach. Technocratic conceptions of curriculum as document and associated rational management models of curriculum-making are analyzed and critiqued. Attention also is given to reasons for their persistence. Then, a critical alternative is offered that highlights the continuing social construction and reconstruction of curriculum in classroom practice — curriculum as a contextualized social process.

Chapter 3, 'Beyond Hidden Curriculum?' extends the critique of conventional curriculum conceptions by challenging both mainstream and radical treatment of 'hidden curriculum'. The challenge is intended to draw attention to and initiate examination of curriculum context. The question of interest is not whether a curriculum has been hidden (or by whom, from whom, or how) but what is to be found and what difference it might make. What is to be found, I suggest, are constraints and opportunities as well as seemingly contradictory messages communicated by the social organization and relations of schooling — the structural context of curriculum. The impact depends on the messages communicated, their congruency with other messages outside schooling, and how they are mediated by students.

Brief examples of curriculum practice have been interwoven into Chapters 2 and 3 in order to illustrate and 'bring to life' the conception of curriculum as a contextualized social process. In Chapter 4, 'Curriculum Practice', the emphasis is reversed to focus on studies of curriculum practice in relation to previously introduced themes. Of the five field studies considered here, two address ongoing curriculum practice, and three examine curriculum practice confronted with change efforts. These studies are referred to again in later chapters on structural context, the State, and curriculum policy and planning.

Part II more closely examines the context of curriculum and reform efforts. With a conception of curriculum as a contextualized social process, curriculum change necessarily entails contextual change. While curriculum and context are mutually determining, curriculum change is more likely to follow than precede contextual change. Particular attention is paid to systemic or structural context and to the State because of their seeming importance and relative neglect. Chapter 5, 'Curriculum and Structural Change', provides an overview of education systems and features that tend toward stability and change, followed by consideration of implications for curriculum practice and reform. Questions of structural influence on curriculum knowledge are of particular concern.

Chapter 6, 'The State and Curriculum Controls', is an extended excursion that draws on diverse theoretical accounts and actual cases. Its purpose is similar to that of Chapter 3, 'Beyond Hidden Curriculum?' insofar as I try to make sense of the concept of the State in ways that are helpful to understanding curriculum and school practice. Whereas I find hidden curriculum an unhelpful distraction, I find a tangible State essential to understanding curriculum control.

Part III takes the prior considerations of curriculum conceptions, practice, and context into the arenas of action and inquiry. The arguments and cases that have been brought to bear in previous chapters are reconsidered and extended in relation to possibilities for future curriculum practice and study. Chapter 7, 'Curriculum Policy and Planning', begins with an analysis of the professionalization and politicization of curriculum policymaking in the US, followed by an examination of cross-national cases and school based curriculum development. In considering implications of context for curriculum relevant policymaking and planning at various levels of the education system, I attempt to show how various contextual layers interact, especially how education systems mediate State and sociocultural pressures. The concluding section briefly sketches approaches to contextualized curriculum planning.

In Chapter 8, 'Curriculum Knowledge and Knowledge about Curriculum', I contrast typical curriculum knowledge with atypical and oppositional curriculum knowledge and then interrogate the nature and role of knowledge about curriculum in research and reform efforts. After considering paradigmatic differences with respect to knowledge about curriculum, I undertake a critique of critical approaches to curriculum studies. By redirecting questions about curriculum conceptions, practice and change to curriculum studies, my intent is to encourage analysis and critique. My hope is that this volume will contribute, in provocative and constructive ways, to curriculum practice and studies in contexts that are more equitable and humane than that in which it was written.

Notes

1   e.g., H. A. Giroux, *Theory and Resistance in Education* (South Hadley, MA: Bergin and Garvey, 1983); C. Cherryholmes, *Power and Criticism: Poststructural Investigations in Education* (New York: Teachers College Press, 1988).
2   S. Grundy, *Curriculum: Product or Praxis?* (London: Falmer Press, 1987).
3   *Op cit.*, p. 115.
4   *Op cit.*, p. 116.

5 *Op cit.*, p. 142.
6 See, for example, J.J. Schwab, *Science, Curriculum, and Liberal Education: Selected Essays,* ed. I. Westbury and N.J. Wilkof (Chicago: University of Chicago Press, 1978); J.J. Schwab, 'The Practical 4: Something for Curriculum Professors to Do', *Curriculum Inquiry* 13, 3 (1983): 239-265; W.A. Reid, *Thinking about the Curriculum* (London: Routledge & Kegan Paul, 1978).

Chapter 2

Curriculum as Contextualized Social Process

How we conceive of curriculum and curriculum making is important because our conceptions and ways of reasoning about curriculum reflect and shape how we see, think and talk about, study and act on the education made available to students. Our curriculum conceptions, ways of reasoning and practice cannot be value free or neutral. They necessarily reflect our assumptions about the world, even if those assumptions remain implicit and unexamined. Further, concern with conceptions is not 'merely theoretical'. Conceptions emerge from and enter into practice. If, for example, we conceive of curriculum as a document of one sort or another, curriculum studies are likely to be documentary, and curriculum change efforts are likely to focus on document revision and perhaps teacher 'training'. If, in contrast, we conceive of curriculum as a contextualized social process, curriculum studies are likely to be practice-oriented, and curriculum change efforts are likely to focus on contextual change. Or, if our experience has been such that changing a curriculum document has led to little desired change in classroom practice, we may come to reject a documentary conception of curriculum and curriculum change and to seek alternatives.

Most of the efforts to characterize, distinguish, or categorize curriculum conceptions have accepted the dominant technocratic conception of curriculum as document and noted variations on this theme. They have neither identified nor created alternative conceptions.[1] Even those who advocate radical or critical curriculum content and practice tend to accept an essentially technocratic conception of curriculum and curriculum-making.[2] The limits of technocratic approaches and their incompatibility with radical goals seem not to be recognized.

After presenting a critical analysis of the predominant, technocratic conception of curriculum as document and associated rational management models of curriculum-making and considering the persistence of the technocratic view, I introduce a critical conception of curriculum that emphasizes the continuing construction and reconstruction of curriculum in classroom practice — curriculum as contextualized social process.[3] My interest is with curriculum experience and the circumstances of curriculum stability and change.

A major difference between technocratic and critical views is their treatment of context. Technocratic approaches decontextualize curriculum both conceptually and operationally. Conceptual decontextualization has meant separating curriculum as product (e.g., a document such as a syllabus or course of study, a package of materials accompanied by directions for their use) from curriculum policy-making, design, and practice. Operational decontextualization has meant treating curriculum, however defined, apart from its structural and sociocultural contexts as if it were independent of its location in an education system, society and history. A critical approach, in contrast, assumes contextualization of curriculum. Curriculum as social process is created and experienced within multiple, interacting contexts.

Technocratic Curriculum

The prevailing, mainstream conception is a technocratic one that views curriculum as a tangible product, usually a document or plan for instruction in a particular subject. The specificity and detail of the curriculum product can range from a brief outline of topics to be taught and learned, such as a syllabus or course of study, to an elaborate outline accompanied by teacher and student materials (e.g., readings, worksheets, transparencies) and a teacher guide including directions for teaching and testing.

Conceptual Separation

In the mainstream view, curriculum construction is a presumably objective, development project separate from curriculum policy-making and implementation. The project is guided ostensibly by a set of procedures or steps to be followed, usually including: specifying learning objectives to be obtained by students; selecting or creating and arranging the subject matter content, activities and materials; devising means of assessing students' attainment of the specified objectives and providing directions for intended use of the curriculum product. This development task typically is undertaken by curriculum specialists outside the schools or by teacher committees guided by specialists. The curriculum product thus produced is then disseminated for implementation by teachers.[4]

The procedural steps of curriculum development suggest that curriculum is composed of discrete components (e.g., objectives, subject matter, materials) that can be constructed separately, often in a linear sequence, and then assembled to make a coherent curriculum. The procedures are intended to provide efficient management and control of development resources and activities once curriculum policy decisions have been made by others (e.g., legislatures, ministries, school boards). Thus, the procedures are assumed to be value neutral while the curriculum developers are assumed to be disinterested specialists.[5]

These procedures for curriculum development seem to be derived from now dated perceptions of how successful businesses operate, that is, a rational management model.[6] In its simplest form, a rational management model is objectives-focused. Objectives to be obtained by students are specified; then content, activities and accompanying materials are identified or created and finally the means of assessing student attainment of the objectives are devised. Curriculum is conceived largely in terms of a management system; management systems become curriculum forms.[7]

Additional assumptions underlying this conception of curriculum and its construction concern change and rationality. If curriculum is a tangible product, then changing the curriculum means constructing and implementing a different document or package. Change is a function of the curriculum product. Rationality is of the means-end variety, which assumes that ends are set, that means are known or knowable and that the path between them is a direct one. One therefore follows step-by-step procedures to obtain the predetermined end state (i.e., finished curriculum product). This rational approach is seen to provide precision and control over the otherwise disorderly nature of curriculum and teaching.[8] Curriculum construction, thus conceived as a technocratic project of efficiently managing resources to produce a tangible product, gives the appearance of being scientific, which tends to enhance its appeal to administrators, funding agencies and the general public as well as specialists. It conveys images of scientific efficiency, effectiveness, and progress.[9]

Despite continuing and widespread advocacy, observations regarding the use of technocratic conceptions of curriculum and associated rational management models of curriculum development raise questions about their viability. They do not seem to be widely used in practice by national projects, local committees, or individual teachers. Further, the curriculum products produced under their auspices do not seem to be widely used as intended by their developers. Yet, the mainstream view of curriculum and its construction continues to be espoused by, for example, curriculum textbook authors and funding agencies. The discourse appears to have become self-sustaining apart from school and classroom practice.

Evidence that rational management models have not been widely used in practice is provided by studies of curriculum projects[10] and teacher planning.[11] In practice the model tends to be resisted or rejected altogether. Experienced teachers tend to perceive the model as cumbersome and impractical, even though teacher planning appears to be far from simple.[12] Although teachers follow such curriculum planning models when required to do so, most seem to abandon them at the first opportunity. Even when a rational management model is formally mandated and supported, it is not widely or consistently used.[13]

That technocratic conceptions and rational management models of curriculum development are negatively perceived in use and often abandoned should not be surprising insofar as they represent a reconstructed or idealized logic rather than a practical logic-in-use.[14] That is, the advocated procedures do not reflect what actually occurs when curriculum documents are produced. Rational management models of curriculum development are analogous to reified accounts of 'the scientific method' such as the *post hoc*, reconstructed logic often presented as scientific method in school textbooks.

There also is evidence that the curriculum products produced under the umbrella of these models are not widely used or used as intended by their developers. Use of curriculum documents and materials from the 1960s and 1970s national projects in mathematics, science, and social studies in the United States was not widespread.[15] Accounts of use in the US and elsewhere portray considerable discrepancy between intended and actual use, suggesting that new curriculum documents and materials often are adapted to pre-existing beliefs and practices.[16] Explanations of the limited use and misuse of curriculum project documents and materials include reasons similar to those offered to explain rejection of technocratic conceptions and associated rational management models, particularly the mismatch between recommended procedures on the one hand and prevailing beliefs, practices, and school and social conditions on the other. Implicit in the curriculum projects' focus on materials production was the assumption that classroom practices could be changed by changing curriculum documents and materials. Existing patterns of school organization and classroom interaction seem to have been ignored as were underlying values and interests.[17]

While substantial questions have been raised about the viability of the mainstream conception of curriculum and its construction, more serious concerns are that it tends to obscure critical questions of responsibility, value and interest. With respect to value and interest, a technocratic approach seems to be apolitical and nonideological. Curriculum is to be developed according to presumably neutral procedures or decision steps. In effect, we are offered a curious form of problem-solving wherein problems and solutions are predetermined. The problem is usually taken to be that not enough students are learning enough of whatever is considered desirable for them to learn (e.g., calculus, computer programming, commitment to national principles and policies). The solution is to change the curriculum to include or emphasize whatever it is that students are to learn. The model simply specifies the procedures by which this solution is to be obtained. Major curriculum decisions have been abdicated to others.[18]

Attention to the values conveyed by a curriculum (for example, in its selection, organization, treatment, and distribution of knowledge) and the social groups and interests that are served or disserved by those values, would enable careful evaluation of curricular appropriateness and examination of alternatives and their implications.[19] By not explicitly addressing questions of value as well as the conservative values inherent in the technocratic model itself, the technocratic conception of curriculum and its construction tends to perpetuate myths of curriculum neutrality and benevolence.[20] For example, questions about the nature of knowledge tend not to be addressed. The procedures of objective setting, sequencing learning activities, assessing attainment of objectives, and so forth, at least tacitly presume that knowledge is predeterminable. Knowledge is treated as an object that can be reproduced and given (i.e., taught, sold) to students. Students are assumed to have learned when they have acquired the intended knowledge objects. Typically, possession is indicated by reproducing, recognizing, or applying the appropriate knowledge objects on a pencil and paper test. Alternative conceptions of knowledge tend not to be considered because they do not fit the model. In this way, form shapes substance.

Denial of responsibility is evident not only in the technocratic emphasis on procedure but also in the separation of curriculum policy-making, construction, and implementation. Specialists identified as curriculum developers, housed in local, regional, or national offices do not see themselves (nor are they usually seen by others) as responsible for curriculum policy or implementation. Someone else decides curricular goals and practice. The curriculum developer is thus absolved from responsibility for curriculum purposes and practices.

In sum, curriculum is conceptually decontextualized by technocratic models in at least two related ways. One is that curriculum as product and its construction are arbitrarily separated from curriculum policy-making and use. The second is that curriculum and its construction are seen as apolitical or neutral, apart from or above competing social values and interests. An ironic consequence is that curriculum developers are not responsible for the education made available to students, and attention is directed to the curriculum document rather than to classroom practice.

Structural and Sociocultural Isolation[21]

Isolation of curriculum and curriculum construction processes from their structural (i.e., systemic) and sociocultural (i.e., extrasystemic, societal) contexts is especially evident in national curriculum projects.[22] Curriculum produced in national centers, such as the new math and social studies projects of the 1960s in the US, were assumed to be appropriate for students and teachers, schools, and school systems across the country. The features of the US education system and local variations were largely ignored by curriculum developers while sociocultural influences on the shape and substance of the new curricula remained unexamined at least until critical questions were raised by others.

Structural and sociocultural decontextualization can be seen to follow from the technocratic conception of curriculum and its construction. The predetermination of curricular problems and solutions limits sensitivity and responsiveness to context as does the presumed nature of curriculum change. Separation of curriculum products and their development from policy-making and implementation discourages attention to structural conditions while the assumption of value neutrality deflects attention from sociocultural influences. The role of curriculum developer is not to question the curriculum product's feasibility or its desirability. But schools and classrooms are not closed systems, inaccessible to outside influences. Nor are they rational systems in the sense implied by a technocratic view. Rather, they are permeable, social organizations embedded in an education system, society and history.

A technocratic curriculum model could address the contexts in which its products are formed and to be used. Decisions about objectives, subject matter, and so forth could be made with explicit reference to structural constraints and sociocultural pressures, for example. However, to do so would complicate matters and compromise rationality. One response to criticism and resistance to top-down models has been advocacy and trial of local, bottom-up models of curriculum construction.[23] The technocratic procedures are largely unchanged with the exception that decisions are made by local actors. Although local actors might be expected to be more sensitive and responsive to immediate structural conditions and sociocultural influences than distant experts, their sensitivity and responsiveness are likely to remain limited, tacit and unexamined. And, curriculum still is conceived as a tangible product.

Given the widespread decontextualization of curriculum both conceptually and operationally, we ought not to be surprised by continuing discrepancies between curriculum documents and curriculum practice or by repeated disappointment with the effects of technocratic curriculum change efforts. Neither the promised efficiency nor beneficence have been obtained. Rather than attempt to refurbish unworkable and, I believe, inappropriate models, we might well consider alternatives. One such alternative would contextualize and thereby redefine curriculum. It would treat curriculum critically rather than technically, as a contextualized social process.

Before turning to a critical conception of curriculum as a contextualized social process, it is worthwhile to consider briefly reasons for the persistence of mainstream views. Attention to technocratic persistence can suggest problems and possibilities of change.

Technocratic Persistence[24]

Decontextualization of curriculum and the predominance of technocratic conceptions are apparent in the US by the early twentieth century. Curriculum decontextualization, including the separation of curriculum policy-making, design and practice, seems to have begun in the late nineteenth century and to have become established by the 1920s. Contributing factors include (a) the disintegration of public and professional consensus regarding what was to be taught, how, and to whom, (b) the expansion of mass public schooling to include a larger, more diverse student body and (c) the emergence of curriculum specialists as experts in curriculum making.

Disintegration of consensus resulted from the rapid growth of knowledge as well as changes in the US economy and society. It was heightened by mass immigration and internal, rural to urban migration, which dramatically increased the size and heterogeneity of the school population. The traditional public school (especially the secondary school, college preparatory) program and pedagogy no longer seemed appropriate or adequate, either to socialize immigrants or to prepare young people for new occupations.

The perceived need to reconstruct school curricula occurred during a period when social efficiency and scientific management movements were gaining ascendancy in economic and social life.[25] These complementary movements supported specialization and division of curriculum labor, including the emergence of curriculum development specialists, and pushed curriculum conceptions in decontextualized, technocratic directions. Key features of the scientific management that was to provide efficiency have been task analysis and measurement. Task analysis not only facilitated measurement by fragmenting complex acts into presumably discrete elements amenable to quantification but also facilitated the pre-specification and control of curriculum and teaching that was to enhance efficiency. It was assumed that tasks such as curriculum making could be meaningfully decomposed, that the separate elements could best be constructed one at a time and then assembled to create the desired whole. Thus, curriculum came to be seen as a product, or plan for teaching, that was developed according to procedures of task analysis by outside experts and then made available to classroom teachers in various school settings.

Illustrative of these decontextualized, technocratic conceptions and practices is the curriculum work of Bobbitt, Charters, and later, Tyler. Bobbitt, a leading advocate of scientific management in education, and

Charters, were influential in establishing a task analysis approach to curriculum making. For example, in his *The Curriculum* (1918) and *How to Make a Curriculum* (1924), Bobbitt emphasized the precise specification of 'particularized' objectives derived from activity analysis as the central task of curriculum development. Appropriate learning experiences and means of evaluation, he believed, would routinely follow from such analysis and specification. The 'Tyler rationale' with its 'production model' of teaching and learning and behavioral objectives can be seen as an extension of this earlier work.[26] By the late 1940s, a decontextualized, technocratic approach to curriculum and its construction had come to be taken-for-granted. Its origins in a particular time and place were largely forgotten, and it came to be seen as natural or normal. The political and professional interests that contributed to and continue to benefit from this approach (curriculum development specialists, for example) tend to be obscured.

Once established and taken for granted, conceptions and their associated practices are difficult to modify or replace. Having become embedded in daily practice, they are barely visible and thus unlikely to be questioned, challenged, or changed. Other factors contributing to the persistence of a technocratic approach to curriculum and its construction include (a) its compatability with broader cultural themes or aspects of consciousness, (b) its claim to explanation and justification of special interests and (c) its appeal to school administrators.

Berger, Berger and Kellner's[27] conceptualization of modern consciousness is helpful to understanding the persistence of a technocratic approach to curriculum and its construction. Technocratic conceptions and associated practices can be seen as manifestations of a particularly modern consciousness whose primary sources and carriers are technological production and state bureaucracy. Berger *et al.* define consciousness as the historically and socially located and constructed meanings formed in people's interactions with each other and their institutions. This shared consciousness or 'symbolic universe' encompasses interrelated cognitive and normative dimensions, an organization of knowledge and an orientation toward knowledge and action. The organization of knowledge and orientation derived from technological production and state bureaucracy carry over into other areas of life, including education, to form modern technological-bureaucratic consciousness. This 'symbolic universe of modernity' consisting of a 'network of cognitive and normative definitions of reality' provides a common frame of reference shared by most members of a society'.[28]

Among the major themes of the symbolic universe of modernity delineated by Berger *et al.* are: functional or technical rationality, componentiality, makeability and progressivity derived from technological production; and orderliness and taxonomization derived from state bureaucracy. Each of these themes can be seen to make a technocratic approach to curriculum and its construction plausible in the US (and western or modern) setting.

Technical rationality represents the generalization of an engineering mentality to the manipulation of cognitive and social as well as material objects. It carries assumptions of machine-like functioning, reproducible linear process (for example, interchangeable parts in assembly line production), and measurability of output. Technical rationality also is dependent upon the assumption of componentiality, i.e., that 'everything is analyzable into constituent components, and everything can be taken apart and put together again in terms of these components'. These components are seen as 'self contained units' that are 'interdependent in a rational, controllable and predictable way'.[29] Clearly, curriculum and schooling have been deeply affected by the widespread adoption of technical rationality in modern life.

The theme of makeability follows from technical rationality and componentiality. It refers to a 'tinkering attitude' and a 'problem-solving inventiveness' that seeks to maximize output or results, usually on criteria of quantity or cost-effectiveness.[30] Progressivity refers to 'an "onward and upward" view of the world' that expects and favors continuing change and improvement.[31] It can be seen as underlying and reinforcing the makeability theme and contributing to the plausibility of curriculum reform movements such as the new science and mathematics of the 1950s and 1960s, the integrated studies of the 1970s, and the school-based curriculum development efforts of the 1980s.

From state bureaucracy, modern consciousness derives the complementary themes of orderliness and taxonomization. Bureaucracy creates and maintains order and predictability through rationalized procedures, i.e., normal channels. Bureaucratic systems of procedures are typically 'based on a taxonomic propensity' similar to but more arbitrary than the componentiality of technological production.

Phenomena are classified rather than analyzed or synthesized. The engineer puts phenomena into little categorical boxes in order to take them apart further or to put them together in larger wholes. By contrast, the bureaucrat is typically satisfied once everything has been put in its proper box.[32]

Mainstream curriculum conceptions and associated practices can be seen to persist in large part because of their congruence with these technological and bureaucratic themes of modern consciousness. They also gain holding power from the reassurance they appear to offer. Insofar as particular conceptions exemplify cultural themes, they not only derive support from those themes but also serve to dramatize them as cultural ideals and to orient individual and collective action towards their realization. Shared ideals and conceptions offer a feeling of community and a comforting security, i.e., reassurance that the right path is being trod.

Secondly, the mainstream approach persists because it provides an illusion of explanation that serves to direct action and thereby to justify special interest and professional practices. The description of curriculum and its construction that a technocratic approach offers tends to be taken as an explanation of what curriculum is, how it functions, and how it can be changed as if to decontextualize, analyze, and then label the presumed components of a phenomenon is to comprehend and perhaps to control it. Upon closer examination, however, the illusion of understanding fades, and the tautology emerges. A technocratic approach prescibes but does little to explain curriculum practice.

Technocratic prescriptions and language contribute to an aura of professional curriculum expertise by supporting a discourse that is seemingly scientific and barely comprehensible to outsiders and by implying that curriculum specialists have the knowledge and capacity to deal with the problems that they have identified. The interests of curriculum specialists are promoted as their professional identity and claims to expertise are enhanced. Curriculum specialists are the official proprietors and interpreters of conceptions and associated practices to which the uninitiated have little access or right of appeal.

A third factor contributing to the persistence of the mainstream approach to curriculum and its construction is appeal to school administrators beyond that provided by general cultural congruence and apparent explanation-justification of current practice. This appeal stems from the widespread if implicit assumption that teachers are poorly prepared and/or overburdened, the desire for control over programmatic as well as other aspects of the schools, and the seemingly tangible and feasible nature of a technocratic approach. The assumption that teachers are unable to deal directly with curriculum matters and, therefore, are in need of expert, external direction has been evident since the emergence of curriculum specialists as an identifiable professional group. In 1926, for example, Harold Rugg observed that although teachers should be the 'true educational intermediary' and the curriculum (i.e., course of study accompanied by suggested instructional materials and activities) should 'stand merely as a subordinate element in the educational scheme', most teachers were unable to take worthwhile curriculum initiatives. Consequently, he looked to 'the construction of curriculum which shall as fully as possible overcome the handicaps of the present situation' as the 'greatest hope for improvement in our generation'.[33] Despite improvements in the education of teachers and the conditions of schooling (e.g., smaller classes, availability of more instructional materials), distrust of teachers continues. Witness efforts, especially since the 1960s, to produce 'teacher-proof' curriculum packages and technologically guided curriculum systems.[34]

If teachers cannot be trusted in curriculum matters, then administrators aided by outside experts must take charge. As previously noted, a technocratic approach to curriculum and its construction offers at least the illusion of control and orderliness if not efficiency. Administrators can meet their curriculum responsibilities by hiring a curriculum specialist or consultant to develop or revise documents, with or without teacher participation, or by purchasing presumably self-contained curriculum packages or systems. The procedures are straightforward and relatively easy to do through what have become normal channels in most US school districts, and the outcome is a tangible product that can be displayed for interested publics. Later, if the new curriculum is not used as intended by teachers or does not yield the desired student outcomes, blame is heaped on teachers or students, reinforcing the assumption of teacher inadequacy and the perceived need for even more technocratic control.

These sources of technocratic persistence should not be taken as evidence of technocratic inevitability. Rather, they point to the social construction of current curriculum conceptions and associated practices and to their cultural and political as well as historical embeddedness. What has been socially constructed can be reconstructed though not without effort and due consideration of the circumstances of both.

Critical Curriculum

Conceptual Integration

Curriculum construction is an ongoing social activity that is shaped by various contextual influences within and beyond the classroom and accomplished interactively, primarily by teachers and students. The curriculum is not a tangible product but the actual, day-to-day interactions of students, teachers, knowledge and milieu. The curriculum encompasses what others have called curriculum practice or the curriculum-in-use. Curriculum as product or object, the conventional view, is seen as one aspect of the context that shapes curriculum practice.

This is not to discount planning and product development but to suggest modifications of their purpose and perceived relation to curriculum; planning involves crucial choices regarding the selection, organization, treatment and distribution of knowledge to be made available to students. Prior planning, however, regardless of how it is undertaken, at best provides an inert curriculum skeleton. Curriculum comes to life, so to speak, as it is enacted. If our curriculum concern is with what students have an opportunity to learn, and perhaps also how they are enabled to learn it, then we ought to focus on classroom practice, not previously documented intentions. In an analogous situation, the evaluation of experienced or student teachers for example, supervisors typically observe teachers teaching; they do not simply review the teachers' written plans or stated intentions.[35]

It may be that, in some education systems, schools and classrooms, there are few differences between curriculum documents and curriculum practice either because there is widespread agreement about what is to be taught and how, or because the education system allows schools and teachers little or no discretion. This is not the case in the US and, I suspect, not often the case elsewhere, particularly in pluralistic societies and nations with relatively open, decentralized education systems. Across the US, similarities in curriculum practice are considerable in the absence of an official, national curriculum document. Both similarities variations in curriculum practice are less likely to be associated with curriculum documents than with different structural and sociocultural circumstances.

This alternative, critical conception of curriculum shifts attention from intention to realization, from plan to practice. The focus is on what knowledge and learning opportunities actually are made available to students, how they are created, and what values they reflect and sustain. Here, responsibility is shared, not evaded. Viewing curriculum in this manner as a contextualized social process gives explicit notice to critical philosophical, social and political questions regarding what is taught, how and to whom. It does not merely celebrate practice.[36]

A contextualized social process view of curriculum and its construction reflects a critical rather than a technical rationality. Critical rationality is characterized by wide-ranging questioning as well as grounding in logical argument and empirical data. It entails probing beneath surface appearances and questioning claims, evidence and proposals, such as those for technocratic approaches to curriculum. Technical concerns do not become ends in themselves; instead, they serve both debunking and generative purposes, for example, in questioning data on curriculum change. The questioning and probing associated with critical rationality extend beyond the immediate situation in time and space to historical antecedents and larger contexts. Critical rationality can further curriculum understanding and reconstruction by illuminating contradictions that point to tensions or strains that might become loci for change (e.g., the contradiction between programmed instruction and creative or critical thinking goals).

Curriculum as contextualized social process encompasses both subject matter and social organization and their interrelations. Social organization, including teacher and student roles (and their attendant rights and obligations) and patterns of interaction, provides a setting for academic activities that can extend or constrain students' learning opportunities. Recitation activities, for example, reflect the super and subordinate roles of teachers and students respectively, and the limited communication patterns found in many classrooms. Learning opportunities are constrained by the recitation organization insofar as students are discouraged from pursuing ideas, raising questions, or offering personal observations. Social organization and academic activities also communicate normative messages including the meaning of knowledge, authority, responsibility, work and success as will be illustrated in subsequent chapters.[37]

The curriculum knowledge or subject matter of interest here is primarily but not solely academic (e.g., mathematics, history). It also includes the personal, social, and world knowledge that is communicated or otherwise made available to students and what might be characterized as knowledge about knowledge — its nature, sources, limits and change. While knowledge typically is treated as an object or commodity to be acquired, that is not the intention here. Curriculum knowledge as the knowledge made available to students refers to opportunities to constuct, reconstruct, or critique knowledge. Knowledge selection and organization refer both to the information that is communicated directly and the opportunities that are provided for students to create and critique knowledge. The selection and organization of curriculum knowledge can be purposeful or tacit as seems to be the case when teachers and students follow a textbook. Knowledge treatment refers to what others have distinguished as pedagogy or instruction; it also includes the playing out of assumptions about the nature of knowledge. Knowledge distribution refers to the kinds of knowledge opportunities made available to different groups of students.

Where the technocratic approach is fragmented, the critical conception of curriculum and its construction is integrated. It does not separate curriculum policy-making, construction and implementation as a linear sequence of events. Instead, it posits dynamic interaction among policy, planning, enactment and their structural and sociocultural contexts.[38] In other words, curriculum is constructed and reconstructed in situated practice. Whereas a technocratic view puts curriculum as instrumental to classroom practice, a critical view sees curriculum as existing in practice, not independent of it. Further, a technocratic view tends to be prescriptive of practice while a critical view is interpretive and questioning.

From a critical perspective, curriculum causality and change are complex and problematic. Causality and change (or stability) are seen to involve the interplay of biographical (personal and professional), structural and sociocultural factors over time. Curriculum construction and reconstruction both reflect and respond to their immediate and more distant contexts as illustrated in several recent field studies and described in Chapters 4 and 5.[39] It is to an exploration of the structural and sociocultural contexts of curriculum that I now turn.

Structural and Sociocultural Contextualization[40]

Contextualization is inherent in the alternative conception of curriculum and its construction just offered. Context both situates and shapes curriculum;

thus, changing a curriculum involves changing its context. It remains to elaborate the nature of relevant contextual settings and influences. Recognizing that context is widely acknowledged but largely uncharted territory — not unlike the 'new world' of fifteenth century European maps and perhaps for good reason — I proceed with caution. The complexity and elusiveness of context make it difficult to 'pin down' and link empirically to a particular curriculum. What follows, then, is a tentative sketch; these outlines are yet to be worked out fully, either theoretically or empirically. Meanwhile, illustrations from recent field studies are provided in Chapter 4, and ideas introduced here are further developed in Chapters 5 and 6.

First, the nominal context is not necessarily the relevant context of curriculum. Nominal context refers to what is 'out there' that might influence curriculum, in other words, the environment at large. That environment includes social, political, economic and demographic conditions that are translated into constraints, demands and priorities, by groups with diverse and often conflicting interests. In addition, events within and outside the schools are potential context for subsequent curricular activity, and within the education system, each organizational layer (e.g., state or provincial department of education, school) is potential context for curricular activity nested within it. Relevant context, in contrast, refers to those aspects of the nominal context that can be shown to actually influence curriculum in a particular instance, directly or indirectly. Compared to other education sectors such as teacher education, the relevant context of school curricula is extensive.

Distinguishing between structural or systemic and sociocultural or societal contexts is in part an attempt to make context more manageable. It is also and more importantly intended to call attention to the education system context of curriculum, which tends to be overlooked in curriculum discourse and taken for granted in curriculum practice, particularly in the US. Critical theoretical work, for example, typically treats curriculum in relation to larger sociocultural dynamics such as economic and gender relations but neglects its more immediate setting, in effect leapfrogging the intervening structural context of curricula. Education systems are not simply conduits that convey or reflect and thus reproduce larger societal patterns. The structural context is important because it both mediates extrasystemic sociocultural influences and generates curriculum experience. A similar argument is offered by Archer in rejecting correspondence/reproduction theories of schooling and [any] theory or approach which treats the boundary of the educational system as unimportant by holding that any kind of social factor or force penetrates education directly. Instead concrete processes of social interaction are what cross the boundary between education and society. Outside influences do not flow into the system by an equivalent of osmosis (this would be to abandon human agency for holistic metaphysics). They have to be transacted.[41]

An important feature of curriculum context is its variability or fluidity. The relevant curriculum context varies over time and with the curriculum of interest and the local situation within the national milieu. Variability can be seen in the presence of particular context factors, their relative strength or intensity, and their interaction (e.g., aggregation, conflict). For example, in the US, recent decades have witnessed alternating demands for 'basic skills' and 'higher order thinking'. Differences in the numerical strength and activism of extremist religious groups from one community to the next provide another example.[42]

In sum, the relevant structural and sociocultural contexts of curriculum are multifaceted and fluid. While nested one within another, they also are overlapping and interacting. As a consequence, there is no generic curriculum context, no fixed set of parameters or invariant grid that can be imposed on any curriculum. Instead, potential aspects of curriculum context can be identified and their relevance to a particular curriculum can be illustrated.

System as Structural Context

Social systems are typically described in terms of their form and their process or mode of operation. I treat form and mode of operation as structure, defined as the established roles and relationships, including operating procedures, shared beliefs and norms (i.e., tradition, culture). The structure of an education system conditions outsiders' interaction with and participants' interaction within it.[43]

A system consists of two or more interrelated components (e.g., legislature and judiciary in political system, school and state or provincial department of education in education system) and associated roles and patterns of interaction, which can be simple or complex; complex components often constitute subsystems. For example, classrooms and the elementary and secondary schools that house them constitute subsystems of most national education systems. As subsystems of a national education system, elementary and secondary education and their curricula are subject to the structural conditioning and social interaction of the larger system as well as their own internal dynamics. Viewing the education system as the structural context of curriculum thus directs attention to the roles, relationships, patterns of activity and culture of interacting system components.[44]

With few exceptions, access to formal education was severely limited until the nineteenth century. Ownership and control were frequently in the hands of families, community organizations, or religious bodies who provided facilities, hired and supervised teachers and determined programs of study. Distinguishable mass education systems emerged along with the modern nation-states that supported them. (On the State and system-State relations, see Chapter 6.) National systems of mass education have been a means of nation building, especially of:

1 defining and providing socialization for national citizenship and incorporating diverse populations;[45]
2 preparing workers for the economy; and
3 conferring credentials that allocate individuals to different positions in
   society.[46]

National education systems thus serve societal, political, economic and stratification functions as well as the more often recognized individual demands for enlightenment, practical skills, and/or status.[47] In so doing, education systems exert controls on curriculum knowledge, through curriculum policymaking and by shaping the conditions of curriculum practice (see Chapters 5 and 7).

Although the historical experience of national systems of formal, mass education has been marked by conflict and discontinuity, several long-term trends can be identified: (a) expansion and extension to serve more people for longer periods of time, and (b) more specialized and differentiated educational provisions, accompanied by (c) increasing complexity, bureaucratization and standardization. Another historically rooted but not inevitable feature of education systems that has major consequences for curriculum is conservatism. Given the purposes for which national education systems were established, it is not surprising that their structure tends to foster cultural transmission and societal continuity. Once a national identity and tradition have been established, with the help of the education system, a major function of the education system is to perpetuate that way of life. In several instances this century where the education system has been used by political leaders to support radical change (e.g., People's Republic of China, Cuba), it can be seen as functioning to sustain revolution. The education system, even in these cases, was used to conserve, not to bring about, a new order. This is not to argue that the observed conservatism of national education systems is historically inevitable, but that change more often originates outside the system.

Education systems also tend toward self-perpetuation. System participants and beneficiaries have a stake in its maintenance and perhaps also its expansion. Curriculum change efforts that are seen as strengthening or extending the education system (or one of its subsystems) are more likely to be embraced than those that appear to weaken or reduce it or that otherwise challenge its operation or underlying values.

Curriculum relevant differences across education systems include the nature and extent of bureaucratic co-ordination and control, (de-)centralization, and boundary clarity and permeability. These and other features of education systems are made reasonable by their cultural traditions. By culture I mean operating procedures, shared meanings and beliefs, and norms including goals and priorities. It is not uncommon to find shifting priorities or simultaneous pursuit of a multiplicity of seemingly conflicting goals within an education system or subsystem (e.g., efficiency, equity, quality), especially within large systems in heterogeneous societies.

Understanding a curriculum and how it might be changed requires understanding the culture of the education system, which may involve several subcultures associated with occupational groups (e.g., teachers, administrators), subsystems (e.g., elementary education, teacher education), and regions (e.g., urban, rural, midwest) as well as racial-ethnic, religious, socioeconomic and gender groups. The curriculum relevant aspects of these cultures may be overlapping or distinct, compatible or antagonistic. Shared meanings, beliefs and norms that constitute a teacher subculture, for example, include teacher conceptions of knowledge, their expectations for student learning, and their perceptions of the school community and parental expectations. That there is variation in the teacher culture from school to school as well as within schools means that it cannot be taken for granted or ignored in studies of curriculum practice or in change efforts. As a number of studies have documented, change efforts that 'do not consider the underlying patterns of school belief and conduct . . . may only rearrange the technological surface'.[48]

Because education systems tend to be open rather than closed systems, the context of curriculum is not solely structural. Unlike self-sufficient or closed systems, education systems are dependent on their environment and thus sensitive to environmental influences. Dependence on government funding, for example, usually means government influence if not control of how its funds are used. The US education system, for example, is quite permeable, providing relatively easy access for powerful interest groups. The tradition if not the practice of local, public control of elementary and seconday education serves to encourage efforts of external groups to influence the contours and course of schooling including and often especially, curriculum. The permeable character of the US education system makes it highly susceptible to external influences (i.e., sociocultural context) and perhaps also helps to explain why structural context is too often overlooked.

Sociocultural Context

The relevant sociocultural context of curriculum consists of those extra-systemic demographic, social, political, and economic conditions, traditions and ideologies, and events that influence curriculum and curriculum change. Influence can be direct or indirect; the latter may involve the education system as mediator.

The sociocultural context often provides the impetus for curriculum change (e.g., computer literacy). At times, education systems seem more responsive to sociocultural expectations and demands than to those of their clients or participants (e.g., students, teachers). This may be a function of 'the external legitimation, definition, and control of their internal processes',[49] stemming from what Meyer and Rowan describe as widespread acceptance of 'the schooling rule' whereby education is defined as 'a certified teacher teaching a standardized curricular topic to a registered student in an accredited school'. Referring primarily to the US experience, they conclude that

> schooling is thus socially defined by reference to a set of standardized categories, the legitimacy of which is publicly shared. As the categories and credentials of schooling gain importance in allocation

and membership processes, the public comes to expect that they will be controlled and standardized. The large-scale public bureaucracy created to achieve this standardization is now normatively constrained by the expectations of the schooling rule. To a large degree, then, education is coordinated by shared social understandings . . . the legitimacy of schools and their ability to mobilize resources depend on maintaining congruence between their structure and these socially shared categorical understandings of education.[50]

With a few notable exceptions, it appears that the sociocultural context is less conservative (or at least more heterogeneous and turbulent) than the structural context.[51] As a result, external demands for change are often moderated within the system. Both acknowledged problems and desirable but difficult to attain goals are likely to be redefined and acted upon in ways that are system maintaining rather than reformist.

The structural and sociocultural contexts of curriculum are better seen as overlapping and interacting, nested layers than as separate concentric circles. The structural context, nested within the sociocultural context, does not always have clear-cut or stable boundaries. Whatever the system boundaries, they are rarely impermeable. Nesting also occurs within each context (e.g., subsystems nested within the national education system, communities within states or provinces). Further, over time, experiences with prior curriculum and change efforts are potential context for subsequent ones.

Putting curriculum in context necessitates reformulation of curriculum conceptions and reconstruction of curriculum practice, including the practice of curriculum theorizing, research, design and change. While avoiding the reductionism and impotence of technocratic approaches to curriculum and its construction, contextualization is not without problems such as complexity, situational contingency and risk (of the unfamiliar and of retaliation by vested interests in the *status quo*). These human, social-structural problems are not amenable to technical solutions.

Implications

Juxtaposing technocratic and critical approaches to curriculum and its construction reveals important differences in conceptions and associated practices with different social and political as well as pedagogical implications. Among the differing and interrelated implications of the two approaches are those concerning (a) teacher and curriculum specialist roles, (b) the nature of knowledge made available to students and (c) social control, conflict and change. Technocratic approaches to curriculum and its construction foster reliance on experts and expert knowledge. Teachers (and students) are assumed largely incapable of curriculum planning or enactment in the absence of direction or assistance from curriculum specialists and so-called change agents. The teacher is cast as a manager or passive implementor of expert designs. In effect, technocratic approaches contribute to what has been characterized as teacher de-skilling.[52] A critical approach, in contrast, by highlighting situated teacher-student interaction, assumes and fosters active, reflective and responsible teacher roles. It also suggests modification of curriculum specialist, especially curriculum developer and change agent, roles.

In the US, most teachers are neither as dismal nor as enlightened as they are portrayed by technocratic and critical approaches to curriculum and its construction. The continuing education and teacher education reform movement began in the early 1980s with a wave of state level regulation consistent with a technocratic approach.[53] The mid and late 1980s have witnessed a countertrend toward teacher empowerment and/or professionalization that is potentially compatible with a critical approach. A strong movement for teacher empowerment could overcome the resistance of established experts and administrators and the inertia of tradition.

One's conception of curriculum and associated practices also carries implications for the knowledge made available to students. While there is no one-to-one correspondence between approach and the nature and treatment of knowledge in curriculum, a technocratic approach tends to foster transmission of presumably expert knowledge, often in fragments amenable to behavioral objectives, sequencing and standardized testing. So-called individualized programs such as IGE (Individually Guided Education, developed at the University of Wisconsin R and D Center) and IPI (Individually Prescribed Instruction, developed at the University of Pittsburgh R and D Center) in the US, and mastery learning, programmed and computer assisted instruction, are prime examples. As a result, knowledge in the form of correct answers is predetermined and often trivialized; academic-intellectual integrity is lost. There is little or no room for either teacher or student personal knowledge, creativity, or critique that might lead to comprehension let alone knowledge generation or reconstruction.

Memorization of correct answer and mastery of discrete skills take precedence over open-ended inquiry or reflective thinking. Attempts to include the latter in technocratic curriculum typically result in mechanized inquiry sequences (a series of steps to be followed in order to arrive at a predetermined conclusion or 'discovery') or isolated thinking 'skill' development exercises. There are problems in planning for thinking or inquiry that technocratic approaches simply cannot accommodate. These include provision for student generated questions as well as student hypotheses and interpretations, and conclusions not anticipated or condoned by the curriculum developers. In addition, national curriculum documents cannot provide opportunities for experiences beyond the classroom to generate questions, test hypotheses, or act on conclusions. A packaged curriculum cannot anticipate local possibilities.

While a critical approach offers no guarantee that the nature and treatment of knowledge in curriculum will be constructivist, it does hold potential for alternative knowledge forms and processes including knowledge generation or reconstruction by teachers and students. The extent to which this potential is realized depends on both teachers' capacity and contextual supports.

Whereas a technocratic approach attempts to foster both knowledge and social control and thereby minimize conflict, a critical approach acknowledges conflict, which is seen as an impetus for change, and fosters intellectual and social empowerment. In contrast to critical approaches, technocratic approaches to curriculum tend to be alienating, distancing teachers and students from knowledge and curriculum, from their own teaching and learning. Alienation, in turn, results in the perceived need for further control to overcome technocratically generated resistance and classroom conflict.

Related to these differing postures toward control and conflict are different attitudes towards curriculum and social change. A technocratic approach tends towards the perpetuation of the *status quo* within and outside the schools. Although the particular facts or skills to be learned or the means by which they are to be taught might be altered in a new curriculum document, the technocratic curriculum form with all its previously noted limitations remains intact. Consequently, change is necessarily within the existing system. Even if that system were equitable and humane, a technocratic approach to knowledge would constrain human possibility. A critical approach is not so limited; its normative aspects support curriculum, system, and social change consistent with human dignity and possibility and with social justice. Further, such change is seen as interrelated. If curriculum is viewed critically as a contextualized social process, then curriculum change is a function of contextual change. Curriculum is unlikely to change in the absence of supportive structural changes, which are unlikely to be initiated in the absence of external pressures or supports. This line of reasoning indicates the futility of trying to bring about substantive curriculum or other reform simply by substituting one curriculum document for another. Further implications of a critical conception of curriculum are explored in subsequent chapters.

Notes

1 For example, see E. Eisner and E. Vallance (Eds.), *Conflicting Conceptions of Curriculum* (Berkeley, CA: McCutchan, 1973); E. Vallance, 'A Second Look at *Conflicting Conceptions of Curriculum*', *Theory into Practice* 25 (1986): 24–30.

2 For example, see M. W. Apple, *Ideology and Curriculum* (London: Routledge & Kegan Paul, 1979); J. Goodman, 'Teaching Preservice Teachers a Critical Approach to Curriculum Design: A Descriptive Account', *Curriculum Inquiry* 16, 2 (1986): 179–201.

3 This conception of curriculum is similar to, but more encompassing, than what others have called curriculum-in-use or curriculum practice.

4 To make the presentation manageable, I have synthesized particular instances to present a composite that reflects the spirit and substance if not the particulars of individual cases. Also, while acknowledging differences in the form and substance of curriculum activities (e.g., at national, state or province, and local district, school, and/or classroom levels), I do not find consideration of such differences germane to the exploration of the broader question of curriculum meanings and implications; conceptions span organizational levels.

5 The mechanization of curriculum construction and the separation of curriculum policy-making and development inherent in the technocratic view stand in contrast to a craft view of curriculum construction. A craft view implies a holistic conception of curriculum products as well as an appreciation of creativity in their construction. Craftsmanship acknowledges both technical skill and personal preference in curriculum construction. The values and particular aims of the curriculum developer as artisan are seen to guide the imaginative use of procedure and technique. Procedure is thus subordinated to purpose, and the curriculum artisan is personally involved in determining both. From a craft perspective, curriculum construction as technical project is not unlike painting by number. The

craft view, however, still views curriculum as a tangible product. Similarly, a deliberative approach to curriculum also views curriculum as a tangible product. See W. A. Reid, *Thinking about the Curriculum* (London: Routledge & Kegan Paul, 1978).

6 In *Basic Principles of Curriculum and Instruction* (Chicago: University of Chicago Press, 1949), Ralph W. Tyler offered the best known rational management model of curriculum development, which was subsequently elaborated by others. While perhaps the most influential, Tyler was not the first to propose a rational management model of curriculum development in the United States. A student of Franklin Bobbitt, Tyler seems to have revived and refurbished ideas current in the 1920s. See M. L. Seguel, *The Curriculum Field: Its Formative Years* (New York: Teachers College Press, 1966). On misconceptions of how successful businesses operate, see T. J. Peters and R. H. Waterman, Jr., *In Search of Excellence* (New York: Warner Books, 1982).

7 A dramatic example is provided by the Individually Guided Education (IGE) curriculum reform in T. S. Popkewitz, B. R. Tabachnick and G. Wehlage, *The Myth of Educational Reform* (Madison: University of Wisconsin Press, 1982). An example of a rational management model of curriculum construction is provided by J. E. Davis, *Planning A Social Studies Program: Activities, Guidelines, and Resources* (Boulder, CO: Social Science Education Consortium, 1983, rev. ed.).

8 See, e.g., M. W. Apple, 'Curricular Form and the Logic of Technical Control', in *Cultural and Economic Reproduction in Education,* ed. M. W. Apple (London: Routledge & Kegan Paul, 1982), pp. 237–274; W. A. Reid, *Thinking about the Curriculum,* 1978, *op cit.*

9 See T. S. Popkewitz, 'Educational Reform as the Organization of Ritual: Stability as Change', *Journal of Education* 164 (1982): 5–29.

10 For example, W. A. Reid and D. F. Walker (Eds.), *Case Studies in Curriculum Change* (London: Routledge & Kegan Paul, 1975); G. W. F. Orpwood, 'The Reflective Deliberator: A Case Study of Curriculum Policymaking', *Journal of Curriculum Studies* 17, 3 (1985): 293–304.

11 For example: G. McCutcheon, 'Elementary School Teachers' Planning for Social Studies and Other Subjects', *Theory and Research in Social Education* 9 (Spring 1981): 45–66; P. L. Peterson, R. W. Marx and C. M. Clark, 'Teacher Planning, Teacher Behavior, and Student Achievement', *American Educational Research Journal* 15 (1978): 417–432.

12 McCutcheon, G. W. (1981) *op cit.*

13 D.C. Neal, A. J. Pate and A. B. Case, 'The Influence on Training, Experience, and Organizing Environment of Teachers' Use of the Systematic Planning Model', paper presented at the annual meeting of the American Educational Research Association, Montreal, Canada, April 1983.

14 A. Kaplan, *The Conduct of Inquiry* (San Francisco: Chandler, 1964).

15 M. Fullan and A. Pomfret, 'Research on Curriculum and Instruction Implementation', *Review of Educational Research* 47 (1977): 335–397; R. E. Stake and J. A. Easley, *Case Studies in Science Education, Vol. I: The Case Reports, Vol. II: Design, Overview, and General Findings* (Urbana, IL: Center for Instructional Research and Curriculum Evaluation, University of Illinois, 1978).

16 For example: N. Boag and D. Massey, 'Teacher Perspectives on Program Change', *Theory and Research in Social Education* 9 (Fall 1981): 37–59; C. Cornbleth, 'Old versus New Curriculum Materials Use in Science and Social Studies', *Curriculum Perspectives* 2 (1982): 25–33; D. Hamilton 'The Integration of Knowledge: Practice and Problems', *Journal of Curriculum Studies* 5 (1973): 146–155; S. B. Sarason, *The Culture of the School and the Problem of Change* (Boston: Allyn and Bacon, 1971).

17 Rather than not working, at least as intended by their developers, technocratic curriculum change efforts can be seen as effectively serving to sustain and reaffirm existing beliefs and practices, that is, to maintain and legitimate the *status quo.*

18 H.M. Kliebard, 'Systematic Curriculum Development, 1890–1959', in *Value Conflicts and Curriculum Issues,* ed. J. Schaffarzick and G. Sykes (Berkeley: McCutcheon, 1979); Reid, *Thinking about the Curriculum,* 1978, *op cit.*

19 See H.M. Kliebard and B. M. Franklin, 'The Course of the Course of Study: History of Curriculum, in *Historical Inquiry in Education*, ed. J. H. Best (Washington, DC: American Educational Research Association, 1983), pp. 138–157.

20 Other models of curriculum and its construction, such as a craft model (see Note 5) or Walker's naturalistic model, do attend to normative assumptions and implications. However, they still view curriculum construction largely as a product development task. See D.F. Walker, 'A Naturalistic Model for Curriculum Development', *School Review* 80 (1971): 51–65.

21 The character and features of structural and sociocultural contexts are treated briefly here, elaborated in the next section, and further explored in subsequent chapters.

22 Even more dramatic examples are found in cases of international transfer of curriculum products. See, e.g., J. G. Lee, D. Adams, and C. Cornbleth, 'Transnational Transfer of Professional Knowledge: Adopting a US Teaching Innovation in Korea', *Journal of Curriculum Studies* 20, 3 (1988): 233–246.

23 During the past decade, so-called school based or school centered curriculum development and change have received increased attention and trial. See, for example, J. Eggleston (Ed.), *School-Based Curriculum Development in Britain* (London: Routledge & Kegan Paul, 1980); S. Lindblad, The Practice of School-

Centered Innovation: A Swedish Case', *Journal of Curriculum Studies* 16 (1984): 165–172.

24 Much of this section draws on and extends the interpretation offered in C. Cornbleth, 'The Persistence of Myth in Teacher Education and Teaching', in *Critical Studies in Teacher Education,* ed. T.S. Popkewitz (London: Falmer Press, 1987), pp. 186–210.

25 R.E. Callahan, *Education and the Cult of Efficiency* (Chicago, University of Chicago Press, 1962).

26 H.M. Kliebard, 'Persistent Curriculum Issues in Historical Perspective', in *Curriculum Theorizing: The Reconceptualists,* ed. W. Pinar (Berkeley, McCutchan, 1975).

27 P. Berger, B. Berger and H. Kellner, *The Homeless Mind: Modernization and Consciousness* (New York: Vintage, 1973).

28 *Ibid,* pp. 108–109.

29 *Ibid,* p. 27.

30 *Ibid,* p. 30.

31 *Ibid,* p. 113.

32 *Ibid,* p. 49.

33 H. Rugg, 'The School Curriculum and the Drama of American Life', in *Curriculum-Making Past and Present,* 26th Yearbook of the National Society for the Study of Education, Part I, ed. H. Rugg (Bloomington, Il: Public School Publishing Co., 1926), pp. 3–6.

34 Recent trends such as teacher involvement in school based curriculum development in Britain and calls for teacher empowerment or professionalization in the US may be modifying (or reflect modification of) the inadequate teacher assumption. Such trends suggest possible points of entry for alternative approaches to curriculum and its reconstruction.

35 A more dynamic, iterative view of planning would not limit planning to preactive plan-making. Rather, planning would be seen as a process of intentionally designing and effecting change in the structure, program, and/or impact of educational systems and organizations'. Here, planning is a continuing process; initial plans are modified in practice. Change is planned, and plans are changed. See D. Adams and C. Cornbleth, *Planning Educational Change* (manuscript in progress).

36 My position that classroom (or curriculum) practice is to be understood and interrogated, not taken as given or desirable, is compatible with that argued by I. F. Goodson in *The Making of Curriculum* (London: Falmer Press, 1988), Chapter 2. However, we differ in where we place emphasis and how we treat history. Where Goodson's focus is on 'preactive curriculum' or publically stated

intentions, mine is on curriculum-in-use or what actually occurs in school classrooms. Neither discounts the other.

With respect to curriculum history, Goodson's interest is in the historically located, social construction of preactive curriculum whereas mine is in the historically located, social construction of classroom practice. The history of interest to me is broader and perhaps less deep than Goodson's insofar as I see curriculum as shaped by structural and sociocultural contexts of which 'preactive curriculum' is only one part. For example, while I agree with Goodson that 'Understandings of the making of curriculum should help provide cognitive maps of the antecedent purposes and structures which precede and locate contemporary practice' (p. 16), I include past practice or classroom traditions as well as 'struggles over the preactive definition of curriculum' (p. 15) among the relevant antecedents. Also, I see preactive curriculum as influencing or shaping rather than setting 'parameters for interactive realization and negotiation in the classroom and school' (p. 16). This latter difference may well reflect differences in US and UK experience. In sum, our differences are complementary ones akin to movements between foreground and background, although we might well dispute which is which.

37 See, e.g., C. Cornbleth and W. Korth, 'Teacher Perspectives and Meanings of Responsibility', *Educational Forum* 48, 4 (1984): 412–422.

38. Cf, W. A. Reid, 'The Changing Curriculum: Theory and Practice', in *Case Studies in Curriculum Change,* ed. W. A. Reid and D. F. Walker (London: Routledge & Kegan Paul, 1975), pp. 240–259.

39 E.g., C. Cornbleth, 'Socioecology of Critical Thinking' (paper presented at the American Educational Research Association in Chicago, April 1985); C. Cornbleth, W. Korth and E. B. Dorow, 'Creating the Curriculum: Beginning the Year at a Middle School' (paper presented at the American Educational Research Association in Montreal, 1983); L. M. McNeil, *Contradictions of Control: School Structure and School Knowledge* (New York: Routledge & Kegan Paul, 1986); T. S. Popkewitz, B. R. Tabachnick, and G. Wehlage, *The Myth of Educational Reform* (Madison: University of Wisconsin Press, 1982).

40 This and the following section draw on prior work on the contexts of US teacher education policy change and of educational planning. See C. Cornbleth and D. Adams, 'The Drunkards's Streetlamp? Contexts of Policy Change in US Teacher Education', in *Governments and Higher Education: The Legitimacy of Intervention*, ed. Ontario Institute for Studies in Education/Higher Education Group (Toronto, OISE, 1987), pp. 314–344; D. Adams and C. Cornbleth, *Planning Educational Change* (manuscript in progress).

41 M. S. Archer, 'Educational Politics, A Model for their Analysis', in *Policy-Making in Education*, ed. I. McNay and J. Ozga (New York: Pergamon, 1985), p. 41.

42 How context is identified can be seen as another source of its variation. For example, are relevant contextual factors those perceived and reported by curriculum participants and/or those that appear to an observer to have influenced curriculum activity? As indicated previously, empirically linking curriculum and context is neither simple nor straightforward.

43 M. S. Archer, *Social Origins of Educational Systems* (London: Sage, 1984). While the literature on systems and systems analysis is extensive, there has been relatively little theoretical or empirical work on education systems as system is meant here. The conventional distinction in organizational and systems theory between formal structure and process obscures the dynamic nature of structure in action. My position is compatible with that of Katz and Kahn, among others, for whom 'A social system is a structure of events or happenings rather than of physical parts and it therefore has no structure apart from its functioning'. (D. Katz and R. L. Kahn, *The Social Psychology of Organizations* (New York: John Wiley, 1966, p. 31.) Also, see A. Giddens, *Central Problems in Social Theory* (Berkeley: University of California Press, 1979); M. S. Archer, 'Morphogenesis versus Structuration: On Combining Structure and Action', *British Journal of Sociology* 33, 4 (1982): 455–483. The conceptualization of system presented here is compatible with Gouldner's portrayal of natural (non-organic) as opposed to rational systems and Scott and Meyer's 'societal sector'. (A. W. Gouldner, 'Organizational Tensions', in *Sociology Today*, ed. R. K. Merton, L. Bloom and L. S. Cottrell, Jr. (New York: Basic Books, 1959); W. R. Scott and J. W. Meyer, 'The Organization of Societal Sectors', in *Organizational Environments*, ed. J. W. Meyer and W. R. Scott (Beverly Hills, CA: Sage, 1983, pp. 129–153.)

A further point is that the conception of education system offered here is a non-organismic one. That is, while education systems are treated as real (i.e., having an independent existence that is observable, analyzable, and perhaps measureable), I do not endow them with purpose or action apart from the people who occupy roles in the system or influence it from outside. Individuals and groups have purposes and take action; systems do not. Social systems do not have lives of their own. See M. Keeley, 'Realism in Organizational Theory: A Reassessment', *Symbolic Interaction* 6, no. 2 (1983): 279–290. Thus, I reject, as overly deterministic, conceptions of structure as external, controlling '"objective" features of social organization that exist apart from culture and the consciousness of participating actors' or apart from the intentions and actions of participants. (D. Rubenstein, 'The Concept of Structure in Sociology', in *Sociological Theory in Transition*, ed. M. L. Wardell and S. P. Turner (Boston: Allen & Unwin, 1986), pp. 80–94.) At the same time that structural factors are recognized and respected, so too is human agency. I am assuming a dynamic interaction between structure and agency in time and place that is compatible with Mills' macro conceptualization of the interaction of history, biography, and social structure. (C. W. Mills, *The Sociological Imagination* (New York: Oxford University Press, 1959).)

44 My focus here is on the national rather than classroom, school, or other levels of the education system. The nature and influence of state or provincial, school district, school, and classroom level structural context are illustrated in Chapters 4 and 5.

45 On the US experience, see D. Tyack, *One Best System* (Cambridge, MA: Harvard University Press, 1974) and R. F. Butts, *The Revival of Civic Learning* (Bloomington, IN: Phi Delta Kappa, 1980); on England and France, see M. Archer, 1984, *op cit.*; for a worldwide view, see J. Boli, F. O. Ramirez and J. W. Meyer, 'Explaining the Origins and Expansion of Mass Education', *Comparative Education Review* 29, 2 (1985): 145-170.

46 The language of this listing reflects the structural/functionalist paradigm of most government officials and social scientists. From a critical paradigm, one would speak of (a) maintaining the cultural hegemony of dominant groups, (b) supporting capitalist (or other) relations of production, and (c) rationalizing social and economic inequities.

47 See, e.g., R. Collins, 'Some Comparative Principles of Educational Stratification', *Harvard Educational Review* 47, 1 (1977): 1-27.

48 T. S. Popkewitz, 'Educational Reform and the Problem of Institutional Life', *Educational Researcher* 8, no. 3 (1979): p. 8.

49 J. W. Meyer 'Conclusion: Institutionalization and the Rationality of Formal Organizational Structure', in *Organizational Environments*, ed. J. W. Meyer and W. R. Scott (Beverely Hills, CA: Sage, 1983): p. 269.

50 J.W. Meyer and B. Rowan, 'The Structure of Educational Organizations', in *Organizational Environments*, ed. J. W. Meyer and W. R. Scott (Beverly Hills, CA: Sage, 1983): p. 84.

51 See, e.g., R. G. Corwin, 'Models of Educational Organizations', in *Review of Research in Education*, Vol. II, ed. F. N. Kerlinger and John B. Carroll (Itasca, IL: Peacock, 1974), pp. 249-295.

52 M. W. Apple, 'Curricular Form and the Logic of Technical Control', 1982, *op cit.*

53 See C. Cornbleth and D. Adams, 'The Drunkard's Streetlamp?' 1987, *op cit.*

Chapter 3

Beyond Hidden Curriculum?

In school, students seem to learn much that is not publicly set forth in official statements of school philosophy or purpose, or in course guides, syllabi and other curriculum documents. This learning, which includes information, beliefs, and ways of behaving, is often attributed to a 'hidden curriculum' of schooling.[1] With few exceptions, this hidden curriculum is portrayed as a powerful, detrimental force that undermines the professed commitment of the schools to foster intellectual development and a democratic community. Attention to a hidden curriculum is often associated with critiques of the authoritarianism and inequities of primary and secondary schooling in politically democratic societies.[2] But, while 'hidden curriculum' is an intuitively attractive phrase, one that gives the appearance of accounting for the complexity of how schools affect students and why schools resist change, it tends to label more than to explain.

It may be that the usefulness of the concept of hidden curriculum as a vehicle for criticism depends in part on a degree of amorphousness that precludes close scrutiny. The possibility of a pernicious hidden curriculum, however, demands careful attention to its operation and influence. And when we give it this attention, the questions of interest are not whether a hidden curriculum is hidden — by whom, from whom, or how — but what is to be found and what difference it might make for the experience and study of curriculum and schooling.

In this chapter, I begin with the claims made in the name of hidden curriculum and then turn to the evidence that might support the concept and the claims. Following this review, I offer an alternative interpretation and implications for curriculum studies, extending the conceptual framework introduced in Chapter 2; here, the emphasis is on contradiction, mediation and context. When curriculum is viewed as a contextualized social process, the social organization and relations of schooling are highlighted and interrogated. Hidden curriculum becomes a vestige of documentary conceptions of curriculum.

Interpretive Claims

The phenomena referred to as constituting the hidden curriculum are tacit in so far as their presence is unseen and often taken for granted rather than directly acknowledged and examined — for example, the segmentation of the school day and programming into fixed time periods for supposedly separate subjects. These phenomena also appear to be both complex and changing, with varying features and messages, academic and social, across time and place.[4] In addition, the phrase, 'hidden curriculum', implies some sort of conspiracy — for which the evidence is not at all compelling. As Vallance suggests, 'the hidden curriculum became hidden by the end of the nineteenth century simply because the rhetoric had done its job'.[4] By the turn of the century, the schools' explicit 'assertive socialization' function had become sufficiently established that it could be taken for granted; upon rediscovery, it was assumed by many to have been hidden. For these reasons, it would seem more appropriate, at this point, to consider the *implicit curricula* of schooling rather than a hidden curriculum.

Implicit curricula consist of the messages imparted by the classroom and school environment and the interaction with and within them. In a McLuhanian sense, the medium is a large part of the school's message, perhaps the predominant message. And the messages of implicit curricula might complement, contradict, or parallel the explicit curriculum of reading, writing, mathematics, science, social studies and other subjects. Among the outcomes attributed to implicit curricula messages are individual and societal effects that foster conformity to national ideals and social conventions while maintaining socio-economic and cultural inequalities. Individual students are assumed to acquire prevailing world views, norms, and values as well as predefined and usually subordinate roles in authority relationships. Collectively, such effects are seen as serving a social control function by perpetuating existing social structures and the ideologies that support them. The elements of implicit curricula identified as exerting these influences range

43

from features of texts and other curriculum materials to teacher-student relationships and school policies and routines. But, while there is diverse evidence suggesting the presence and operation of implicit curricula, documentation of specific effects on students, individually and collectively, remains sketchy. Implicit messages have tended to be equated with effects.

Empirical Evidence

Structural or social organizational aspects of a school's implicit curricula include the arrangement of time, facilities, materials, and examinations as well as established roles and relationships. The school program not only provides opportunities for learning certain subjects, but it minimizes opportunities for learning others. In this way, it communicates what is considered important and to be taken seriously by teachers and students — for example, that history, which usually is required, is more important than music, which usually is optional if available at all. What counts as worthwhile knowledge is also indicated by time allocations, the sequencing of subjects, the number and range of facilities and materials provided and the examination practices. In US elementary schools, for example, reading and language arts usually are scheduled daily for approximately two hours in the morning, followed by mathematics. In contrast, social studies and science usually are scheduled two or three times per week, for less than an hour, and most often in the afternoon.[5] If events require a change in schedule, social studies and science are more likely to be abandoned than is reading. In addition, fewer facilities and materials (e.g., textbooks, workbooks, audio-visual media and computers) typically are available for these subjects, and they are not emphasized on routinely administered standardized tests or in special assistance programs.

Further, the compartmentalization of the school program into separate subjects suggests that knowledge is not or should not be integrated and that school knowledge is different and separate from everyday life. The degree of program flexibility is yet another aspect of implicit curricula. To the extent that the explicit curriculum is standardized, at least on paper or through examinations, the message might be communicated that knowledge is given, handed down by authorities, and not to be questioned by the uninitiated.

Just as the questions, 'What is selected for inclusion in the curriculum as a whole?' and 'How is it treated?' reveal aspects of a school's implicit curricula, similar questions asked of specific subjects and of the textbooks and other materials used within subjects reveal additional implicit messages. Although textbooks are seen primarily as repositories and conveyors of subject matter, they communicate more than information. For example, texts that minimize social and intellectual diversity and conflict[6] or that legitimize existing political and economic institutions[7] and selected cultural values[8] not only offer misleading notions of social science and history but also might foster support for currently dominant groups and the *status quo*.

Insofar as texts are treated as the sole or most authoritative sources of knowledge rather than as inevitably biased summary interpretations, they can contribute to the reification of knowledge, dependence on authority and denial of personal experience. Anyon's[9] comparative investigation of what counts as knowledge in US elementary schools in different socioeconomic status communities found that students, particularly in working and middle class communities, tend to believe that knowledge is something to be acquired primarily from teachers, books and other authorities. For example, in her interviews with eighty fifth-grade students concerning the nature and source of knowledge, most students said that they could acquire knowledge — by 'doing pages in our books and things', by 'doing your work in school' but that they could not create knowledge.

Another illustration of students' perceptions regarding school knowledge comes from a field study of a two and one-half week 'Europe unit' in a seventh-grade US social studies class.[10] Interviews with students following daily observation of their class revealed students' perception of the importance of notes. It appeared that the 'skills' that the teacher saw herself as emphasizing served to facilitate the acquisition, retention, and reproduction of presented information rather than active student thought. Student comments about notes included:

> I take my notes home when she gives them to us . . . She always writes them on the board . . . the important stuff, she puts on the board so we can remember, and we make sure we have all those notes when we're done.
>
> She writes notes on the chalkboard. You have to write them down on paper.
>
> Make sure you get every note that she gives you.

Notes are given, not taken. Knowledge has been reified, to be transmitted from textbooks and teachers to students, like the passing of the baton in a relay race. Thus, messages about the sources and nature of knowledge as well as subject matter information may be communicated to students.

A further illustration of the treatment of knowledge is the multiple choice question, which often appears on practice exercises and tests. Regardless of the topic, both the questions considered worth raising and the alternative responses are presented to the student. Students are directed to choose from those options provided by authorities (e.g., teacher, textbook author, examiner), only one of which presumably is correct. Thus, students are presented with an illusion of choice[11] that can be viewed as preparation for the limited definition and practice of freedom that they are likely to encounter in adult society where problems often are defined by others and decisions are made by selecting from predetermined alternatives.

At a broader level, aspects of implicit curricula include school or school district policies, routine procedures and rituals, roles and authority relationships, and the array of extracurricular activities and services available to students and the community. Policies, procedures, and rituals include the grading system, ability grouping or tracking practices and patriotic or other ceremonies. Among the messages that might be communicated by these features of school life are the desirability of competition, meritocracy, efficiency and unquestioning national loyalty. To the extent that a school's social organization is hierarchical, characterized by differentiation of policymaking, supervisory, and implementation roles, for example, it might communicate parallel messages regarding authority relationships, rational management and compliance. Extracurricular activities and services may provide affiliation, independence, and success opportunities for students, thus moderating the impact of other aspects of schooling and making them more palatable. Or, they simply may extend the school's contribution to stratification and the socialization of students for adult roles.

Even when the social organization of the school, or classroom within a school, appears to be 'open', other messages may be communicated. Open classrooms and schools, characterized by flexible use of time and space and some form of individualization, may offer little more than an aura of freedom and equality.[12] Their implicit curricula may be quite similar to those of traditional schools and classrooms.

Similarly, other organizational arrangements cannot be taken at face value. Peer tutoring programs, for example, can foster co-operation or exacerbate academic status differences among students. Neither individualization nor mastery learning-criterion referenced evaluation necessarily eliminates competition as indicated by observations of students racing through sequentially organized programs to get ahead of their peers (e.g., by completing more activity cards, by moving from the gold to the blue reading book).

Vivid illustration of the differential messages that might be communicated by apparently similar organizational and programmatic arrangements is provided by Popkewitz, Tabachnick, and Wehlage in their study of exemplary Individually Guided Education (IGE) elementary schools.[13] Although all six schools were model implementers of the IGE curriculum management reform, there was considerable variation in the substance of teaching and learning and the implicit messages communicated, prompting Popkewitz *et al.* to distinguish among illusory, technical and constructive conditions of schooling. (Illusory, technical and constructive schooling are described further in Chapter 4).

Within the schools' organizational arrangements, patterns of interaction, especially among teachers and students, communicate additional messages. For example, several classroom studies suggest that elementary teachers tend to stress an institutionally sanctioned core of values including punctuality, orderliness, task orientation and acceptance of authority. This management core[14] is evident in both traditional and open classrooms[15] and as early as kindergarten.[16]

Interviews with suburban US, middle school English, science, and social studies teachers regarding their priorities[17] provide further illustration of the prominence of these core values. While the teachers' concerns were wide ranging, aspects of a 'management core',[18] usually mentioned under the rubric of responsibility, were quite salient. For example, the teachers indicated that student responsibility, by which they meant doing the work and/or doing it well and on time, was most important for gettting good grades in their classes. Also noted as important were class participation and effort, which mean showing interest, co-operation, and working to potential as perceived by the teacher.

Although there is diverse evidence suggesting the presence and operation of implicit curricula, documentation of specific effects on students remains sketchy. Some evidence regarding the impact of implicit curricula relevant to social education can be found in the political socialization and citizenship education literature.[19] While explicit curricula transmit some political information to some students, they do not appear to substantially influence political attitudes or participation. School and classroom climate and student participation in extracurricular and school governance activities, however, do seem to be important influences. For example, a classroom setting in which controversial issues are freely discussed and students believe they can influence classroom events shows a consistently strong relationship with political and participatory attitudes, including higher political efficacy and trust and lower political cynicism and alienation.[20] Participation in school governance and extracurricular activities also is related to students' political attitudes as is school organization and governance climate; less authoritarian school environments that afford varied opportunities for meaningful student participation are associated with positive political attitudes and behavior. In contrast, regular engagement in patriotic rituals, the use of repetitive worksheets and an emphasis on presumed political facts tend to be negatively related to students' political knowledge and democratic beliefs.[21] Overall, this research suggests that the school milieu and the manner in which classes are conducted, i.e., curriculum and context, have as much or more impact on students' political learning, particularly on their political beliefs and participatory behavior, than do the topics, activities, and materials constituting the formal program.[22]

A major conclusion to be drawn from the evidence regarding implicit curricula is that the primary value of the notion of implicit curricula is that it calls attention to aspects of schooling that are recognized only occasionally and remain largely unexamined, particularly the schools' pedagogical, organizational, and social environments (i.e., their structural and sociocultural contexts, particularly the former), and their interrelations. Thus, although the term, implicit curricula, is more descriptive of these phenomena than is hidden curriculum, it seems preferable to forego both labels and directly examine (a) the constraints and opportunities as well as the seemingly contradictory messages that are communicated by curriculum practice and the school milieu and (b) how they are mediated by students. My purpose in the following sections is to pursue such an examination, thereby extending the conceptual framework introduced in the previous chapter. When curriculum is viewed as a contextualized social process, so-called hidden curriculum or implicit curricula are made explicit and subject to scrutiny.

Contradiction and Mediation

Contradiction and normative variation are inherent in schooling as in other social institutions in heterogeneous or changing societies. Schools proffer contradictory messages and possibilities for interpretation and action. Among the contradictions of contemporary schooling are discrepancies within and between curriculum documents and curriculum practice, discontinuities among the messages of schooling and other social institutions, and the paradox of the schools' role in affording both liberating opportunities and constraints on personal autonomy.

Contradictions between curriculum documents and practice are evident when, for example, cultural (including political and intellectual) diversity is lauded by teachers or textbooks as contributing to the vitality of a democratic society, but students are rewarded, informally or with higher grades, for conforming to their teacher's notion of the good student or citizen. Curricular inconsistencies are apparent when, for example, social studies texts laud freedom of speech as a hallmark of political democracy but ignore or denigrate contemporary dissenters. More broadly, schools and curriculum are often seen as the agency for mitigating historic social and economic inequities by providing all individuals with equal opportunity for 'life, liberty, and the pursuit of happiness'.[23] Yet equal opportunity often means unequal treatment, for example, tracking, pull-out compensatory programmes, differential provision of seemingly similar programmes within and across schools.[24] In addition, variation in messages regarding what constitutes appropriate adult work roles and relationships to authority have been found to differ with the perceived socio-economic status of the school community in ways that could perpetuate status differences.[25] Variation is also evident within schools. In one classroom, for example, the message might be that students are to think for themselves, while in another students are effectively free only to agree with the authority represented by the teacher or textbook.

Normative variations and contradictions extend beyond the school to discontinuities among the messages communicated by schools and other social institutions. Concurrent influences on students and teachers include family, peers and media.[26] Contradictions are obvious when, for example, school curricula communicate the value of compliance with authority while television and film portray heroes who flout convention and established authorities. Not infrequently, schools communicate particularistic local values in conflict with more cosmopolitan national ideals.[27] In this regard, the social control exercised by US schools may serve less as 'the handmaiden of industrialization' than to maintain eighteenth and nineteenth century rural notions of community and moral virtue against the perceived diversity and corruption of urban-industrial society.[28] Consistent with this view are the recurrent movements in the US to restore 'local control' of schooling and curriculum. Part of the present movement in the US for changes in schooling appeals to the restoration of a narrow morality and patriotism as protection against the degradation of encroaching 'secular humanism'. It would seem that the potency of the messages communicated by curriculum and school experience depends in part on their compatibility with the messages communicated by other social institutions and personal experiences.

The literature that is critical of schooling tends to focus on those aspects that might constrain and control individuals and thereby contribute to legitimating and maintaining existing social structures. But there also are aspects of curriculum and schooling that are potentially liberating. In so far as they enable students to develop socially valued knowledge and skills, i.e., cultural capital, or to form their own peer groups and subcultures, they may contribute to personal and collective autonomy and to possible critique and challenge of existing norms and institutions. However, student groups whose values and norms conflict with those dominant in middle-class schools and serve to moderate their impact,[29] or to obviate it altogether,[30] may, in effect, serve to sustain racial-ethnic, economic, and gender inequities and dominant social interests.[31] Schools are neither the all-powerful instruments of cultural and economic reproduction that some have claimed them to be nor the prime sources of emancipation as others have promised. Yet, while schools are neither, they provide opportunities for both, i.e., for domination and for resistance or transformation.[32]

These examples of contradiction point to more profound social contradictions of which curriculum is an integral part. At issue are questions of the relation of individual and society, as well as questions of cultural transmission versus cultural transformation and of equity and justice. Thus, contradictions in the relation of the individual and society are realized in the competing conceptions of individuality and individualization of schooling that underlie classroom practice.[33] Individual differences are social constructions that are constituted and played out in social circumstances; context and interaction, in effect, define individuality. It is ironic perhaps that, in schools that profess to celebrate the individual, the individual student has little voice in the determination of what differences matter, how they are to be assessed, or how assessments are to be interpreted and acted upon.

These contradictions and resulting tensions might be viewed as disenabling to students and others trying to make sense of school experience or to determine which messages are operative in a particular situation. Alternatively, contradictory messages might cancel each other out, effectively communicating little except ambiguity and uncertainty. Some students might learn that they cannot trust what others say and do, that throughout life they will experience contradictions and that there is little or nothing they can do to resolve such contraditions to their benefit. The conventional wisdom suggests, for example, that more schooling provides access to better jobs. When better jobs — or any jobs — are unavailable, students are likely to see through the schools' facade and become more cynical. Other students probably do not take the schools' messages very seriously and thus are not bothered by contradiction. For them, the school already lacks credibility compared to the street, their homes or work. Textbook notions of human freedom or dignity, for example, are easily dismissed as unrealistic or irrelevant. Cynicism borders on learned helplessness insofar as these students expect and accept that just the opposite — constraint and indignity — are 'the way it is' and likely to be in their foreseeable future.

It is also possible that contradictions are seen as a normal aspect of human experience and, as such, offer choices regarding which messages to act on or even opportunities to create one's own interpretations. Whether contradictions within schooling and its relation to the wider society become impetus to critical redefinition and reconstruction depends, in part, on how contradictory messages are mediated by teachers, students, and other school personnel. By mediation I mean the interpretative process by which people make sense of or create meaning from experience. Mediation is an intervening and linking process between messages on the one hand and meanings and actions on the other.

In schools, mediation occurs in at least two interrelated ways, one organizational and the other individual and collective. Schools as organizations mediate among community and wider sociocultural values and the experiences that are made available to students. External interests are thus filtered through structural arrrangements. Structural mediation, however, does not directly shape students' school experience and learning. Nor does it completely shape the further mediation by teachers as professionals and individuals and by students as individuals and group members. An adequate account of schooling and curriculum would accommodate both forms of mediation and the dynamic relations between them.

Neither functionalist nor structuralist conceptualizations are adequate to this task. Implicit in both functionalist and structuralist social theory are the assumptions that schools reflect the larger society and that the schools' messages are transmitted in such a manner that they are accepted by most students. Nominal messages are taken to be effective, and, by implication, students are viewed as passive receptors or helpless victims. However, not all messages are effectively transmitted, and students differentially mediate curriculum and school experience, both individually and collectively.[34] Underlying the concept of mediation is the assumption that people, including students, are active participants in the creation and interpetation of their social environments and actions. But students are not independent agents; they are shaped by history and culture, through prior personal experience in that history and culture, and by the immediate social relations and practices of schooling. The relationship of individual, history, and setting is a dynamic one that is neither mechanistic nor predetermining.

Illustrations of student mediation of school experience are abundant, including their differential interpretation of the relative importance of school subjects, the appropriate roles of men and women and the meaning of particular teaching behaviors. Teacher praise, for example, may be experienced as rewarding and to be sought after by one student and as embarrassing and to be avoided by another. Most students appear neither to adopt intact nor completely reject the various messages of schooling. Between the extremes of commitment and rebellion are options ranging from detached acceptance and accommodation, to resistance, redefinition and subversion. As Waller has convincingly argued, some conflict between students and their teachers and schools is inherent in 'the condition' of compulsory, mass instruction. Even in, 'the orthodox school, old-style', students:

> inevitably attempted to establish their own social order independently
> of teachers . . . The social order which the teacher worked out in
> advance and attempted to establish could never be quite complete . . .
> In the interstices . . . there sprang up spontaneous life of students.
> There was always a loophole, and life always found the loophole . . .

The conflict that always arose between the teacher definitions and the pupil definitions...was made more severe by the fact that the students never quite accepted the teacher-ordained social order as one of the unalterable facts of life.[35]

Many students, for example, seem to become adept at 'playing school', that is, keeping up appearances, and seem to go along in order to gain advantage without internalizing the school's values or views of the world.[36] For example, in her study of an 'effective' inner-city elementary school, Felsenthal found that a student's school success, i.e., grades, depended as much or more on attitudes and behavior as on academic ability or performance and that students were well aware of the importance of proper attitude and good behavior.[37] In response to the interview question, 'How do you earn grades for your report card?' fifth and sixth graders' comments included:

If you want to earn good grades you got to hand in your work on time. You got to sit up straight and don't talk to no one.

You have to be quiet, be a nice student and know how to write and read and stuff.[38]

Other students may develop sophisticated forms of defiance, enabling them to avoid both subordination to school norms and getting into trouble with school authorities. They approach their school situation in ways not unlike the speeding motorist on the lookout for radar traps; instead of becoming more law-abiding, they become more adept at law-breaking. Given that schooling is only one of several influences on students and that these influences are mediated, how students differentially filter and act on messages conveyed by curriculum and schooling cannot be ignored in efforts to understand curriculum and school experience.

The Irony of Context in Isolation

It has been suggested that curriculum and school experience are complex and dynamic, comprised of contradictions and tensions, and always mediated by students and others within their social, structural and historical circumstances. This conception has compelling implications for curriculum studies, several of which are briefly explored here. (Further implications of a critical perspective for curriculum studies are considered in Chapter 8.)

What are needed are ways of understanding the contradictions inherent in and the mediation of curriculum and school experience — ways that enable us to comprehend the multidimensionality and dynamics of curriculum and context, avoiding both decontextualized micro-analyses of a curriculum facet and leaps of faith from such accounts to sociocultural explanations. To examine curriculum or context in isolation from each other is to use an inappropriate lens, with the possibilities of spurious conclusions — not unlike someone examining an interstate highway with a microscope and concluding that it does not go anywhere. An escape from the irony associated with studying context in isolation suggests contextualized inquiry rather than inquiry into context *per se*. Structural and sociocultural contexts are considered in relation to and interacting with curriculum phenomena. External relationships as well as internal patterns are examined. What is background in one instance may be foreground in another.

Neither conventional empirical-analytic nor interpretive research paradigms seem adequate. The pitfalls of 'abstracted empiricism' have been well documented.[39] Studies of school phenomena out of their context of time, place, and personal experience — history, social structure, and biography — can be misleading. Similarly, a reduction of context to discrete variables such as demographic characteristics, organization charts and dyadic interactions tends to be distorting. It is not sufficient merely to substitute social 'traits' for psychological ones. Social class, for example, is not simply a category representative of the distribution or possession of factors associated with occupation and income; it might superficially describe, but it does not explain. To categorize people in this way is also to suggest permanence and attribute status to the individual, obscuring the influence of history and social conditions and the possibility of change. The value of the concept of class lies in its indication of a differential and dynamic *relationship* among people and their social situations. It is a complex relationship of relative power and autonomy, which involves, for example, not only the nature of one's work but also other institutions including schooling and the use of goods, services and culture. Similarly, gender is much more than an independent variable with various correlates. It is 'a pattern of *relations* among people . . . an extensive and complex pattern, woven through all the institutions they live in . . . and shapes their lives at every level'.[40] The explicit and implicit contributions of curriculum and schooling to the perpetuation or dismantling of disabling sex-role stereotype are clearly more complex and subtle than matters of textbook content or athletic opportunities.

The presupposition that curriculum and schooling are embedded in contradictory contexts necessitates modification of conventional notions and study of causation. Complexity and mediation preclude neat causal laws and prediction. Explanation must be sought in terms of multiple reasons. Explanatory inquiry would take into account historical processes, structural conditions including roles and relationships, patterns of social interaction with and within those structures, and the actions of individuals as they contribute to the perpetuation or alteration of social situations, specifically curriculum and school experience. Such inquiry is both historical and rooted in concrete experience as it seeks to uncover structural and sociocultural arrangements that shape human relationships, actions and meanings. Although arguments that simply equate implicit messages with effects might be useful for critique of the seemingly antidemocratic and anti-intellectual features of curriculum and schooling, they simply offer tautologies or non-falsifiable theories that neither demonstrate nor explain the claimed oppression or how it might be mitigated.[41]

Our methods (i.e., concepts and procedures) of inquiry also need to be *critical* — to question or make problematic those aspects of schooling commonly accepted as normal or natural so as to reveal layers of meaning that are not usually part of our everyday awareness. In other words, our inquiries ought to probe beneath the veneer of supposedly self-evident and self-justifying assumptions and practices and enable us to expose the contradictions and possibilities inherent in historically- and culturally-formed school circumstances. Such inquiry is necessarily interpretative as well as material, incorporating participant conceptions and acknowledging our own values. What is called for, then, is inquiry that is sensitive to context and contradiction, including meanings to participants, and critical of prevailing school practices and illusions that impede realization of human potential and social justice. A hidden curriculum is not merely to be made visible but is to be interrogated as to its nature and function. The embeddedness and reciprocity of curriculum and context are made accessible with a focus on features of schooling that can be altered to enhance personal development and democratic community. Existing conditions are not taken as the limits of what might yet be.

Whereas conventional research naively aims to be apolitical, critical inquiry is explicitly normative. The former tends toward reification and, consequently, a conservatism that is accepting of the *status quo* and at least implicitly supportive of its continuance in the interest of technical control or practical understanding. In contrast, the interest of critical inquiry holds the potential of being emancipatory. To see through the facades and pretensions or schooling can be liberating, enabling us to 'reduce our collaboration with the accidents of birth and circumstance. Our perception of the whole and our relationship to it can be changed and enlarged with such vantage points'.[42] Critical inquiry can thus serve as a catalyst for change, not only to explain but also to reveal inherent contradictions in the structure of schooling and how repression or dissatisfaction can be alleviated by altering underlying structural conditions.[43]

Empirical investigations of (explicit and implicit) curriculum and school effects, as illustrated earlier, have had an individual focus. That is, investigators have sought evidence of effects on individual students and then aggregated their data, usually with the intent of identifying generalizable relationships. This approach is not surprising given the empirical-analytic paradigm and individual psychological orientation of most educational research. Another theoretical approach, one that seems particularly well suited to the concept of implicit curricula and the concerns of scholars who pursue it, is one that explores societal effects. In analyzing the effects of education, Meyer finds individualistic-collective socialization and allocation theories inadequate and posits a legitimation theory of 'the institutional impact of education on social structure' that distinguishes four categories of legitimating effects of education.[44] Along the knowledge dimension of his two-by-two matrix (knowledge and personnel effects by elite and mass audience) are categories of:

1 'authority of specialized competence' (elite), which 'does not simply allocate people to a fixed set of positions in society' but 'expands the authoritative culture and the set of specialized social positions entailed by this culture';[45] and
2 'universality of collective reality' (mass), which 'creates the assumptions of a national culture', thus expanding 'the social meaning of citizenship, personhood, and individuality'.[46]

Along the personnel dimension are modifications of more familiar categories of:

3 'elite definition and certification' (elite), which 'defines the nature and authority of the elite roles themselves — helping to create the categories of personnel as well as to designate the particular occupants of these categories';[47] and

4 'extension of membership: nation-building and citizenship' (mass), which expands 'both the meaning of citizenship and the set of persons who are seen as citizens', thus opening 'new possibilities for citizens — in particular, new claims for equality which can be made on society'.[48]

The value of Meyer's formulation here is two-fold. First, it directs attention to societal effects of education as an institution, such as cultural formation and nation-building. Second, it highlights generative effects of education in creating new knowledge and social roles. How curriculum and context contribute to such effects are important questions for critical inquiry. In what ways does curriculum as a contextualized social process contribute to cultural formation as well as transmission? What is the nature of this cultural formation? What implications might be drawn for curriculum and social change?

If concern with the anti-intellectual and undemocratic features of schooling is to be more than a wringing of hands or inspirational oratory, then prevailing notions of hidden curriculum are better put to rest. Beyond hidden curriculum, we might well engage the complexity and contradictions of curriculum as a structurally and socioculturally contextualized social process with critical studies and enlightened action.

Notes

1 Although Philip W. Jackson is acknowledged as the first to use the term 'hidden curriculum' in the US in *Life in Classrooms* (New York: Holt, Rinehart & Winston, 1968), the presence of what has become known as hidden curriculum was identified earlier by others. In *Experience and Education* (New York: Macmillan, 1938, p. 48), for example, John Dewey referred to the 'collateral learning' of attitudes that occurs in schools that may have more long-range importance than the explicit school curriculum. While Elizabeth Vallence ('Hiding the Hidden Curriculum: An Interpretation of the Language of Justification in Nineteenth-Century Educational Reform', in *Curriculum and*

Evaluation, ed. A. A. Bellack and H. M. Kliebard (Berkeley, CA: McCutchan, 1977)) has provided historical perspective regarding its origins, the hidden curriculum of contemporary schooling remains a notably elusive phenomenon. Also, see R. Dreeben, 'The Unwritten Curriculum and Its Relation to Values', *Journal of Curriculum Studies* 8(1976): 111–124; J. Martin, 'What Should We Do with a Hidden Curriculum When We Find One?' *Curriculum Inquiry* 6 (1976): 135–151; E. Vallance, 'The Hidden Curriculum and Qualitative Inquiry as States of Mind', *Journal of Education* 162 (1980): 138–151.

2 See, for example, H. A. Giroux and A. N. Penna, 'Social Education and the Classroom: The Dynamics of the Hidden Curriculum', *Theory and Research in Social Education* 7, 1 (1979): 21–42.

3 See J. Anyon, 'Social Class and the Hidden Curriculum of Work', *Journal of Education* 162 (1980): 67–92; J. Anyon, 'Social Class and School Knowledge', *Curriculum Inquiry* 11 (1981): 3–42; M. W. Apple and N. R. King, 'What Do Schools Teach?' *Curriculum Inquiry* 6 (1977): 341–358; R. Dreeben, *On What Is Learned in School* (Reading, MA: Addison-Wesley, 1968); R. Fielding, 'Social Education and School Change: Constraints of the Hidden Curriculum', in *Social/Political Education in Three Countries: Britain, West Germany and the United States*, ed. I. Morrissett and A. M. Williams (Boulder, CO: Social Science Education Consortium, 1981); J. Henry, 'Docility or Giving the Teacher What She Wants', *Journal of Social Issues* 11 (1955): 33–41. J. Henry, 'Attitude Organization in Elementary School Classrooms', *American Journal of Orthopsychiatry* 27 (1957): 117–133; P. W. Jackson, 1968, *op cit.*; N. V. Overly, ed., *The Unstudied Curriculum: Its Impact on Children* (Washington, DC: Association for Supervision and Curriculum Development, 1970); B. R. Snyder, *The Hidden Curriculum* (New York: Knopf, 1971).

4 E. Vallance, 1977, *op cit.*, pp. 601–602.

5 I. R. Weiss, *Report of the 1977 National Survey of Science, Mathematics, and Social Studies Education* (Research Triangle Park, NC: Research Triangle Institute, 1978).

6 M. W. Apple, 'The Hidden Curriculum and the Nature of Conflict', *Interchange* 2, 4 (1971): 27–40; T. S. Popkewitz, 'The Latent Values of the Discipline-Centered Curriculum', *Theory and Research in Social Education* 5, 1 (1977): 41–60; M. P. Riccards, 'Civic Books and Civic Virtue', *Child Study Journal* 2, 2 (1972): 67–74.

7 J. Anyon, 'Elementary Social Studies Textbooks and Legitimating Knowledge', *Theory and Research in Social Education* 6, 3 (1978): 40–55; J. Anyon, Ideology and United States History Textbooks', *Harvard Educational Review* 49, 3 (1979): 361–386.

8 C. A. Bowers, 'Cultural Literacy in Developed Countries', *Prospects* 7, 3 (1977): 323–335.

9 J. Anyon, 1981, *op cit.*

10 W. Korth, C. Cornbleth, and J. DeAngelis, unpublished study, University of Pittsburgh, 1981.

11 E. Smollett, 'Schools and the Illusion of Choice: The Middle Class; and the Open Classroom', *This Magazine* 7, 4 (1973): 10–13.

12 B. Bernstein, *Class and Pedagogies: Visible and Invisible* (Paris: Organisation for Economic Co-operation and Development, 1975); T. J. Czajkowski and M. King, 'The Hidden Curriculum and Open Education', *Elementary School Journal* 75, 5 (1975): 279–283; E. Smollett, 1973, *op cit.*

13 T. S. Popkewitz, B. R. Tabachnick and G. Wehlage, *The Myth of Educational Reform* (Madison, WI: University of Wisconsin Press, 1982).

14 M. LeCompte, 'Learning to Work: The Hidden Curriculum of the Classroom' *Anthropology and Education Quarterly* 9, 1 (1978): 23–37.

15 B. Bernstein, 1975, *op cit.*; A. M. Bussis, E. A. Chittendon and M. Amarel, *Beyond Surface Curriculum* (Boulder, CO: Westview, 1976); M. F. Klein, 'The 39th School', unpublished manuscript, University of Southern California, 1980; M. LeCompte, 1978, *op cit.*

16 M. LeCompte, 'The Civilizing of Children: How Young Children Learn to be Students', *Journal of Thought* 15, 3 (1980): 105–127.

17 C. Cornbleth and W. Korth, 'Teacher Perspectives and Meanings of Responsibility', *Educational Forum* 48, 4 (1984): 413–422.

18 M. LeCompte, 1978, *op cit.*

19 See, for example, L. H. Ehman, 'The American School in the Political Socialization Process', *Review of Educational Research* 50, 1 (1980): 99–119; C. Cornbleth, 'Citizenship Education', in *Encyclopedia of Educational Research*, ed. H. E. Mitzel (New York: Macmillan, The Free Press, 1982).

20 On an 'implicit civics curriculum', see W. D. Hawley, *The Implicit Civics Curriculum: Teacher Behavior and Political Learning* (Durham, NC: Duke University, Center for Policy Analysis, Institute of Policy Sciences and Public Affairs, 1976).

21 J. V. Torney, A. N. Oppenheim and R. F. Farnen, *Civic Education in Ten Countries* (New York: Wiley, 1975).

22 Note that this research assumes individual effects of implicit curricula that collectively affect society. An alternative approach is suggested in the last section of this chapter.

23 For example, M. Carnoy and H. M. Levin, *Schooling and Work in the Democratic State* (Stanford: CA: Stanford University Press, 1985).

24 See, for example, J. Oakes, *Keeping Track: How Schools Structure Inequality* (New Haven, CN and London: Yale University Press, 1985).

25 See, for example, J. Anyon, 1980, 1981, *op cit.*; J. L. Kapferer, 'Socialization and

the Symbolic Order of the School', *Anthropology and Education Quarterly* 12 (1981): 258–274; K. Wilcox, 'Differential Socialization in the Classroom: Implications for Equal Opportunity', in *Doing the Ethnography of Schooling: Educational Anthropology in Action*, ed. G. Spindler (New York: Holt, Rinehart and Winston, 1982).

26 See R. W. Connell, D. J. Ashenden, S. Kessler and G. W. Dowsett, *Making the Difference: Schools, Families, and Social Division* (Sydney: Allen & Unwin, 1982).

27 For example, A. Peshkin, *Growing Up American: Schooling and the Survival of Community* (Chicago: University of Chicago Press, 1978).

28 B.M. Franklin, *Building the American Community* (London and Philadelphia: Falmer Press, 1986).

29 For example, R. W. Connell *et al.*, 1982, *op cit.*; P. A. Cusick, *Inside High School* (New York: Holt, Rinehart & Winston, 1973).

30 For example, P. E. Willis, *Learning to Labour: How Working Class Kids Get Working Class Jobs* (Teakfield, UK: Saxon House, 1977).

31 For example, L. Weis, ' "Thirty Years Old and I'm Allowed to Be Late": The Politics of Time at an Urban Community College', *British Journal of Sociology of Education* 7, 3 (1986): 241–263.

32 For example, H. A. Giroux, *Theory and Resistance in Education* (South Hadley, MA: J. F. Bergin, 1983).

33 T. S. Popkewitz, 'The Sociological Bases for Individual Differences: The Relation of Solitude to the Crowd', in *Individual Differences and the Common Curriculum*, Eighty-second Yearbook of the National Society for the Study of Education, Part I, ed. G. D. Fenstermacher and J. I. Goodlad (Chicago: University of Chicago Press, 1983).

34 See L.H. McNeil, 'Negotiating Classroom Knowledge: Beyond Achievement and Socialization', *Journal of Curriculum Studies* 13 (1981): 313–328.

35 W. Waller, *The Sociology of Teaching* (New York: Wiley, 1932), pp. 309–310.

36 On 'strategic compliance,' see C. Lacey, *The Socialization of Teachers* (London: Methuen, 1977).

37 H. Felsenthal, 'Factors Influencing School Effectiveness: An Ecological Analysis of an "Effective" School', paper presented at the annual meeting of the American Educational Research Association, New York City, March 1982.

38 *Ibid.*, p. 10.

39 C. W. Mills, *The Sociological Imagination* (New York: Oxford University Press, 1959); E. G. Mishler, 'Meaning in Context: Is There Any Other Kind?' *Harvard Educational Review* 49 (1979): 1–19.

40 R. W. Connell *et al.*, *op cit.*, pp. 33–34.

41 See, for example, C. Cornbleth, 'A Reaction to "Social Education in the Classroom: The Dynamics of the Hidden Curriculum" ', *Theory and Research in*

Social Education 8, 2 (1980): 57–60; H. A. Giroux, and A. N. Penna, 'Response to Cornbleth', *Theory and Research in Social Education* 8, 2 (1980): 61–64.

42 T. S. Popkewitz, *Paradigm and Ideology in Educational Research: The Social Functions of the Intellectual* (London: Falmer Press, 1984), p. 194.

43 See B. Fay, *Social Theory and Political Practice* (London: Allen & Unwin, 1975) on the relation of critical theory and practice.

44 J. W. Meyer, 'The Effects of Education as an Institution', *American Journal of Sociology* 83, 1 (1977): 55–77, p. 65.

45 *Ibid.*, p. 67.

46 *Ibid.*, p. 69.

47 *Ibid.*, p. 68.

48 *Ibid.*, pp. 69–70.

Chapter 4

Curriculum Practice

The focus here is on field studies of curriculum or classroom practice for the purpose of 'bringing to life' ideas introduced in previous chapters, particularly the critical conception of curriculum as contextualized social process. A related purpose is to foreshadow the consideration of education system/structural conditioning and change in Chapter 5 and of the State and politics of curriculum control in Chapters 6 and 7.

The selection of classroom and school based field studies is not an arbitrary one. Empirical-analytic or conventional quantitative studies typically focus on one or a few classroom events such as teacher questions or student time-on-task. Relatively few examine classroom interaction between teacher and students or among students. They simply cannot (and do not intend to) convey the breadth, complexity, or dynamics of classroom processes. In addition, their purpose is to generalize findings across settings, which necessitates ignoring, controlling, or 'averaging out' context factors. Context that here is taken to be crucial to understanding curriculum and change is seen as a threat to external validity in conventional educational research.[1]

The field studies that I draw on represent a range of methodologies, spanning interpretive and critical research paradigms. All provide a rich description of classroom and curriculum processes although their researchers-authors may not have framed their studies or interpretations in curricular terms or with particular attention to context or critique. Where context or critique is 'thin', I take the liberty of suggesting further interpretations or questions that might be pursued in order to better understand curriculum practice. Two of the studies examine on-going curriculum practice while three studies examine curriculum practice in relation to change efforts. Finally, if I devote more space to studies in which I have had a part, it is not because they are better but because I have access to more relevant data from my own work than from others'.

Creating the Curriculum

'Creating the Curriculum: Beginning the Year in a Middle School'[2] was a follow-up to an earlier, more quantitatively oriented field study of classroom activities that was conducted with English, science, and social studies teachers in a suburban US, public middle school.[3] Despite the school staff's apparent seriousness of purpose, many of the academic tasks presented to students seemed trivial to us. For example, while 90 per cent of class time was spent in academic activities, only 21 per cent was devoted to comprehension or reasoning tasks as distinguished from information acquisition or reproduction tasks.[4] Interested in how the curriculum came into being, we returned the following year to investigate how teachers and students created their curriculum at the beginning of the school year. After briefly introducing the school site, participating teachers, and study procedures, I describe the first day of school and then present our analysis of the curriculum that was created, with particular attention to social organization and academic learning opportunity. Observations regarding social organization and academic learning opportunity are presented separately and then interrelated in an interpretation of the kinds of messages communicated by and the apparent implications of this case of curriculum practice.

The study site was a seventh-eighth grade middle school. The school serves all the students in the district, which includes three communities adjacent to a north-eastern US city. The 530 students represented a range of socioeconomic backgrounds; although some students qualified for free lunches, the large majority were middle-class, and almost all were white. Students' standardized test scores were reported to be at or above national norms, and there were no apparent student behaviour or faculty morale problems at the school. While old, the school building was well maintained, and hallways were colorfully decorated with student murals. The residential neighborhood immediately surrounding the school also was old and unpretentious but well maintained.

All nine of the twelve teachers from the previous study who remained at the school were willing to participate in the follow-up study. Six were selected on the basis of subject area, grade level, and class schedule so as to include one seventh and one eighth grade class for each of the three subject areas (English, science, and social studies). With one exception (seventh grade English), the teachers were male. All but one (eighth grade English) had more than ten years of teaching experience. They impressed us as career teachers, that is, teachers who believe their work is important, enjoy most of it most of the time, and intend to remain in teaching.

Data were obtained by means of (a) daily observation of the six classes during the first week of the school year and one observation per week for each of the next three weeks, (b) monitoring activities in the school office and (c) informal interviews with staff members. These data were supplemented with information obtained from school documents (e.g., student handbook, daily absence sheet and announcements) and the previous year's extended observation-interview study.[5]

A dominant impression of the first day of school was orderliness and calm. When the first busloads of students arrived, Dave[6], the seventh grade social studies teacher, was on bus duty as last year, coffee cup in hand, welcoming and directing students. Inside the school, it seemed like any day except that there were fewer teachers in the workroom drinking coffee or running off dittos; most were in the halls, greeting familiar students and asking new ones if they needed help finding their homeroom. Separate orientation assemblies for seventh and eighth grade students were held in the gym during an extended homeroom period. At these assemblies, students were welcomed back to school, informed of key school rules, and urged to assume responsibility by co-operating (following the rules), paying attention and participating in class and making an effort to do well. Then, classes proceeded on a modified schedule with relatively few interruptions from the office or from lost or late students. The school bureaucracy was operating smoothly.

The teachers' major goal during the first days of school seemed to be to create a personal image and classroom atmosphere — as if setting the stage for a play that they would be starring in and directing. The means they employed and the images they created varied considerably. Illustrative of the differences among teachers are the following teacher comments to their students on the first day of school:

> This is my room. I am the king, and you are the subjects. (eighth grade science teacher)

If you don't aggravate me, I won't aggravate you . . . As long as you do what I tell you, we'll get along fine. (seventh grade social studies teacher)

You are very important to me. If you are worried, see me. I want you to be successful this year. (seventh grade English teacher)

Despite striking differences in style, there were significant commonalities in the messages communicated by the six teachers as they attempted, with apparent success, to establish their preferred image and classroom atmosphere. Two messages predominated: (a) teachers should be obeyed, and students would benefit from accepting and meeting teacher standards; and (b) students should not worry about subject matter learning and grades, at least not at this time. All six teachers appeared to us as acting in what they saw as their students' best interests. They presented themselves as knowledgeable helpers and expected their students to trust them.

While the teachers were assertive in creating a classroom social organization, they seemed to be easing students into academic activities. For the most part, academic demands were minimal, consisting of reviews or introductions such as a discussion of 'What's science?' and 'What do scientists do?' in the seventh grade science class. The implication was that if students make an effort, they will get passing grades; school is to be taken seriously, but not everyone is expected to do well academically. Only Harry placed any emphasis on academic learning, telling his eighth grade English class on the first day of school that 'Basically, we're going to learn in here — writing, reading, and grammar'. He emphasized that this might be the students' 'last chance' to learn basic skills such as spelling and writing and that basic writing and reading skills are important for any job.

Social Organization and Academic Learning Opportunity

Efforts to create classroom social organizational groundrules, usually in the form of behavioral or procedural regulations, were quite explicit during the first weeks of school as were the rules themselves. In contrast, academic expectations remained less clear, at least less clearly academic in any traditional sense.

Students seemed to anticipate and accept that establishment of classroom social rules would be initiated and controlled by the teacher. For example, on the first day of school, students in the seventh grade social studies class talked among themselves as they entered the room. When the bell rang and Dave entered, they were seated and silent, looking up at him expectantly. After six or more years of school experience, students seemed to know what is expected of them.

For the most part, rules were presented matter-of-factly by the teachers, sometimes written on the chalkboard, and usually explained or justified. Being on time and having your materials so class can start when the bell rings means that time is not wasted getting ready to work. Gary, the eighth grade social studies teacher, told his students, 'It is your job. Bring the tools of your trade to class. What would you think of a plumber who arrived without tools?'

Several teachers also indicated the consequences of noncompliance with classroom rules (i.e., detention for being late to class). Gary warned his students that he would 'blow up' if they interrupted a speaker or disrupted a presentation. Emphasizing that students were not to go behind his desk where he kept a variety of science laboratory supplies, Wally, the seventh grade science teacher, told students that anyone who did would end up with 'a long skinny neck with [my] fingerprints on it'. Such exaggerated threats and humor seemed to have a double message — 'I mean what I say', but 'I'm not a bad guy'. The teachers also used humor to make commands more palatable and deter possibly hostile student reactions. Asking students to speak up so that he could hear them, Gary commented, 'People [like me] who lose their hair are old and hard of hearing'. In additon to presenting and explaining rules, and sometimes indicating the consequences of noncompliance, the teachers reviewed rules with students, and, in some classes, the rules appeared on quizzes.

The patterns of interaction that emerged in the six classes were clearly teacher dominated. Teachers initiated interactions with the expectation that students would respond. Usually, teachers addressed the class as a whole. Private teacher interactions with individual students were infrequent in most classes, and student-student interaction was discouraged.

During these first days of school, students seemed generally accepting of the teachers' rule announcements and follow-up tactics. Most students did not appear either surprised or resentful; from their facial expressions, some seemed a bit amused at times. Students accepted the teachers' claim to set the rules and wanted to know the groundrules.[7] They were not consulted about the rules nor did they take any initiative in this regard. They waited for the teachers to tell them what to do (or not to do), when, where and how. Although students were not consulted, their compliance and acceptance of the teachers' authority 'implicates them in the joint construction of the social world of the classroom'.[8] Teachers cannot establish authority without student consent; in effect, students have power to grant or deny teacher authority. In the classes we observed, students did not deny teacher authority. They did, however, engage in minor rule violations (e.g., talking without permission, not turning in homework on time) as if to test the limits of the teachers' tolerance, i.e., the circumstances where the announced rules were the actual, operating groundrules.

In contrast to the explicit classroom social organizational groundrules, substantive academic expectations remained largely implicit and somewhat vague. Teachers seemed concerned not to overwhelm students academically. Academic-social contrasts were most apparent in the seventh grade social studies class. While Dave was adamant that students behave as he directed, he encouraged students to ask questions about assignments and generally presented himself as their academic helper. On the third day of school, for example, after indicating the difficulty and importance of the topic (the earth's rotations and revolution around the sun), he said, 'If I lose you say something. Don't let me go on', and he responded helpfully to student questions. He also was receptive to student questions that went beyond the assignments and to student disagreement regarding the 'right answer'.

Along with the nondemanding nature of the academic tasks, the pace of activities in the science and social studies classes was slow, particularly during the first week. Seatwork-worksheet activities, for example, often were teacher directed in a step-by-step manner with comments such as 'don't write in the answer until I tell you', 'one part at a time', and 'just hold up for a second'. Ample time was provided for students to complete other in-class reading and writing assignments. Students who finished early were advised to 'get a magazine or find something to do'. The English classes, in contrast, moved at a brisker pace, perhaps because many of the activities involved review of previously studied subject matter (e.g., grammar, dictionary use).

Despite subject area differences, 'basic' skills were emphasized in all the classes, for example, vocabulary in science and social studies, spelling and grammar in English. Study skills such as outlining and map and graph reading also had high priority. Importantly, skills were often addressed in isolation from subject matter. For example, during the second and third weeks, students in the seventh grade social studies class were reading and constructing bar, line, circle, and pictographs. One set of graphs in their workbooks showed the average annual income of black and white families in the US, 1964-1976, clearly illustrating the increasing gap between them. In a review activity, workbook questions about the graphs were answered without any mention of the substance and implications of the information presented. Also, while comprehension tasks were not uncommon in these classes, only one instance of student involvement in reasoning or problem-solving tasks was observed. Here too, skills were separated from subject matter insofar as students were solving puzzles unrelated to the physical science they had been studying.

Grading procedures usually were described in detail by the teachers. All six used a point system in which each assignment was worth a certain number of points, and report card grades were determined on the basis of the total number of points students earned, not unlike a factory piecework system or a salesperson's commission. In most classes, tests counted less than in-class and homework assignments.

Consistent with these grading procedures, teachers emphasized 'doing the work' and 'making an effort'. Doing the work usually meant completing written assignments, such as worksheets and outlines, and turning them in on time. Paying attention and participating in class by answering teacher questions also were expected. The implication was that students would be held accountable and that everything counted. The substance and quality of work rarely were mentioned; more often, teachers told students not to worry if they had difficulty with a task. The emphasis on timeliness and effort seemed intended to reassure students that they all could get at least C or B grades. Gary, for example, told his students that none of them had to fail, that no one should get less than a B, and that grades depend on turning in assignments on time. By defining academic expectations primarily in terms of doing the work, the teachers seemed to be establishing standards that most students could meet, thereby increasing the likelihood that both they and their students would be successful. While some students seemed restless at times, no direct student objections or counterproposals to the teachers' academic expectations were observed.

Academic expectations were established in much the same way as classroom social rules — by means of teacher presentation, repetition, explanation, indication of the consequences of noncompliance, and follow-up in the form of reminders, encouragement and exhortation to do the work. However, there was little humor here; work was to be taken seriously. What students were expected to learn was important, their teachers told them, for doing well on achievement tests and in high school and beyond. For example, after asking students what material objects they would 'really like', and suggesting such things as a Rolls Royce, a house with a swimming pool, and a physician's license, Gary continued:

> How do you achieve these dreams? The grades you make from this point on are extremely important. If you graduate from high school with an A average, your chances are better at achieving your goals. Grades are your payment for job performance. Thirteen years in school determine what you will do in 47 years in the labor force.

Students seemed generally accepting of their teachers' academic expectations. That most students did take their teachers, if not the work, seriously was indicated by their many questions about grading procedures and assignments (e.g., 'Should we copy that (what was written on the chalkboard) in our notebooks?') and their doing the work.

Congruence between academic expectations and learning opportunities on the one hand and social organization on the other was quite evident in these classes. The social groundrules provided an environment conducive to doing the work. If students did not bring a pencil and notebook to class, for example, they could not get their work done. With the exception of the seventh grade science class, which was more loosely organized, the classes became highly structured and teacher-directed. Teacher defined and enforced orderliness and work became the norm.

Classroom academic and social organizational groundrules were supported and encouraged by the school administration and documents such as the staff and student handbooks. In describing what they expected students to learn, the principal and assistant principal used the phrase, 'academic responsibility', by which they meant following the rules and doing the work, the assumption being that as a result the school would run smoothly and students would learn what they needed to know. Apparent consensus regarding school goals and practices served to realize and maintain them. The modesty, neatness, and care of the school building and surrounding neighborhoods appeared to be reflected in the curriculum being created in these classrooms.

At the organizational level, the emerging groundrules and routines enabled the school to operate smoothly and students to learn what adults believed was important for them to know, i.e., what was needed to do well on achievement tests, in high school and at anticipated adult jobs. Parents and school district administrators appeared to be satisfied, even pleased, with the school. We did not encounter any questioning of school goals or means of achieving them. The language and practice of academic responsibility and preparation for the future seemed congruent with community expectations. Assuming that the beginning of the school year establishes a backdrop for what follows, how did it seem to extend, constrain and shape subsequent social and academic learning opportunities? What messages were communicated to students, and what purposes were served?

Limited Opportunity, Conservative Message and Purpose

The teachers' management of their classrooms seemed to provide an orderly social environment that was relatively predictable and comfortable for both teachers and students. Establishing routines, for example, reduced demands on the teachers' attention, enabling them to get down to business and attend to other matters such as students' difficulties and concerns. Once rules and routines were established, they tended to be maintained by participants' shared expectations and sense of mutual obligation. If relatively stable interaction patterns had not been established, then teaching-learning opportunities might have been limited by recurring management problems, and much less class time could have been spent with academic activities.

The teachers' emphasis on order and personal control, on students following rules and directions, resulted in clearly differentiated super- and subordinate teacher and student roles. Emerging activity patterns were highly structured by the teachers. An orderly flow of teacher-directed activities seems to have had several benefits: (a) there was ample and equal opportunity for students to learn something (e.g., since students were to be seated quietly with their materials on their desks when the bell rang, academic activity could and usually did begin immediately); (b) some degree of privacy and security within the classroom group was provided to individuals; and (c) student compliance allowed the teacher to assist individual students while the others were 'working'.

At the same time, learning opportunities were constrained, and student academic initiative, while usually tolerated, generally was not encouraged. The priority given to an orderly flow of activities seemed to discourage divergent thinking and reasoning about academic matters and the expression of student ideas and beliefs except during assigned creative writing periods in English. Much of the time in class was spent in modified recitation (teacher questions, student answers, and teacher elaborations) and individual seatwork, both intended to foster the acquisition, recall and application of factual information. Also, the slow pacing of academic activities in most classes may have limited students' opportunity to learn. Among the messages that might be communicated by these management and instructional practices are that one's own thoughts and feelings are unimportant, that patience and passive compliance are rewarded while initiative and originality are not, and that learning (or work) occurs primarily in situations structured and supervised by others.

The priority that teachers gave to establishing and maintaining their authority in the classroom social order appears to have precluded open-ended, interactive activities. Also militating against such activities were the grading system and the prevailing definition of success in terms of making an effort and doing the work. It is more difficult to demonstrate effort and assign points to work accomplished in the absence of predetermined right answers.

Except for tests, students seldom knew in advance what academic tasks or subject matter their teachers had planned for them, and specific academic expectations other than doing the work were seldom explicit. As a result, there seemed to be little sense of continuity or movement toward meaningful academic goals. The clear implication was that students should trust the teacher to know and do what was best for them and that they should follow wherever the teacher led. In these ways, the teachers seemed to be encouraging dependency. For the most part, the responsibility that students were expected to assume was limited to that delegated and defined by teachers. Also, to some extent, the teachers may have been fostering intellectual mediocrity. Students could succeed in school by making an effort and doing the work. Teachers generally did not seem to expect or want more than this. The intent seemed benevolent — to reassure students and encourage them to try. Yet, the teachers also appeared to be communicating low expectations.[9]

Meanings given to authority, work, and success further illustrate the seemingly constraining nature of the curriculum created in these classrooms.[10]

Authority was claimed by the teachers largely on the basis of personal expertise and assertion. It was implicitly and broadly defined as the right to decide, supervise and evaluate classroom activity. Teacher demands, moderated by humor, justification and expression of concern for students appeared to be accepted as reasonable by most students. Authority was a characteristic or right of some teachers (i.e., those who worked hard and earned it), which was inaccessible to students. Here, as in Dreeben's analysis of school experience and authority,[11] students had ample opportunity to learn how to cope with and make the best of subordinate positions in authority relationships, but they had little opportunity to learn to assume authority and responsibility for themselves.

Regarding work, it was not uncommon for teachers to compare students to employees. 'I'll treat you as if this were your job and I'm your employer', Mike told his students on the first day of school. Much of the work that students were to accomplish was mechanistic in form and substance — more like that of factory or office personnel than of managers, professionals, or artists. Students were expected to do the work but not to participate in its planning or evaluation; they had little voice in deciding what they would do, how they would do it, or the basis on which it would be evaluated. Also, while schoolwork was to be taken seriously, it was not presented as enjoyable or satisfying in itself, but as a means to future, usually material rewards. Generally, it was presented as instrumental to survival in a routinized and sometimes hostile adult world. Norms of orderliness, timeliness and effort also were justified in terms of preparation for adult work. It seems that the activities, interactions, and sentiments that constitute schoolwork and, by implication, foreshadow adult work, come to be taken for granted and accepted not only as the way things are but also as how they should be.[12]

The operative definition of success at the middle school reflected the meanings given to authority and work. School success was defined primarily in terms of points earned for grades and promotion to the next grade level. School success, in turn, would lead to adult success on the job and material comfort. The prevailing message was that quality of school life and life after school depends on the quantity of things possessed (e.g., points, automobile) and that survival and success defined in these terms are achieved by fitting in and making the best of one's situation, not by trying to change it. Although not necessarily contrary to students' present and future interests, the messages about authority, work and success are conservative of the *status quo*. In a sense, we were witness to the middle class schooling itself.

Overall, the knowledge that was made available to students was fragmented rather than integrated. Basic skills and facts were acquired separately, and skills seldom were used to comprehend or interrogate information. Fragmentation thus limited the power of the knowledge that students acquired. Fragmentation combined with teacher direction seemed to encourage student dependency by suggesting that students could not learn on their own, without teacher guidance, and that students could not generate or create knowledge. In addition, the slow pacing of academic activities and the emphasis on effort or doing the work more than on learning limited the breadth and depth of knowledge that students might acquire either on their own or with teacher guidance. Clearly, teacher mediation of knowledge was pervasive and constraining.

This study paid more attention to the curriculum and its construction as a social process than to curriculum context. Our focus was on the establishment of classroom social organization, including teacher and student roles, patterns of interaction and norms that seemed to shape what students had an opportunity to learn and how they were enabled to learn it. Curriculum documents appeared to play a minor role in this process. None of the teachers relied on or even followed a single textbook. Multiple instructional materials, including teacher-made materials, were used frequently. Curriculum practice in each classroom appeared to be shaped less by courses of study, textbooks, or official mandates than by institutionally sanctioned teacher beliefs and teacher-student interactions. Among the contextual factors shaping curriculum in this school, the congruence of teacher priorities and practices with administrative and community expectations is particularly striking. Major shortcomings of this account of curriculum are its failure to examine historical antecendents to the observed present and its failure to probe the structural and sociocultural contexts of curriculum beyond the school and its immediate community. In other words, understanding of the curriculum in this school is hampered by its limited contextualization.

Curriculum and Control

In Contradictions of Control, McNeil examines links between school organization and priorities on the one hand and the selection, organization, and treatment of social studies knowledge on the other.[13] Her work well illustrates how school and school district levels of structural context influence curriculum practice. Drawing on her field studies of social studies teaching in four seemingly typical US public high schools, she shows how curriculum knowledge is largely a function of school organization and administrative emphasis on either controlling students or educating them.

While 'defensive teaching' was observed at all four schools, it was more common at the two schools where administrators distanced themselves from curricular concerns, providing little academic support for teachers, and gave priority to controls on students and, less overtly, on teachers. Defensive teaching 'cut across differences in teachers' individual political and pedagogical philosophies and across formal definitions of variations in student abilities',[14] suggesting that its occurrence was more a function of school context than individual 'style'. According to McNeil, when

> administrative personnel expend most of the staff's time, meetings and resources on discussions of hall order, discipline and numbers of course credits earned, teachers respond with overt but usually reluctant compliance on those goals, but reduce effort and aim for only minimal standards in their actual teaching.[15]

In such structural contexts, McNeil found that teachers

> choose to simplify content and reduce demands on students in return for classroom order and minimal student compliance on assignments ... they teach 'defensively', choosing methods of presentation and evaluation that they hope will make their workload more efficient and create as little student resistance as possible.[16]

Defensive teaching, which controls students by controlling classroom knowledge, is characterized by (a) fragmentation or reducing information, such as New Deal programs, to lists, (b) mystification or presenting a complex or controversial topic, such as the Federal Reserve System or socialism, as important but unknowable, (c) omission, for example, of contemporary events in US history, and (d) defensive simplification or seeking 'students' compliance on a lesson by promising that it will not be difficult and will not go into any depth',[17] that is, 'the ritual of seeming to deal with the topic'.[18] Analysis of relationships between school organization or administrative context and the occurrence of defensive teaching revealed a parallel between administrators' attempts to gain minimal compliance from teachers and teachers' settling for minimal compliance from students. In those schools where administrators devoted most of the schools' staff time and resources to maintaining order and to attending to such details as course credits, the administrators paid less attention to the academic quality of teaching. The content of the curriculum was clearly secondary to the maintenance of order. Teachers in these schools tended to expend minimal effort in the classroom; frequently this was deliberate and was explained by the teacher as retaliation for or reluctant accommodation to administrative pressure for precision in paperwork, extra hall monitoring, or extended meetings related to such matters as graduation requirements.[19]

In contrast, at the school where administrators most supported teaching and provided incentives for instructional quality,

> teachers responded by demanding more of themselves in the presentation and preparation of lessons. They felt, and demonstrated, less of a wall between their personal knowledge and the 'official' knowledge of the classroom. They developed entire courses, used original handouts and continually collected and re-designed materials. They used fewer lists and provided more extended descriptions, more opportunities for student discussion, more varieties of learning experiences . . . [20]

At another school, a strong social studies department chair mediated administrators' preoccupation with student control and supported meaningful teaching and learning. However, the teachers tended not to take advantage of the opportunity to teach other than defensively. The presence of some variation in school structural context and associated curriculum practice across the four sites indicates both the importance of school structural context and its variability within a decentralized education system.

The contradiction that McNeil's studies and analysis highlight is that efforts to improve schooling by means of regulation or control have the opposite effect of encouraging defensive teaching and minimizing meaningful learning. Her account of the school organizational and administrative aspects of the structural context of social studies curriculum vividly illustrates their influence on what students have an opportunity to learn in their social studies classes.

> Defensive, controlling teaching does more than make content boring; it transforms the subject content from 'real world' knowledge into 'school knowledge', an artificial set of facts and generalizations whose credibility lies no longer in its authenticity as a cultural selection but in its instrumental value in meeting the obligations teachers and students have within the institution of schooling. The potential richness of such content as historical events, and their interpretations and the conflicts inherent in economic systems, are flattened into . . . lists, slogans and mystifications . . . [21]

While giving more attention to the historical and structural context of the school than did 'Creating the Curriculum', *Contradictions of Control* also fails to probe the structural and sociocultural contexts of curriculum much beyond the school and its immediate community. Ironically, the focus on school structural context may result in overestimating its influence on curriculum practice. McNeil's teachers appear to be largely reactive rather than active or proactive in shaping their teaching situations. One wonders whether these teachers are truly victims of an overwhelmingly oppressive school organization and administration, simply poor teachers who would or could not take advantage of a more supportive teaching situation if it were provided, or perhaps just exhausted veterans who have given up fighting 'the system'. In any event, their apparent passivity or acquiescence is disturbing.

Reforming Curriculum Reform

Whereas the two cases just presented were concerned with on-going curriculum practice, this one and the two that follow deal with curriculum practice in relation to change efforts. In *The Myth of Educational Reform*, Popkewitz, Tabachnick, and Wehlage show how six US public elementary schools adapted the IGE (Individually Guided Education) curriculum management reform to their own situations and purposes.[22] All six schools had been identified as model implementors of the IGE reform.[23] However, school personnel used IGE in very different ways compatible with their local school and community contexts. They did not simply adapt the IGE program to reach a common goal; they adapted both the IGE technology and its stated goals in ways that helped to conserve differing prior conditions in the schools. The authors characterized these conditions of schooling as illusory, technical and constructive. These differences are explained in terms of the interrelated social contexts of the schools: a pedagogical context, an occupational context of teaching and a social/cultural context.[24]

Pedagogical context consists of 'the daily practices and discourse of classroom life and the patterns of this activity which produce conceptions of school work and knowledge'.[25] What are the underlying assumptions and routine operating procedures that define what counts as worthwhile knowledge or learning and what constitutes appropriate classroom tasks? The IGE study clearly revealed different answers to this question.

Constructive schooling (one school) 'emphasizes multiple ways by which children can come to know about the world . . . how knowledge is created . . . Knowledge is treated as permeable and provisional, ideas as tentative, and often ambiguous'.[26] In the constructive school, students were offered opportunities to pursue their own interests, engage in a variety of activities, and examine a broad range of knowledge and possibilities. Learning activities were designed to foster students' interpersonal and communication ability, and students were expected to demonstrate independence and initiative as well as responsibility. Comprehension rather than memorization was valued, with curriculum knowledge often being integrated across subject boundaries and related to students' experiences. It was assumed that knowledge is tentative, that there are multiple ways of learning and knowing, and that different perspectives ought to be considered. For example, along with government structures and processes, students in a constructive school might examine various meanings of democracy and possibilities of economic and social as well as political democracy.

Technical schooling (three schools) emphasizes procedures to enhance efficiency. 'Knowledge was standardized; all important ideas and skills were measurable and expressed in a discrete, sequenced form . . . technologies and procedures rose to the status of values'.[27] Students in technical schools typically were offered a preplanned series of activities intended to produce measurable competencies that could be recorded as students demonstrated mastery of them, often by completing worksheets. Curriculum knowledge was limited, for the most part, to presumably discrete skills and bits of information. Official learning (what counted for grades) tended to be mechanical and unrelated to students' experiences, the apparent assumption being that knowledge is standardized and that right answers can be predetermined. Students were expected to strive to attain the objectives set for them — within the bounds of explicit discipline and management procedures intended to promote efficiency.

Illusory schooling (two schools), in contrast, provides little academic or subject matter knowledge as

> children and teachers engage in the rituals and ceremonies of reading, writing, and arithmetic, but in practice the lessons contain many instances in which the substance of teaching is not carried through. What occurs is an emphasis on form *as* substance . . . . The discourse of schooling emphasizes co-operation, hard work, respect for property, and delay of gratification — qualities that teachers in illusory schools believe are not taught at home and have to be built into the school before any 'real academic' learning can take place.[28]

For example, students in illusory schools might recite the Pledge of Allegiance daily but rarely if ever engage in examination of the concepts of republic, liberty, or justice.

Occupational context 'refers to the teaching occupation as a social community which maintains ideologies and mechanisms of legitimacy',[29] for example, beliefs about how young people develop and learn, about how best to teach various skills and subjects, and about how to adapt teaching to the perceived needs of different student groups.[30] Teachers assert that, as professionals, they know what is best for their students' learning. Occupational context, which shapes pedagogical context, is shaped in turn by social/cultural context as well as by teacher associations and collective experience.

Social/cultural context refers to the community in which a school is located and 'the manner in which a community's social/cultural and economic orientations, sensibilities, and awarenesses affect school practices'.[31] It also includes 'social demands which reflect both local concerns and larger social and cultural issues'.[32] In all six schools, the teachers' and administrators' perceptions of community lifestyles, occupations, values and expectations influenced their adaptation of the IGE reform. According to Popkewitz:

> In two of the three technical schools, for example, there was an emphasis on teaching the functional skills, responsibility, and

discipline that teachers believed would enable the children to succeed in the blue-collar or low-status service occupations of their parents. The intellectual and social point of view in the constructive school responded to the professional social and cultural orientation of a community in which interpersonal control, facility with language, and responsiveness to the subtle nuances of interpersonal situations are important. The illusory schools, located in poor communities, reflected the pedagogical ideology of pathology and therapy [i.e., the belief that the problems these students brought to school made academic teaching and learning impossible].[33]

Although differences among the schools were related to socioeconomic variations among the six communities, the schools did not simply mirror the economic situation of their location; there was not a one-to-one correspondence between SES and school practices. Technical schools for example, were found in a poor rural community, a working-middle-class suburb, and an affluent, religiously-oriented, business community. Further, different conditions of schooling were found in communities of similar SES; a technical school was found in one poor, working-class community and an illusory school in another. The technical school was located in the rural South where 'extended family relations went back for generations, and the school represented a valued communal feeling . . . teachers had a sense of optimism that children could be taught technical skills and knowledge'.[34] The illusory school was located in a medium size, northern industrial city where there was little sense of communal obligation and 'the teachers viewed the neighborhood's culture as pathological'.[35] Thus, religion, geographic location, and community continuity or stability as well as SES appear to be influential aspects of social/cultural context that shape conditions of schooling.

The focus of *The Myth of Educational Reform* is on classroom practice and change. Curriculum is treated as a contextualized social process, and the treatment of context extends beyond the individual teacher and classroom to the collective school culture and the school community. The purpose is not merely to describe supposedly exemplary practice but to probe beyond surface appearances and stated intentions in order to account for substantial differences in the learning opportunities made available to students in the six schools. The explication of occupational and social/cultural context links the immediate situation of the schools to larger social issues such as mobility, meritocracy and reproduction. Sociocultural context is emphasized while structural context is relatively underdeveloped. Whereas McNeil separates administrators and teachers and emphasizes the influence of administrative context on teaching practice, Popkewitz *et al.* seem to view school administrators and teachers as being similarly influenced by common, largely external, forces.

Critical Thinking and Curriculum

In the mid-1980s, I participated in a multi-year, collaborative (school district and university) project to reorient the social studies curriculum of a northeastern US, urban school district to foster critical thinking. My role was that of university consultant and co-ordinator of a field study that sought to understand how project teachers interpreted critical thinking in their conversation and classroom practice. We were interested in what occurred 'in the name of critical thinking' and what might account for the observed interpretations, to inform both the on-going project and understanding of curriculum change. Aspects of context that emerged as particularly salient were the teachers' pre-existing beliefs and teaching practices (Popkewitz *et al.*'s pedagogical and occupational contexts or teacher/school culture), the conditions of classroom teaching and school district goals and policies.[36]

The stated purpose of the Critical Thinking Project was to help students think critically and communicate critical thought through reading, discussion and essay writing in social studies. Initially, the Project Steering Committee composed of teachers and supervisors, in collaboration with university staff and consultants, focused its energies on creating diagnostic essay tests and rating guides to assess students' ability to communicate critical thought. The priority given to the essay tests was consistent with the school district leadership's belief in mastery learning and assessment-driven instructional improvement. Sustained attention to how critical thinking, discussion and writing might be fostered in classroom practice came towards the end of the Project's second year in the spring of 1984.

Meanwhile, a small field study was undertaken during 1983–84 involving nineteen teachers, most of whom were Steering Committee members, to learn what was common practice in their social studies classes and how they conceived of critical thinking. At this point in the Project, we did not expect to find much critical thinking or teaching for critical thinking if for no other reason than that the curricular aspects of critical thinking had not been emphasized.

The Critical Thinking Project was piloted by fifth, eighth, and eleventh grade social studies teachers (the grades in which US history was taught) in thirteen elementary, middle, and high schools during 1983–84. Nineteen teachers and classes from eight schools (four teachers from two elementary schools, eight teachers from three middle schools, and seven teachers from three high schools) voluntarily participated in the field study. Fifty-nine classroom observations were obtained consisting of both narrative description of classroom events and coding of selected dimensions of classroom activities (e.g., nature and treatment of subject matter, number of substantive student questions). Individual interviews were conducted with all nineteen teachers after the classroom observations had been completed.[37]

Meanings Given to Critical Thinking

The language of critical thinking was prominent during our fall classroom observations and notably absent in the classes we observed the following spring. In the fall, teachers introduced students to 'the Project' and to critical thinking, especially what came to be called the 'elements' of communicating critical thought in essay writing: topic statement, evidence and examples, explanation, conclusion. Teachers also provided opportunities for students to practice identifying these elements and writing their own essays. The explicit attention to critical thinking may have been the teachers' way of showing that they were 'doing' critical thinking.

By spring, the last of the Project essay tests had been administered and scored, the school year was nearing its end, and critical thinking may have lost its salience, particularly for the high school teachers who seemed concerned with 'getting through' as much subject matter as possible in the time remaining. It also is possible that, at least in some classes, critical thinking as the teachers interpreted it had become a way of life and was no longer labelled as such. Consistent with this possibility, more critical thinking and teaching reflecting the elementary teachers' descriptions were evident in the classes we observed during the spring than the previous fall.

Four somewhat different meanings of critical thinking were distinguished in the teachers' talk and classroom practice, three of which emphasize skills.

There were no systematic differences in teacher interpretations by school level or by length of Project participation.

For eight of the nineteen teachers, critical thinking meant one or more skills or abilities, particularly organizing information and one's own ideas, analyzing information, and inferring or going beyond given information. Four teachers linked general skills, particularly analyzing, organizing, and explaining, to broader but somewhat fuzzy conceptions such as 'thinking things through', 'thinking your own thoughts out', and 'thoughtful thinking, not just off the top of their heads'. More integrated but formulaic conceptions of critical thinking were offered by four teachers: 'forming an opinion and defending your position', 'analyze a problem, give your opinion and reasons why', 'evaluate, categorize, and examine evidence in order to draw conclusions or develop opinions', and 'to analyze and evaluate a situation or problem and come to a conclusion'. In contrast, three of the teachers offered vague descriptions without reference to specifics: 'a new way of looking at things . . . logical way of thinking', 'adult way of thinking', and 'to make decisions about things in life, fairly logically'. None of the teachers repeated or paraphrased what became the official Project description of critical thinking: questioning the ideas one encounters, a dynamic process of questioning and reasoning, of raising and pursuing questions about our own and other's claims and conclusions, definitions and evidence, beliefs and actions.

As a group, the teachers had more to say about teaching for critical thinking. Most often, they described it in terms of questioning and helping students learn the 'elements' of communicating critical thought. These elements were widely accepted by the teachers as reasonable and worthwhile although some teachers initially had objected to the essay writing emphasis and questioned whether this was a social studies or an English-writing project.

Whether they saw critical thinking as skills, skills in relation to some kind of 'thoughtful thinking', a means of reasoned decision-making, or something essentially undefined or undefinable, none of the teachers specifically mentioned skepticism or student questioning of the ideas they encounter. In only one class did we observe the teacher actively encouraging students to question the ideas and events being considered (US government policies and actions in Grenada and Lebanon during the fall of 1983). In other classes, students did occasionally raise unsolicited substantive questions that seemed to reflect critical thought or skepticism that might lead to critical dialogue. These student initiatives usually were dealt with briefly by the teacher. Although one teacher did modify an essay writing assignment to incorporate a student idea (that the US population may reflect neither a 'salad bowl' nor a 'melting pot' but some combination), instances of student questioning were not pursued as opportunities for critical thinking. Overall, the meanings given to critical thinking in the teachers' talk and classroom practice were characterized by fragmentation, mechanization, and a product orientation.

Fragmentation.

Critical thinking was fragmented into skills and elements. A common critical thinking task across elementary, middle, and high school classrooms was to present students with a topic statement or conclusion and ask them to find evidence in their textbooks to support it. For example: 'Conditions on a slave ship bringing Africans to America were terrible'. (fifth grade); 'Indians moved across North America for many reasons'. (eighth grade); 'Jefferson claimed that his election marked a revolution'. (Eleventh grade). Only in the last instance were students asked to find evidence contradicting as well as supporting the given statement.

The explaining, analyzing and organizing skills that teachers talked about also tended to appear separately. Explaining usually meant responding to a teacher follow-up question requesting evidence, reasons, or further elaboration of a student's comment or answer to a prior teacher question. While emphasizing and providing practice in using evidence and explanation, these instances typically were not tied to a larger question or process. Analyzing and organizing usually meant completing a chart prepared by the teacher or making notes of evidence and examples to be used in writing an essay.

Mechanization

Mechanization refers to the highly structured and teacher directed nature of critical thinking tasks and to the teachers' tendency not to pursue student initiatives. Most, but not all, of the questions that teachers posed had answers that they considered to be correct or desirable. For the most part, students were to analyze, organize, compare, and/or explain in order to reach the teacher's conclusions. In only one case (the previously mentioned eleventh grade class dealing with Grenada and Lebanon) did the teacher acknowledge the tentativeness of his own beliefs and the importance of students making up their own minds. Similarly, there was only one instance (the previously mentioned fifth grade class dealing with immigration to the US resulting in a salad bowl or melting pot) where the teacher modified a task to accommodate a student's point of view.

Fragmentation and mechanization also are suggested by summary data describing the classrooms we observed during the fall of 1983. Across school levels, 90 per cent of class time was spent in academic activity, and two-thirds of this time was spent in a modification of the conventional recitation characterized by teacher questions, student responses and teacher elaboration of student responses. No time was spent in sustained (two minutes or more) discussion or dialogue characterized by students raising as well as responding to open-ended questions and interacting directly with one another. Only 4 per cent of academic activity time, all at the high school level, involved reasoning tasks. Across school levels, 15 per cent of academic activity time involved divergent application tasks (e.g., taking and supporting a position); most academic activity time was spent with tasks involving the acquisition or recall of information in essentially the same form as it was presented or the direct application of given information.

Curriculum knowledge most often consisted of presumably factual information in contrast to concepts or issues. This information usually was treated as fixed or certain rather than tentative. In this context, it is not surprising that students raised less than two substantive (in contrast to procedural) questions per class. The number of substantive student questions per class varied considerably, however, from none in twenty-three classes to ten or more in three classes.

Product orientation.

In addition to fragmentation and mechanization, the meanings teachers gave to critical thinking were characterized by a product orientation. Emphasis was placed on producing a coherent essay, i.e., a well organized written response to a given question, containing a topic statement, evidence and examples, explanation, and a conclusion. Essay writing, not critical thought or dialogue, was sought and rewarded by most teachers.

These meanings given to critical thinking served to adapt it to 'regular' lessons and curriculum knowledge in most classes. Rather than incorporating critical thinking into everyday teaching and learning, and thus significantly modifying curriculum practice, most teachers tended to teach critical thinking as they did other subject matter — in a fragmented, mechanistic manner that yields right answers or tangible products.

Understanding Teacher Interpretations

The pilot teachers we talked to and observed seemed to take critical thinking seriously and to support the Project, albeit with some reservations. Their interpretations of critical thinking and teaching, however, differed considerably from the conception and teaching framework envisioned by the university consultants and eventually introduced in the Steering Committee meetings and Project materials. How might we understand the teachers' interpretations? This is not a question of why the teachers did not adopt the Project interpretation; it is why the teachers seemed to interpret critical thinking and teaching as they did and the implications for curriculum change.

The meanings that teachers gave to critical thinking and teaching are best understood within their structural and sociocultural contexts, not simply as individual or personal constructions. The teachers' pre-existing beliefs and practices, the conditions of classroom teaching and the school district's goals and policies all seem to have shaped the teachers' interpretations.

Pre-existing beliefs and practices.

In the US, social studies and school goals are customarily separated into categories of knowledge, skills and attitudes or values. When critical thinking appears, it usually has been as a subset of the skills category.[38] Not surprisingly, the teachers accepted and sustained the knowledge-skills-attitude language and the accompanying belief that critical thinking consists of a collection or arrangement of skills. Their fragmentation of critical thinking and teaching is compatible with this belief and other beliefs about students and teaching heterogeneous classes.[39] It also is possible that the teachers had had little prior exposure to and experience with critical thinking as raising and pursuing questions about the ideas one encounters. In this case, it would be unreasonable to expect them to model and promote such critical thought in their classrooms.

When asked about conditions hindering their efforts to foster critical thinking, the teachers most often mentioned problems with students. These included students not being accustomed to critical thinking, the difficulty of teaching large classes with a wide range of student abilities and interests, and the particular difficulty if not impossibility of poor readers and 'learning disabled' students learning to think critically. The way to deal with these problems was to go slowly and not expect too much too soon. Again, the fragmentation of critical thinking into more manageable skills makes sense.

Conditions of classroom teaching.

Prevailing classroom practices in social studies and other subjects, such as teacher led question and answer with teacher elaboration, can be assumed to prevail because they are compatible with the conditions of classroom teaching. It is unlikely that practice will change significantly without concomitant change in classroom conditions. These conditions encompass expectations or demands that teachers obtain student acquiescence to content coverage if not mastery, in an orderly manner,[40] and foster student adherence to norms such as orderliness, busyness, efficient use of time and acceptance of teacher authority.[41] Critical thinking as intended in the Critical Thinking Project is incompatible with several of these conditions or expectations. Critical thinking is more likely to involve depth rather than breadth of subject matter 'coverage', discussions appear less orderly than recitations and perhaps less efficient, and critical thinking rejects the presumption of the teacher as knowledge authority.

Meeting these demands with a group of twenty to thirty students or more (or five to six classes of twenty to thirty students), given a limited physical space and time schedule is a formidable challenge. Time is further limited, our teachers noted, by student absenteeism, frequent pull-out programs, and special events. Preparation and teaching for critical thinking is time consuming, and there is not enough time in the school schedule to do all that is expected. Such competing demands on teachers' and students' time and energy were the second most often cited condition hindering teachers' efforts to foster critical thinking.

The teachers' interpretations of critical thinking and teaching are compatible with these classroom practices and situational demands. Fragmentation and mechanization make critical thinking manageable. Individual seatwork and whole class, question and answer with teacher elaboration activities that emphasize information acquisition, recall, and application enable teachers to manage content coverage and maintain order simultaneously. In contrast, critical thinking as raising and pursuing questions about the ideas one encounters interrupts content coverage and challenges authority. It often is 'messy', and it does take time.

School district goals and policies.

The school district's goals and policies also can be seen to have contributed to the meanings teachers gave to critical thinking, particularly its product orientation. A major, if not the primary, district goal over the past several years had been to improve student achievement as measured by standardized and other tests. Considerable class time was spent in testing, and test scores were widely publicized. The assumption was that the importance attached to test scores would focus and improve teaching, which in turn would improve student achievement.

The Critical Thinking Project essay tests were part of the district's testing program. Although intended to be diagnostic, the tests seemed to be viewed by teachers as accountability measures that could be used against themselves and their students. Other student achievement test scores (e.g., Metropolitan Achievement Test) had been published in the local newspaper by school and grade level, and perhaps the Critical Thinking Project essay test results would be publicised as well. There was widespread teacher concern that students perform well on the tests, and to this end most teachers provided more opportunity, support, and instruction for essay writing than for critical thought or dialogue. Once again, the teachers' interpretation of critical thinking and teaching can be seen to make sense under the circumstances.

School district goals and policies, in turn, appear to have been shaped at least in part by the larger education system and sociocultural context. The Critical Thinking Project was undertaken in the midst of a nation wide movement for 'school improvement' and just prior to the calls for educational excellence. Both accountability and 'higher order thinking' were among the prominent themes of the period in both the public and professional press. Accountability was defined largely in terms of student test scores. Higher order thinking, variously defined, was a reaction to the previous back-to-basics emphasis and a response to student assessment results (e.g., NAEP, National Assessment of Educational Progress) showing that students performed poorly on tasks requiring more than recall or algorithmic application.

Given the prevailing definition of accountability and the state of assessment, especially standardized tests, the calls for accountability and higher order thinking clearly were contradictory unless higher order thinking was defined in readily measurable terms. The Critical Thinking Project can be seen as one school district's way of dealing with these contradictory 'demands'. Although the school district rejected existing multiple-choice tests of critical thinking in favor of its own locally developed essay tests, it mediated contradictory messages in ways that were detrimental to critical thinking.

Further considerations.

More generally, the meanings teachers gave to critical thinking and teaching can be understood in terms of their practicality.[42] Critical thinking as skills and elements of essay writing is practical in the context just described. Objectives are easily stated, communicated and tested; practice activities and tasks are relatively easily incorporated into existing lessons. Critical thinking has been made congruent with established practice. It also has been made relatively safe.

Fragmentation and mechanization serve to maintain teacher control over student behavior and curriculum knowledge. Student questioning and critical dialogue, in contrast, require teachers to relinquish some control over classroom communication patterns and the topics and viewpoints considered. In so doing, teachers risk classroom disorder and venturing into socially or politically sensitive areas. During the interviews, the one teacher who commented on the subversive potential of critical thinking did so with an approving grin. The other teachers seemed not to recognize or acknowledge this possibility. As most of the teachers interpreted critical thinking, there was little cause for concern about upsetting the *status quo* within or outside their classrooms.

Interpreting critical thinking as skills and elements also can be seen as minimizing ambiguity and associated risks for both teachers and students.

Doyle[43], for example, suggests that students attempt to negotiate academic tasks to low levels of ambiguity and risk in order to enhance their positions in the classroom performance-for-grades exchange. It seems likely that teachers also would attempt to reduce ambiguity and risk for themselves.[44] In the present case, low ambiguity means that role and task expectations are clear; low risk means that chances for success are good. Critical thinking as skills and elements comes closer to satisfying these criteria from both teacher and student vantage points than does critical thinking as raising and pursuing questions about the ideas one encounters.

While the meanings teachers gave to critical thinking entailed some changes in classroom tasks and norms (e.g., more writing assignments and requests for evidence and reasons to support 'answers'), teacher and student roles and patterns of classroom interaction remained essentially unchanged. Thus, critical thinking was rendered workable within the context of pre-existing teacher beliefs and practices, classroom conditions and school district goals and policies.

Curriculum Co-optation

Despite important differences between Popkewitz *et al.*'s IGE study[45] and the critical thinking field study (e.g., scope, nature of intended curriculum change, prior identification of study sites as exemplars of change, focus on teacher-classroom or school), it is noteworthy that, in both, intended curriculum changes were adapted or co-opted to mesh with existing circumstances. Curriculum practice did change, at least on the surface. The IGE and critical thinking languages were adopted by teachers, as were 'new' activity formats and grading procedures. Yet, beneath this appearance of change, the substance of teaching and learning persisted much as it had before the introduction of IGE or the Critical Thinking Project.

These are not cases of overt teacher resistance but of the persistent interplay of contextual influences including (a) teachers' pre-existing beliefs and practices (Popkewitz *et al.*'s pedagogical and occupational contexts), (b) the conditions of classroom teaching, (c) school district goals and policies and (d) social/community milieu. Interpretation in both studies emphasized (a), less as individual teacher attributes than as collective, situationally and historically shaped orientations. Differential emphasis was given to the other factors. Popkewitz *et al.* emphasized the role of social/cultural or community milieu in shaping curriculum practice while I emphasized classroom conditions and school district policies (although neither school nor school district contexts were examined in depth).[46] In both cases, however, it is clear that these sociocultural and structural context influences did not operate independently or directly enter into classrooms, but were mediated, individually and collectively, by teachers and other school personnel. The teachers in the IGE study interpreted community circumstances and expectations in terms of their pedagogical and occupational ideologies and responded to those interpretations. Similarly, the teachers in the critical thinking study interpreted school district testing policies in accountability terms and responded by emphasizing essay test writing rather than critical thinking and discussion.

Individual, collective and organizational experience or history also plays a major role in curriculum persistence and change. For example, prior experience with curriculum reform shapes response to subsequent reform efforts. A disappointing experience can leave a residue of wariness or bitterness that mitigates against future change. Further, historically shaped conceptions and practices of schooling, curriculum and teaching are not easily modified to accommodate reforms such as critical thinking.[47] Although the circumstances and purposes that gave rise to particular practices may be forgotten or have changed, the practices tend to persist. Greater awareness of history in curriculum studies and reform efforts could extend understanding in ways that lessen history's hold on the present as well as the likelihood of repeating past mistakes or reinventing squeaky wheels.[48]

School-Based Curriculum Change?

A final study to be considered here can be interpreted as illustrating the impact of structural context beyond the school on curriculum practice. It also suggests some of the limits to school-based curriculum development, which is being advocated as an alternative to top-down models of curriculum change.[49] Farrar's analysis[50] of the structural and sociocultural contexts of school-based reform efforts highlights the often competing perspectives, interests, and actions of classroom teachers, school and school district administrators, state policymakers and the courts. On the basis of year-long field studies of school-based improvement and effective teaching programs in five urban high schools across the US, she concluded that, in addition to cultures and organization 'antithetical to the purpose of school-based improvement programs',[51] urban high schools operate within an environment that limits their capacity to improve teaching and learning.

> State mandates, district policies and procedures, court requirements in de-segregation cases, the interests of bargaining units and the claims of diverse interest groups with a voice in education compete and interact such as to supercede, countermand or undermine school authority. De-centralizing authority to the schools was considered key to the success of school-based programs, but the formal as well as informal authority of external groups and organizations has had the effect of re-centralizing responsibility (and control) to the district or state level.[52]

As a result, the schools have little discretion for self-improvement but increasing accountability for externally imposed improvement outcomes. They are made

> responsible for the effective implementation of policies established by others — a top-down reform strategy whose failure helped promote current ideas that reforms should be developed at the school level.[53]

One example of external, structural context influence on school-based curriculum improvement efforts involved a group of teachers who had designed and implemented 'a program to provide more attention to students' academic and social development by clustering them in small, stable groups that were taught by cross-disciplinary teaching teams'. The next year, school district administrators

> introduced a new city-wide curriculum and testing program, which detailed curriculum content and schedules in several subject areas. Teachers felt that the new curriculum was sufficiently restrictive that they could not continue team teaching across disciplines without risking low test scores for failure to cover prescribed content. They subsequently abandoned team teaching, although they believed that students were 'falling through the cracks' again for lack of team attention to individuals' academic problems.

According to Farrar, the teachers

> not only regretted what they considered time mis-spent on curriculum design for team teaching; they also felt that the district's curriculum was not demanding enough in the amount of reading and essay writing it required. The schools' improvement program subsequently stalled as teachers subordinated their curriculum and teaching priorities to those assigned by the district.[54]

Farrar's study prompts questions about the impact on curriculum of structural and sociocultural context factors beyond the school level. If the previously cited studies had looked outward — beyond the classroom, school, school district and local community — what might have been found that would enhance their accounts of curriculum practice and change? To posit that curriculum exists within an education system and society is rather simply done. To explicate the linkages, theoretically and/or empirically, is much more challenging. It is towards this goal that the following two chapters are directed.

Notes

1 These points are elaborated in C. Cornbleth, 'Research on Context, Research in Context', in *Handbook of Research on Social Studies Teaching and Learning*, ed. J. P. Shaver (New York: Macmillan, in press).
2 C. Cornbleth, W. Korth, and E. B. Dorow, 'Creating the Curriculum: Beginning the Year in a Middle School', paper presented at the annual meeting of the American Educational Research Association, Montreal, April 1983.
3 W. Korth and C. Cornbleth, 'Classroom activities as settings for cognitive learning opportunity and instruction', paper presented at the annual meeting of the American Educational Research Association, New York City, March, 1982.
4 *Ibid.*
5 Data collection and analysis procedures are detailed in C. Cornbleth *et al.* (1983) *op cit.*
6 All proper names are pseudonyms.
7 Cf., C. Edelsky, K. Draper and K. Smith, 'Hookin' 'Em In at the Start of School in a "Whole Language" Classroom', *Anthropology and Education Quarterly* 14 (1983): 257–281.

8 A. G. West, 'Participant Observation Research on the Social Construction of Everyday Classroom Order', *Interchange* 6, 4 (1975): 35–43, p. 39.

9 See C. Cornbleth and W. Korth, 'Teacher Perspectives and Meanings of Responsibility', *The Educational Forum* 48 (1984): 413–422.

10 They also can be seen as making the hidden curriculum explicit.

11 R. Dreeben, 'Schooling and Authority: Comments on the Unstudied Curriculum', in *The Unstudied Curriculum: Its Impact on Children*, ed. N. V. Overly (Washington, DC: Association for Supervision and Curriculum Development, 1970).

12 Cf., T. S. Popkewitz and G. Wehlage, 'Schooling as Work: An Approach to Research and Evaluation', *Teachers College Record* 79 (1977): 69–85.

13 L. M. McNeil, *Contradictions of Control: School Structure and School Knowledge* (New York: Routledge & Kegan Paul, 1986).

14 *Ibid*. p. 178.

15 *Ibid*. p. 160.

16 *Ibid*. p. 174.

18 *Ibid*. p. 175.

19 *Ibid*. p. 177.

20 *Ibid*. p. 177.

21 *Ibid*. p. 191.

22 T. S. Popkewitz, B. R. Tabachnick, and G. Wehlage, *The Myth of Educational Reform* (Madison: University of Wisconsin Press, 1982).

23 IGE is a systems approach to school reform developed at the University of Wisconsin Research and Development Center in the 1960s and implemented in numerous elementary schools in the 1970s. It is based on the assumption that increasing delivery system efficiency will increase students' chances of success in school and society. Increasing efficiency, according to the IGE model, involves systematically sequencing and implementing behaviorally stated objectives and continuously evaluating student mastery of them. Individualization is accomplished by means of a nongraded unit organization, with each unit consisting of approximately 100 students and four to five teachers plus aides. Within each unit, students are grouped and regrouped on the basis of their progress in attaining the stated objectives. By linking a belief in individualism with faith in the rationality and effectiveness of scientific management, the IGE model is congruent with societal expectations for school efficiency, accountability and meritocratic reward. IGE is further assumed by its developers to provide a universal, nonideological model for elementary school reform.

24 See also, T. S. Popkewitz, 'The Social Contexts of Schooling, Change, and Educational Research', *Journal of Curriculum Studies* 13 (1981): 189–206.

25 *Ibid*, p. 190.
26 *Ibid*, pp. 193–194.
27 *Ibid*, p. 193.
28 *Ibid*, p. 194.
29 *Ibid*, p. 190.
30 What Popkewitz *et al.* characterize as pedagogical and occupational context often are seen as major dimensions of school or teacher culture. McNeil might see pedagogical and occupational contexts as a function of a school's structural or administrative context. Alternatively, occupational context can be seen as influenced by but also partially (or largely) independent of the structural context of a particular school. In the latter case, the 'defensive teaching' McNeil observed could be attributed to both school administration and occupational aspects of structural context.
31 T. S. Popkewitz (1981) *op cit.* p. 190.
32 *Ibid*, p. 198.
33 *Ibid*, p. 200.
34 *Ibid*, p. 202.
35 *Ibid*, p. 202.
36 School-level differences were not apparent as was the case in the McNeil and Popkewitz *et al.* studies. However, their schools were located in different school districts and regions of the US; here, all the schools were in the same school district.
37 Further description of the field study procedures can be found in C. Cornbleth, 'Socioecology of Critical Thinking', paper presented at the annual meeting of the American Educational Research Association, 1985.
38 See, for example, the National Council for the Social Studies position statement, *Essentials of the Social Studies* (Washington, DC: NCSS, 1981), which categorizes the essentials as knowledge, democratic beliefs, thinking skills, participation skills and civic action. The thinking skills category has four subcategories: data gathering, intellectual, decision making and interpersonal.
39 See C. Cornbleth, 'Critical Thinking and Cognitive Process', in *Review of Research in Social Studies Education: 1976–1983*, ed. W. B. Stanley (Boulder, CO: Social Science Education Consortium, 1985), pp. 11–63.
40 I. Westbury, 'Conventional Classrooms, "Open" Classrooms and the Technology of Teaching', *Journal of Curriculum Studies* 5 (1973): 99–121.
41 M. LeCompte, 'Learning to Work: The Hidden Curriculum of the Classroom', *Anthropology and Education Quarterly* 9 (1978): 22–37.
42 See, e.g., W. Doyle and G. Ponder, 'The Practicality Ethic in Teacher Decision-Making', *Interchange* 8, No. 3 (1977): 1–12.

43 W. Doyle, 'Academic Work', *Review of Educational Research* 53 (1983): 159–199.

44. See, e.g., J. K. Olson, 'Teacher Constructs and Curriculum Change', *Journal of Curriculum Studies* 12 (1980): 1–11.

45 T. S. Popkewitz *et al.* (1982) *op cit.*

46 This is not to argue the correctness of one or the other study or interpretation, but to suggest that context is not constant; the nature and impact of context factors vary across situations.

47 Cf., J. W. Meyer and B. Rowan, 'The Structure of Educational Organizations', in *Organizational Environments*, ed. J. W. Meyer and W. R. Scott (Beverly Hills, CA: Sage, 1983), especially their concepts of 'the schooling rule' and 'shared social understandings' introduced in Chapter 2 of this volume.

48 See, e.g., D. Hamilton, *Towards a Theory of Schooling* (London and New York: Falmer Press, forthcoming), especially Chapter 2, 'On the Origins of the Educational Terms Class and Curriculum', and T. S. Popkewitz, 'History in Educational Science: Educational Science as History', (University of Wisconson-Madison, Department of Curriculum and Instruction, September 1986).

49 See, e.g., J. Eggleston, *School-Based Curriculum Development in Britain* (London: Routledge & Kegan Paul, 1980); A. Hargreaves, 'The Rhetoric of School-Centred Innovation', *Journal of Curriculum Studies* 14 (1982): 251–266. School-based curriculum development is examined further in Chapter 7.

50 E. Farrar, 'Environmental Contexts and the Implementation of Teacher and School-Based Reforms: Competing Interests', paper presented at the annual meeting of the American Educational Research Association, New Orleans, April 1988.

51 *Ibid*, p. 4.

52 *Ibid*, pp. 5–6.

53 *Ibid*, p. 6.

54 *Ibid*, pp. 10–11.

Part II
Contexts of Curriculum and Reform

Chapter 5

Curriculum and Structural Change

Existing conditions tend to support existing practices. As illustrated by the studies presented in the previous chapter, desired curriculum changes are unlikely to occur in unsupportive or antagonistic contexts. Curriculum reform requires compatible contextual change. It is the education system or structural context of curriculum that is of interest here. I focus on an intermediate or mid-level of the education system — the school — because that is the immediate layer of the structural context of curriculum, encompassing individual classrooms, teaching teams or departments. While schools can be changed from within, especially in decentralized systems, school level structural change usually is a function of further systemic and sociocultural change. In a sense, the school is a pivotal location linking the local, classroom curriculum and the macro, national education system.

My purpose is not to advise would-be reformers how to bring about curriculum change by altering structural context. Rather, it is descriptive-explanatory and involves examination of how the school shapes curriculum and, in turn, how schools are shaped by their location in a national education system. Although others have noted the context dependence of curriculum and of the impact of curriculum change efforts,[1] there has been little theoretical work on the contextual dynamic that addresses the multiple layers of education systems.

Of particular concern are questions of systemic or structural influence on curriculum knowledge: what selections and organizations of knowledge are made available to students? How is knowledge treated? Which knowledge is made available to whom? Who benefits, individually and collectively, from a particular selection, organization, treatment and distribution of knowledge? How these questions should be answered continues to be contested.[2] My concern here is less with answers than with how both the questions and answers are contextually fashioned.

These questions about curriculum knowledge as a social form located in larger social-structural relations are important for at least two reasons related to the functions of education. One is that curriculum knowledge contributes to cultural transmission or transformation at the societal level and to social reproduction or mobility for individuals and groups. Witness, for example, the attention given to schooling and curriculum in nation-building and the continuing detates in the US and elsewhere about educational equity and excellence (e.g., science and technology education for global economic competitiveness).

The second, related reason involves the relation of knowledge and power. Power resides not only in individuals and groups but also and perhaps more importantly in social organizations, institutions and systems both in their formal or authoritative roles and relationships (e.g., Minister of Education, school principal and teacher) and in their historically shaped and socially shared conceptions and understandings (e.g., curriculum, teaching). In modern societies, power increasingly operates through the definition of these conceptions and understandings as well as the definition of appropriate patterns of communication including rules of reason and rationality, i.e., Foucault's 'regimes of truth'.[3] While people fill roles, enter into relationships and participate in the prevailing discourse (in the course of which they may perpetuate or modify them), the roles, relationships, and discourse precede the individuals who enact them. An especially pertinent example is that of curriculum and curriculum specialist and the present effort to reorient curriculum understanding and practice. Knowledge is empowering insofar as knowledge of conceptions, patterns and rules gives access to power. Further, self-conscious knowledge enables their redefinition. To the extent that curriculum and curriculum studies unreflectively carry the prevailing discourse, they become elements of social regulation.

After examining aspects of the operation of education systems, I consider their implications for curriculum practice and change. The examination of education systems draws freely but not entirely on Archer's historical study of the English and French education systems.[4] Ideas and propositions introduced here are briefly illustrated and then further developed in Chapters 6 to 8.

Contextual Dynamic: System Stability and Change

As noted in Chapter 2, the relevant structural and sociocultural contexts of curriculum are multifaceted and variable. While nested within one another, they also are overlapping and interacting. As a consequence, there is no generic curriculum context, no predeterminable set of parameters or invariant grid that can be imposed on any curriculum. With respect to the education system as structural context, this means that there is no generic system model that can illuminate curriculum practice or change across time and place. Instead, we can point to and theorize particular instances of system operation and change that seem to affect curriculum and be relevant to other settings. Greater understanding of how education systems function and change would enable fuller accounts of curriculum practice and change over time as well as inform curriculum reform efforts.

Structure has been defined as established roles and relationships, including operating procedures, shared beliefs and norms. In contrast to a static, organization chart view of structure as form or object, the present view is dynamic. What appears to be established at any point in time is neither inevitable nor fixed. It is historically constituted and susceptible to change. Further, structure is not of a single piece but comprises a network of interconnected strands. These strands and their interrelations are characterized by varying degrees of stability and discontinuity, of tension and contradiction.[5] With this view of structure, the focus is on how education systems function more than on their specific features.

It also was suggested that the structure of an education system conditions but does not determine outsiders' interaction with and participants' interaction within it.[6] According to Archer's model, structural elaboration (i.e., change) is the outcome of structurally conditioned social interaction; structural elaboration then conditions subsequent interaction, and so forth.[7] In other words, efforts to change an education system or some aspect of it, either from within the system or outside it, are shaped by the nature of the system. Different strategies would be employed to bring about national or nationwide curriculum change in, for example, more and less centralized systems. In the former, the central authority might be persuaded to undertake and support *national* curriculum change. In the latter, where there is no central authority, *nationwide* curriculum change requires coordinated efforts at the state or provincial and local school district or school levels.

Structural change is given impetus by continuing internal strains and discontinuities (e.g., reproduction versus equal opportunity, central control versus local accountability) as well as by external conditions (e.g., demographic trends) and interests and by internal initiations (e.g., teacher professionalization movement) that induce further strains. Structural relations are thus both powerful and fragile.

Structural strains are evident, for example, in the current movement in the US and elsewhere for teacher professionalization. Professionalization is being defined to include, among other things, a greater teacher voice in school level decision-making about personnel and budget as well as curriculum and students. Such changes in the teacher role necessitate changes in school and school district administrator roles and in teacher-administrator relationships. Opposition from school administrators in some US school districts has resulted in court cases (e.g., Rochester, NY) and other efforts to reassert administrative prerogatives and to slow or stop teacher professionalization.

Structural strains also are evident in continuing efforts in the US to promote a standardized or national curriculum, usually in the name of national security and economic competiveness. These efforts conflict with traditions of state and local curriculum policymaking and adaptation to local conditions or perceived needs. They would change the roles of curriculum specialists and classroom teachers from decision-makers to implementors of decisions made by others and perhaps limit the influence of local communities and interest groups. They also are in tension with aspects of the concurrent teacher professionalization movement that would increase teacher autonomy.

In broad outline, Archer's model of national education system operation and change also seems appropriate to local school and intermediate levels, especially in decentralized systems. For example, the structure of a school conditions teachers', students' and others' interaction within, and outsiders' (e.g., parents, special interest groups) interaction with it. Whether that interaction leads to structural maintenance or modification depends not only on the nature of the interaction but also on the nature of the school level structural conditioning, the structural conditioning of encompassing layers of the education system and extra-systemic influences. US schools, for example, are located within school districts (the local education authority, which may or may not be linked to city or county governments, primarily by budget controls), within states, within the nation. In highly centralized and formally coupled education systems, in contrast, national level structural conditioning is likely to more directly affect structure and interaction at the local level, resulting in greater uniformity throughout the system and less locally initiated change.

The impact of structural conditioning is not necessarily one-way, from higher to lower levels of an education system. Conceivably, structural change at the school or intermediate levels, especially if it is demonstrably successful or widespread, could influence upper levels or the system as a whole. Nor is structural conditioning necessarily constraining. Occasionally, schools are encouraged and offered incentives for structural innovation. In the state of New York in the 1980s, for example, schools and school districts were offered monies and exemption from some state department of education regulations to experiment with mentor teacher-intern programs (induction programs for newly certified teachers) and school-based decision-making, both of which entail changes in teacher and administrator roles and relationships. That seemingly successful models eventually may be mandated statewide is another matter.

National Systems

Since the existing system presumably serves dominant groups reasonably well, they are likely to initiate only minor alterations (e.g., up-dating, refinements intended to increase efficiency). Major, system wide structural changes in education, following Archer's analysis, result from conflict between dominant and subordinate but assertive groups. According to Archer, 'most of the time most of the forms that education takes are the political products of power struggles. They bear the marks of concession to allies and compromise with opponents.'[8] The particular nature of these power struggles is shaped by the existing education system's structural conditioning of social interaction. Power struggles also are shaped by the configuration of resources and interests in the society at a given point in time. Thus, given a particular education system and societal configuration, various strategies for maintenance or change are more or less probable and feasible.

Domination of an education system, in Archer's scheme, is a function of three factors: monopoly, constraint and ideology. Once domination is achieved by means of monopolizing scarce resources (e.g., school facilities and materials, qualified or certified teachers), constraints and ideology are necessary to resolve conflict or quell opposition and thus maintain control. Constraints, which can range from symbolic to coercive, are to prevent others from supplying educational resources or providing educational services. An example in the US would be the state regulations and limits imposed on private schools and parental efforts to provide 'home schooling' for their children.[9] Ideology is to provide legitimation for the existing system and its incumbents and to discourage opposition. A successful ideology will engender positive support and minimize the need for enforced compliance to maintain domination.

Assertion resulting in major structural change is a function of bargaining power, ideology, and instrumental activities, which enable subordinate or oppositional groups to subvert constraints, reject the prevailing ideology, and impair the existing domination. Bargaining power is based on numbers, organization and other resources. It is enhanced by a counter-ideology (e.g., mass rather than elite education, secular rather than religious education, multicultural or multilingual rather than monocultural or monolingual education) that serves to consolidate opposition, gain wider support, and justify oppositional goals and activities by challenging the dominant ideology and offering an attractive alternative. Instrumental activities are aimed at (a) replacement involving the transfer of control from the previously dominant to the successfully assertive group, or (b) competition involving the establishment of alternative education organizations outside the control of dominant groups. The former was accomplished in France and the latter in England by the late nineteenth century, leading to a still highly centralized education system in France and a relatively decentralized education system in England.

Within Systems

Within education systems, structural change is a function of various forms of assertion and negotiation more than large scale competitive conflict. Archer distinguishes three forms of negotiation: internal initiation, external transaction and political manipulation. Internal initiation strategies are undertaken by educators' associations and interest groups and might involve (a) increasing the attractiveness of services offered (e.g., upgrading teacher knowledge or instructional expertise), (b) controlling certification (e.g., the number and qualifications of new teachers or administrators), (c) participating in policy decision-making and administration at various levels and (d) promoting educational values compatible with their perceived interests. Strategies (b) and (c), advanced in the language of teacher professionalization and educational excellence, have been prominent in the US education and teacher education reform movement of the 1980s.

External transactions involve organized interest groups in direct negotiation with incumbent groups for desired changes. One example is corporations providing schools with computers and teacher training in exchange for computer education for students. Another, in the US, is Theodore Sizer's 'Coalition of Essential Schools' that enlists school participation in its version of curriculum and educational reform in exchange for assistance and the status of coalition membership. A third is private foundation grants for special projects.

Political manipulation involves influencing authoritative, usually State or governmental, decisions affecting the education system or some part of it. It is the form of 'negotiation' likely to be undertaken by subordinate groups lacking resources for external transactions, for example, minority groups seeking equal educational opportunity. It also is the most likely form of negotiation in centralized education systems whose structure limits internal initiation and external transactions. While the social system determines who has which assets (e.g., wealth, expertise), the structure of the education system determines what can be done with them.[10]

In the face of efforts to negotiate change, education system authorities (e.g., Ministry or Department of Education officials, school district superintendents) typically seek to maintain or increase their control by means of strategies similar to those previously described as elements of domination. They might try to increase the dependence of teachers and administrators by increasing spending or limiting access to other sources of support such as corporations or foundations. Or, they might try to undermine professional autonomy by means of further regulation (e.g., accountability measures, limits on union activity). Thirdly, they might promote an ideology supportive of their control (e.g., the school principal as instructional leader).

Within Schools

At the school level (and perhaps at higher levels of the education system), in addition to the previously noted forms of negotiation and resistance, several forms of organizational control may be operative to shape curriculum and impede or foster change. These controls can be seen as constraints undermining professional autonomy and possibilities for internal initiation. Here, I draw on Edwards's distinctions among personal, bureaucratic and technical forms of organizational control as illustrated in Zeichner, Tabachnick, and Densmore's two-year field study of prospective and beginning elementary teachers in four US schools.[11] The teachers' perspectives and teaching were found to be shaped not only by their personal characteristics, dispositions and abilities, but also by school organizational controls and cultures. The latter contributed to 'understanding how the first-year teachers learned what was expected of them, how desired behaviors were reinforced, and how organizational sanctions were applied.[12]

Personal control involves direct supervision of teachers' activities by superordinates such as department chairs, principals, or supervisors whose close monitoring increases the likelihood that the teachers 'comply with organizational norms'.[13] Bureaucratic control is embedded in the school's organization or social structure and 'enforced through impersonal bureaucratic rules and hierarchical social relations. Sanctions and rewards . . . are dictated by officially approved policies to which . . . role groups, are held responsible'.[14] Technical control, in contrast, is embedded in the physical organization or 'structure of the labor process, and jobs are designed in such a way as to minimize the need to rely on workers' compliance with impersonal bureaucratic rules' or organizational norms.[15] In teaching, direction of work tasks, evaluation of work, and reward or discipline can be accomplished technically by adoption of instructional packages or by team teaching arrangements.

Zeichner *et al.* found little evidence of personal control of the first year teachers by their principals. Only one principal attempted to obtain compliance by directly monitoring teacher classroom behavior. Bureaucratic control was widespread but unevenly enforced. Although

> there were numerous bureaucratic rules and regulations in each school that attempted to dictate to teachers how and what to teach, procedures for managing pupil behavior . . . and such general activities as when teachers could leave the school buildings . . . the first-year teachers were frequently able to ignore or even to openly

violate bureaucratic rules when they wanted to do so. The self-contained classrooms in three of the four schools together with the minimal amount of personal supervision by principals in these three schools weakened the controlling effects of a bureaucratic organization.[16]

The most pervasive and powerful form of organizational control in these four schools was technical. Technical control 'was exerted through the timing of instruction, the [written] curriculum and curriculum materials, and the architecture of the schools'.[17] It was particularly evident in the one school with a team teaching arrangement 'where the pace and form of instruction, the open architectural plan, the precise time schedules and the performance-based curriculum [and pre-set tests] all made deviation from the preferred patterns of teaching very difficult'.[18] Technical control, however, was neither absolute nor irresistible. Zeichner *et al.* observed that teachers can avoid or redirect aspects of technical control that conflict with strongly held personal goals if they have the requisite political skills.[19] It seems likely that technical and other forms of organizational control would vary in strength and compatibility with other structural elements. Avoiding or redirecting one or another form of organizational control then would hinge on the particulars of the situation and teachers' structural knowledge as well as their individual or collective political skill.

In addition to these formal organizational controls over teaching, Zeichner *et al.* point to the often powerful but tacit, informal teacher, student and school cultures that communicate school ethos, tradition and expectations.

> There was usually one formal school culture, but there were several different and often conflicting versions of the informal school culture within a single school; one or more of these informal school cultures were often in conflict with the officially sanctioned one. It was the interaction of these formal and informal cultures rather than the presence or absence of any particular control mechanism by itself that determined the institutional (i.e., structural) constraints and opportunities presented to each teacher.[20]

Zeichner *et al.*'s analysis of organizational controls and cultures illustrates some of the 'strands' that comprise structure, i.e., the roles and relationships and more or less widely shared and stable operating procedures, beliefs and norms.

It also shows the malleability if not the fragility of structural relations insofar as at least one of the teachers they studied was able to 'buck the system'.

The impact of organizational controls and cultures can be seen in the studies presented in the previous chapter. In our 'Creating the Curriculum', school culture seemed to be a dominant influence on curriculum practice whereas McNeil's *Contradictions of Control* highlighted bureaucratic controls. Popkewitz *et al.*'s *Myth of Educational Reform* illustrated both cultural and, to a lesser extent, technical controls. Interestingly in this case, the potential technical control of the IGE curriculum reform appears to have been mitigated by other structural elements. Technical controls were more evident in our study of the Critical Thinking Project where school district testing was found to be a major factor shaping teachers' interpretations of critical thinking.

Bureaucratization

A further aspect of structure to be considered is bureaucratization. Although bureaucratization or bureaucratic control is not always salient within schools, perhaps because it has become so embedded that it is taken for granted and therefore 'unseen', it does seem to be a major feature of national education systems affecting the operation of school districts or LEAs and schools. (The State bureaucracy and its relation to the education system are considered in Chapter 6.)

The actual rules, roles and relations characterizing a specific bureaucratic organization are less important here than that which Berger, Berger and Kellner refer to as elements of modern 'bureaucratic consciousness' that create and maintain order and predictability by means of rationalized procedures.[21] A key element is orderliness, a scheme of jurisdictional catergories and procedures, 'based on a taxonomic propensity'.[22] Taxonomic orderliness and its appeal are strikingly evident in instructional models such as Madeline Hunter's 'Essential Elements of Instruction', the proliferation of special education categories and programs, and skills-based reading programs.

Categories are defined (e.g., teacher, student, subject, learning disability) so that almost everyone and everything has its proper place and role. Procedures are established for categorizing and for dealing with the categories and their interrelations. For example, there are procedures or rules for teacher certification, for identifying and teaching students with learning problems and for creating or modifying required school subjects. These become known as standard operating procedures, normal channels, or simply 'the way we do things'. Orderliness makes size and complexity manageable. It also engenders uniformity, stability, predictability and the presumption of fairness based on anonymity, i.e., presumably everyone is treated the same.

Related to orderliness is an assumption of 'non-separability of means and ends' wherein means become as or more important than the ends they are supposed to further.[23] National or standardized testing of students, for example, seems to take precedence over teaching and learning. According to Berger *et al.*, 'non-separability serves to legitimate . . . procedures'.[24]

Bureaucratization can be seen both as a response to prior structural conditioning, especially during periods of rapid expansion of an education system, and as a source of subsequent structural conditioning. Once established, bureaucratization tends to impede major structural change because such change cannot be accommodated by standard operating procedures. It requires alteration of those procedures that are the very 'being' of bureaucracy. Thus, major structural change is unlikely to be initiated from within the education system, and external pressures for such change are likely to be resisted or redefined to fit normal channels. It also should be noted that there are few incentives for education system bureaucracies to undertake major structural change. When education is compulsory and national systems of public education face little or no serious competition from independent (private or parochial) schools, there is correspondingly little incentive to increase efficiency or effectiveness or to respond to other demands.

However, bureaucracy is not monolithic. There are various layers of education system bureaucracy (e.g., national, state or provincial, local), which may well carry different interests or priorities, especially in decentralized systems and pluralistic societies. These bureaucratic discontinuities offer opportunities for structural change.

Curricular Implications

Summarizing this exploration of aspects of the operation of education systems, the following implications for curriculum practice and change are offered.

The School as a Pivotal Location

If, as has been suggested, the school is in a crucial position linking local curriculum practice with the national education system, then the school becomes a key site for curriculum maintenance or change efforts. The observed variability and potency of school cultures lends support to this interpretation. Focus on the school, however, does not mean that schools can be transformed without regard for their larger structural and sociocultural settings. Major school level change typically entails (a) complementary change at other sites within a school district or an LEA, (b) further systemic change or accommodation and (c) a supportive or at least tolerant sociocultural milieu. Conditions (a) and (b) reflect the bureaucratic nature and structural conditioning of education systems while (c) acknowledges the dependence of education on external support. The school's importance and its limited autonomy is well illustrated by school based curriculum development, which is considered in Chapter 7.

The Structural Conditioning of Social Interaction over Time

Structural context, both immediate and more distant, shapes curriculum practice, the means employed to maintain the education system and its control of curriculum and other aspects of schooling, and the forms of assertion and negotiation employed to bring about structural and curriculum change. The studies presented in the previous chapter illustrate the impact of aspects of local structural context on classroom and school level curriculum practice.
Additional elements of school and school district or LEA structure that affect curriculum, usually through organizational controls or cultures, include: homework, grading and grouping practices; rituals; extracurricular activities and services; staff and student stability or turnover and teacher and administrator evaluation and assignment policies. Farrar's study can be seen as beginning to link school level interaction to the larger education system, particularly state policies in the US.[25]

Still needed are studies that trace the multiple linkages and competing pressures within education systems and among the education system, State and society. For example, in the US, how are demands for both excellence (e.g., higher academic standards) and attention to so-called at-risk students (i.e., potential dropouts) being articulated by advocates, mediated by education bureaucracies and played out in curriculum practice? More specifically, what is the impact on the knowledge of science (or mathematics or history) made available to different groups of students? Retrospectively, one might examine the experience of nationally funded curriculum materials development projects in the US and other nations during the period of the late 1950s through the early 1970s, with particular attention to the nature and effects of interactions within the education system and among the education system, State and societal agencies. What forms of power have been exercised? How has power circulated? Under what circumstances has desired structural and curriculum change occurred?[26]

Means of system maintenance and forms of assertion and negotiation for change appear to vary with the centralization of the education system and the extent of its internal co-ordination. For example, national bureaucratic controls are more characteristic of centralized systems while personal controls are associated with tight co-ordination whether or not there is a high degree of centralization at the national level.[27] Centralization and co-ordination, however, tend not to be uniform throughout an education system.

The US education system has been described by organizational theorists and sociologists as loosely coupled or organizationally loose.[28] Looseness refers to weak internal co-ordination or control, which gives freedom of action to organizations, groups and individuals within the system. Trends toward standardization and accountability, especially at the state level,[29] make the loose coupling characterization less appropriate today than it may have been a decade or more ago. A more serious problem with the loose coupling characterization is its assumption that coupling or co-ordination is a formal property of education systems. Coupling is used in a mechanistic sense of overt, hierarchical organization with clearly and functionally distinguished and linked levels. It ignores the kind of structural cohesion provided by standard operating procedures, shared beliefs (i.e., social understandings) and norms. It cannot account for the many similarities in curriculum practice and recent educational 'reform' activity across the fifty states.

Importantly, looseness appears to be uneven, with some areas being more (or less) tightly co-ordinated and controlled, formally or otherwise, than others. In the US, actual curriculum practice is subject to less direct or formal system control than is the offering of particular courses, which is subject to less formal control than are teacher and student credentialling. Historically, control of organizational matters has become increasingly rationalized and, to some extent, centralized while formal control of curriculum knowledge and practice has remained relatively weak and diffuse. It seems an article of faith among US teachers that 'you can tell me what to teach but not how to teach it'. Consequently, national or nationwide change efforts tend to focus on managerial or organizational matters and to be largely technical or procedural (e.g., credentialling, accreditation, testing), in part because that is the kind of change over which State agencies and education bureaucracies have the most control.[30] Technical or procedural changes, in turn, can be expected to have curricular impact. Standardized testing, for example, is likely to focus, if not narrow, curriculum practice in the name of 'curriculum alignment' (i.e., teaching to the test).[31]

Similarly, distinguishing between centralized and decentralized education systems seems less helpful to understanding means of curriculum control and possibilities for change than identifying which areas are subject to central control, to what extent control is centralized and how that control is exercised. In other words, what is the nature of central-local curricular relationships in particular cases?[32] Further, decentralization implies the presence of a center that, for whatever reasons, has delegated (and might reclaim) authority.[33] In the case of the US education system, fragmentation may be a more appropriate descriptor. The question then becomes the extent to which and how control of particular parts of the system are fragmented. With decentralization of control of the area of interest, local change would be easier than with centralization, while nationwide change would require action at several sites. With fragmented control, even local change efforts need to address several sources of control with possibly conflicting interests.

These conditions suggest that the occurrence and impact of system maintenance and negotiated change strategies are likely to vary within as well as across education systems. In areas where centralization is high and co-ordination is tight, for example, political manipulation is the more likely change strategy because of structural constraints on internal initiation and external transaction. Finally, regardless of the structural particulars of an education system, past experience or history necessarily shapes present interaction. At times, the historical influence is straightforward as when the prior success of an internally initiated change effort prompts future internal initiations. More often, unacknowledged historical residues become embedded in traditions and day-to-day practices.

Impetus for Structural Change

Whether structural changes originate in systemic strains and discontinuities, external conditions, or negotiations undertaken by dissatisfied groups within or outside the education system, they affect curriculum practice directly or indirectly. Since most structural change is likely to be contested, there usually are opportunities for exploiting, resisting, or redefining curriculum impact. This seems to hold especially when structural change is a response to external conditions and/or political manipulation, that is, when sociocultural forces are mediated by the education system.

School desegregation in the US provides a case in point. The 1954 *Brown v. Board of Education* Supreme Court decision and subsequent federal court orders forced structural change in numerous school districts. Few if any court orders contained curricular specifications for meeting desegregation and equity mandates. These decisions were and are being made at the school and school district level. Meanwhile, the changing mix of majority and minority teachers and students in individual schools immediately affected curriculum practice via student aspirations, teacher expectations and the emergent school culture. Similarly, if the teacher professionalization movement succeeds in bringing about school level structural change, it is not at all clear what the consequences might be for curriculum practice.

Role of Ideology

The importance of ideology to system domination and assertion, to structural and curriculum maintenance and change, ought not to be underestimated by those undertaking, resisting, or studying curriculum change efforts. As has been suggested, ideology plays a major role in justifying and maintaining or gaining support for a position and in delegitimizing opposition. The ideologies of school-based curriculum development and of teacher professionalization are salient contemporary examples. The curricular implications of prevailing and emerging ideologies merit careful consideration of what is involved and who benefits. Probing beneath the surface of often fine sounding slogans may reveal simple self-interest, contradictory possibilities for practice, or very little of substance.

Bureaucratization and Organizational Cultures and Controls

Investment of effort and other resources in curriculum *per se* is apt to show little return in an inhospitable milieu. Where existing organizational controls or cultures are in opposition to desired curriculum practice, curriculum change is more likely when those controls or cultures become the focus of negotiation strategies and ideological work than when effort is directed elsewhere. Further, where structural discontinuities are apparent, their exploitation can increase prospects for desired change.

Bureaucratic systems, with their penchant for orderliness in terms of categories and procedures, are resistant but not impervious to structural change. Seemingly messy or disorderly curriculum practice, such as would be entailed by taking critical thinking or democratic education seriously, is inimical to bureaucracy. Two options for change within existing systems are suggested by the foregoing analysis. One involves taking advantage of discontinuities among bureaucratic layers. A second involves introducing a 'new order' or a new definition of order.

Concluding Note

Across education systems, with few local exceptions, the questions about curriculum knowledge raised at the beginning of this chapter have been answered in ways that favor cultural transmission, social reproduction and limited access to knowledge-related power. Calls for a common cultural literacy or a national curriculum suggest conservative unrest while calls for more democratic and empowering school experience indicate liberal-radical dissatisfaction with the present situation. Given inequalities and differing interests within and outside education systems, tensions and pressures for various and sometimes conflicting changes and for maintenance of the *status quo* are on-going. Curriculum will be continually contested. However, in the absence of structural change, it is unlikely that curriculum practice will change substantially despite the competing rhetorics and reform efforts.

Notes

1 See, e.g., G. Guthrie, 'Current Research in Developing Countries: The Impact of Curriculum Reform on Teaching', *Teaching and Teacher Education* 2, No.1 (1986): 81–89.

2 See, e.g., H. M. Kliebard, *The Struggle for the American Curriculum, 1893–1958* (Boston: Routledge & Kegan Paul, 1986); H. M. Kliebard and B. M. Franklin, 'The Course of the Course of Study: History of Curriculum', in *Historical Inquiry in Education*, ed. J. H. Best (Washington, DC: American Educational Research Association, 1983); I. F. Goodson and S. J. Ball (Eds.), *Defining the Curriculum: Histories and Ethnographies* (London/Philadelphia, 1984).

3 T. S. Popkewitz, *A Political Sociology of Educational Reform and Change*, Chapter 1 (manuscript in progress). Discourse and discursive practices can be seen as part of the structural context as well as the substance of curriculum. Alternatively, curriculum could be seen as discourse, but I am reluctant to reduce everything to discourse.

4 M. S. Archer, *Social Origins of Educational Systems* (London: Sage, 1984).

5 See T. S. Popkewitz, *op cit.*

6 See Chapter 2, p. 28.

7 M. S. Archer, 1984, *op cit.*

8 M. S. Archer, 1984, *op cit.*, p. 2. Also, M. S. Archer and M. Vaughan 'Domination and Assertion in Educational Systems' in *Readings in the Theory of Educational Systems*, ed. E. Hopper (London: Hutchinson, 1971), pp. 56–70.

9 See, e.g., S. Arons, *Compelling Belief* (Amherst: University of Massachusetts Press, 1986).

10 M.S. Archer, 1984, *op cit.*, p. 130.

11 R. Edwards, *Contested Terrain: The Transformation of the American Workplace in the 20th Century* (New York: Basic Books, 1979); K. M. Zeichner, B. R. Tabachnick, and K. Densmore, 'Individual, Institutional, and Cultural Influences on the Development of Teachers' Craft Knowledge', in *Exploring Teachers' Thinking*, ed. J. Calderhead (London: Cassell, 1987).

12 K.M. Zeichner *et al.* (1987) *op cit.*, p. 53.

13 *Ibid.*

14 *Ibid.*

15 *Ibid.*

16 *Ibid.*

17 *Ibid.*, p. 54.

18 *Ibid.*

19 Even so-called personal or individual goals (beliefs, values) are socially constructed and contextually shaped.

20 *Ibid.*, pp. 54–55.

21 P. Berger, B. Berger and H. Kellner, *The Homeless Mind: Modernization and Consciousness* (New York: Vintage, 1973).

22 *Ibid.*, p. 49.

23 *Ibid.*, p. 53.

24 *Ibid.*

25 E. Farrar, 'Environmental Contexts and the Implementation of Teacher and School-based Reforms: Competing Interests', paper presented at the annual meeting of the American Educational Research Association, New Orleans, April 1988.

26 Partial responses to these questions are offered by a few recent studies such as Woolnough's examination of physics teaching in England and Wales. B. E. Woolnough, *'Physics Teaching in Schools 1960–1985: Of People, Policy and Power* (Lewes, East Sussex/Philadelphia: Falmer Press, 1988).

27 In decentralized systems such as the US, bureaucratic controls may be strong at the state, school district, or school levels.

28 For example, K. E. Weick, 'Educational Organizations as Loosely Coupled Systems', *Administrative Science Quarterly* 21 (1976): 1–19.

29 See, e.g., M. W. Kirst, 'State Policy in an Era of Transition', *Education and Urban Society* 16 (1984): 225–237.

30 J. W. Meyer, 'Innovation and Knowledge Use in American Public Education', in *Organizational Environments*, ed. J. W. Meyer and W. R. Scott (Beverly Hills, CA: Sage, 1983), pp. 236–260. This distinction and its implications are explored further in Chapter 7.

31 N. Frederiksen, 'The Real Test Bias Influence of Testing in Teaching and Learning', *American Psychologist* 39 (1984): 193–202.

32 See, e.g., H. Tangerud and E. Wallin, 'Values and Contextual Factors in School Improvement', *Journal of Curriculum Studies* 18, 1 (1986): 45–61, especially pp. 54–57.

33 Late 1980s educational 'reforms' in England can be seen as instances of recentralization.

Chapter 6

The State and Curriculum Controls

Education system conditions that shape curriculum practice and change were described and illustrated in the preceding chapter. That examination is extended in this chapter by directing attention to the nature and role of the State in structural conditioning and change and thus to more explicitly political questions of curriculum control.

The State is part of either the structural or the sociocultural context of curriculum. Where the education system is encompassed by the State (i.e., in highly centralized national education systems), the State can be seen as constituting the superordinate layer of the structural context of curriculum. In nations with federal forms of political organization and formally decentralized education systems such as the US, the State spans both the structural and sociocultural contexts of curriculum. In both cases, the State directly and indirectly shapes curriculum practice and change.

Although a State presence increasingly has been asserted in critical education discourse, too little theoretical explication or empirical illustration has been offered. The intent here is to contribute to needed argument and evidence with specific reference to curriculum. The 'State' is a theoretical construct — an intellectual abstraction — albeit not without empirical referents. To deal meaningfully with the State requires linking the theoretical with concrete cases, not merely offering a detached (i.e., decontextualized) account. My interest in the State is primarily in questions of control of the public education system and of implications for curriculum practice and change. I examine the system-State relationship with particular attention to who influences the education system and how that influence is exercised. Since I am not primarily concerned with the State *per se,* I draw on but am not preoccupied with political theory. After briefly examining the nature of the

State, I turn to system-State relations and questions of control.[1] Further implications for curriculum practice and change are considered in the next chapter, 'Curriculum Policy and Planning'.

Nature and Operation of the State

To ask what constitutes the State is to ask who defines and governs a nation's public sector. The State is comprised of more than government officials but less than the public or citizenry at large; it encompasses 'the totality of public authority in a given society (governmental or otherwise), regardless of the level — national, subnational, or local — at which it may operate.[2] The liberal-democratic State is a shifting configuration of elected government officials and their appointees, government bureaucracy, political parties and politically organized interest groups. The US State, for example, has been characterized as the 'configuration of governance',[3] 'coalitions of control'[4] and an 'organization of coercive power'.[5] The authoritarian State is a more or less stable configuration of government officials and government bureaucracy and of economic, religious, and/or military elites.[6]

The State, be it democratic or authoritarian, is the coalition that exerts its power or control by shaping official or authoritative public policy. Its composition varies from one situation and time to another as changing but overlapping coalitions control different areas and periods of public policymaking.

Curriculum is directly affected by the State in at least two ways. First, it is constrained or enabled by existing public policies in education and other sectors. For example, the Great Society's redistributive policies of the 1960s in the US substantially enabled the design of curricula intended to extend educational opportunities for economically disadvantaged groups. Subsequent State policy changes through the mid-1980s (e.g., toward privatization) cut back or curtailed many of these programs. Second, depending on the nation in question, overall curriculum design is more or less a State endeavor as will be illustrated later in this chapter and in Chapter 7.

Indirect State influences on curriculum are as or more powerful than direct ones. As Evans, Rueschemeyer and Skocpol point out, the State not only mediates external demands and pursues its own interests, but also influences 'the meanings and methods of politics for all groups and classes in society'.[7]

Social cleavages and interest are *not*, as received wisdom too often implies, primordial givens that affect the state through politics 'from without'. Rather, the organizational arrangements of states, the existing patterns of state intervention in economic and social life, and policies already in place all influence the social interests pursued in politics.[8]

In other words, the State shapes educational and other debates, influencing the recognition and definition of problems and the ways in which they are to be resolved. By means of its organizational arrangements, existing patterns of intervention and policies — and its media access and use — the State influences the approach taken to curriculum and the kind of curriculum that prevails. This 'shaping the debate' or 'agenda setting' role of the State is well illustrated by the Reagan administration in the 1980s, particularly its use of the so-called bully pulpit to shape public and professional opinion, as will be shown later.

Longer range, the State also contributes to defining and redefining what counts as education and as acceptable education processes and outcomes, including curricular ones. By direct and indirect means, the State contributes to formulation of the socially shared understandings that serve to standardize and control education such as the 'schooling rule' that defines school, teacher and student.[9] In the absence of formally centralized State control of the education system in the US, an evolving, State influenced if not dominated, national discourse serves as a powerful form of control. Curricular changes and the means by which they are planned are constrained by the operative socially shared understandings. For example, since the national State in the US had no constitutional or traditional, programmatic role in public education, its first major progammatic intervention in elementary and secondary schooling, the 1958 National Defense Education Act, was justified in the name of national security and defense where the State has an unquestioned role.

A related aspect of indirect State influence on curriculum is the State's role as a carrier of hegemonic ideas and values. The national education discourse in the US, with its current emphasis on excellence and technocratic means to its attainment, tends to obscure underlying values and interests. A prime example is the National Commission on Excellence in Education's 1983 report, *A Nation at Risk*.[10] 'Cultural literacy' provides another example, suggesting curriculum knowledge beyond functional or basic skills that incorporates all citizens. The common culture that is to be promulgated, however, turns out to be that of selected western European and American males most of whom died more than a century ago (e.g., M. Adler's *Paideia proposal*, former Secretary of Education Bennett's *James Madison curriculum*). This version of cultural literacy is to reassert 'American values' and transmit 'important truths' about the superiority of 'our' western democratic heritage and way of life. Such cultural literacy is to be made available to all students so that they can share in the American Dream.

Key Actors

So as not to disembody the State, it is helpful to further specify who comprises the coalition of control that constitutes the State, particularly those segments of the State that influence the education system. While key actors will vary to some extent, depending on the issue, potentially relevant individuals and groups can be identified. In the US, within the multi-layered governmental segment of the State (national, state and local), the following are actually or potentially relevant:

1 state and federal judges, especially the federal district judges who hear school desegregation cases and the Supreme Court;
2 the Secretary of Education and his/her appointees, and state level equivalents;
3 appointed Presidential advisors, e.g., the White House staff, and commissions, e.g., the 1983 National Commission on Excellence in Education, and state level equivalents;
4 the Congress and state legislatures, especially state and federal legislative committees that deal with education, e.g., the House Committee on Education and Labor and its Subcommittee on Select Education, the Senate Committee on Labor and Human Resources and its Subcommittee on Education, Arts and Humanities (these are authorizing committees that design programs); the House and Senate Subcommittees on Labor, Health and Human Services, Education and Related Agencies (these are appropriations committees that determine which authorized programs are funded and at what level, subject to allocations determined by the full appropriations committees); 11
5 the mayors and city councils of some large cities who have power over city school distict budgets, e.g., Boston, Buffalo;

6 the political appointees and civil service bureaucrats who staff the above listed units.

In addition to elected and appointed governmental officials and their accompanying bureaucracy, the following potential State actors may act in ways relevant to the education system:

7 professional groups, e.g., American Association for the Advancement of Science, American Association of School Administrators, Council for Exceptional Children;
8 teacher unions, the National Education Association (NEA) and the American Federation of Teachers (AFT);
9 philanthropic foundations, e.g., Carnegie, Casey, Ford, Rockefeller;
10 corporate leaders;
11 organized interest groups, e.g., National Association for the Advancement of Colored People, National Organization for Women, Heritage Foundation;
12 'think tanks', e.g., Brookings Institute, American Enterprise Institute;
13 political parties;
14 lobbyists for any of the above non-governmental groups.

That the coalition of control that comprises the State extends beyond the govenment can be seen, for example, in the movement of corporate executive and professionals in and out of government positions. After leaving government service, many become consultants or lobbyists for private organizations that want to make use of their insider knowledge and possible political influence. Another example is the difference between textbook accounts of how a proposed bill becomes a law in the US Congress and what actually occurs in the political process, or the difference between an organization chart and the circulation of power and actual operation of the organization. A third example is the overlapping membership of the 1980s educational reform report commissions. Almost all included the presidents of the AFT and the NEA and one or more governors and corporate leaders. The eighteen members of the National Commission on Excellence in Education that produced *A Nation at Risk* in 1983 included current or former college and university presidents (4) and professors (2), corporate executives (2), high school principals (2), a high school teacher, a school district superintendent, a school board member, a state board of education member, the National School

Boards Association president, a state commissioner of education, a governor and a foundation executive.

This partial specification of State actors in the US names roles rather than the particular individuals who have filled them and groups rather than their representatives. This is not to denigrate individuals but to suggest that, in the US at least, the role is usually as important as the person. People fill roles, represent groups, and enter into relationships, but the roles, groups and relationships precede and shape the individuals who enact them. In other nations, the character of the person may be as or more important than the role. For example, in accounting for successful planning of educational change in Chile and El Salvador, McGinn, Schieffelbein, and Warwick[12] emphasized the part played by particular, named individuals.

> In both cases a strong, charismatic leader directed the Ministry of Education, received unconditional backing from an energetic president . . . came from outside the educational system, had personal but not partisan political allegiances to the president . . . characterized as decisive men of action rather than thinkers . . . depended on trusted lieutenants skilled in management and from outside the system . . . to implement the changes . . . .[13]

Role incumbents in the US State are more likely to be male than female, white than people of color, middle-class or more affluent than poor, politically moderate to conservative than radical and Republican or Democrat than 'third' party. While there certainly are more and less powerful groups in the US, there is no single class or homogeneous group that has maintained its dominance of the US State over time. The US State cannot be credibly characterized as the instrument of a dominant (i.e., capitalist) class as reproduction theorists claim. The US State is, importantly, what Carnoy and Levin describe as a site of continuing conflict within and between dominant and dominated groups.[14] Following their 'social-conflict theory of the State',[15] the politically democractic US State 'provides space' for struggles for equality, economic security and self-determination by the 'subordinate, relatively powerless groups' that are the product of 'capitalist production, with its inequalities of income and power',[16] patriarchy and racism. The combination of capitalist economy, discriminatory culture and democratic State assures continuing social movements and conflicts within society at large that are played out in the State arena and affect curriculum practice and change.

Organization

State organization varies with national historical experience and prevailing ideology. Three aspects of State organization relevant to education system-State relations are considered here: centralization and coupling within and among levels of governance; coherence within and among public policy sectors and relationship with the national economic system. With greater centralization and tighter coupling, the State is able to exert more direct control over the education system. With greater State policy coherence, there also is likely to be more direct State control of the education system so that its actions are compatible with initiatives in other sectors. The interdependence of the State and the national economic system means that education system actions inconsistent with economic interests are unlikely to be tolerated let alone supported. Rather, the State is likely to act in ways that influence the education system to further perceived economic needs.

Centralization and coupling

The organization of the State can be more or less centralized and tightly coupled. Formal decentralization and loose coupling within or among levels of governance do not preclude a strong State presence. While increasingly nationalized, the US State is not strongly centralized compared to States in other parts of the world. It is a federal State that is relatively decentralized and fragmented, not only by constitutional separation of executive, legislative and judicial government powers and division of national and state government powers, but also by diverse regional, economic and ethnic-racial interests.[17]

The historical experience of state formation in the US differed in important ways from that of European nations — ways that discouraged centralization such that the Nineteenth century US State was integrated primarily by the court and political party systems. Political patronage, for example, limited the establishment of a State bureaucracy until after the introduction of the civil service in the 1880s. And, the integration provided by the major political parties was loose and decentralized as was party organization. The major US political parties continue to be non-hierarchically and loosely organized, shifting coalitions rather than class-based and programmatic as in other nations. It was not until the early decades of the twentieth century that the US experienced widespread State bureaucratization and professionalization, first at local and state levels, spurred largely by piecemeal, middle-class sponsored reforms.[18] State centralization occurred primarily during the Progressive and New Deal periods. In the former, centralization was furthered in the name of modernization and efficiency; in the latter, centralization was to cope with economic and social crisis. In both periods, especially the New Deal, centralization was accompanied by efforts to plan change in education and other sectors.

Since World War II and especially in the last decade, nationalization has been a more prominent feature of the US State than further centralization. With respect to educational and other social policy in the 1980s, national agendas and debates are as likely to direct state and local activity as to result in national programs or mandates. The Reagan administration's rhetoric of decentralization was misleading as will be shown later. Rather than encouragement and support for local initiatives, we find locals being pressed to carry out nationally created preferences. A prime example is educational excellence defined as higher standards for high school graduation, teacher education and so forth.

Coherence

Coherence refers to the compatibility or co-ordination of policies and actions within and among public policy sectors. Coherence appears to be facilitated by higher degrees of State centralization and coupling but does not necessarily follow from them. In the US, social provisions such as Aid to Families with Dependent Children and Medicare-Medicaid as well as education remain disjointed and uneven in operation across the fifty states; separate programs tend not to be interrelated within sectors or related to inititiatives in other sectors. At neither the national nor the state levels is there much co-ordination across educational programs such as bilingual, vocational and special education nor co-ordination of educational with other social welfare programs. There are plans but no co-ordinated planning. The absence of coherence may well reflect what Skocpol characterizes as 'continuing American ambivalence about the role of the state in social provision'.[19] However, the relative lack of centralized planning, shifting alignments of interest and power and ambivalence have not precluded expansion of the US State and public sector in both already established arenas of State activity such as defense and education and new ones such as family life and sexuality.[20] That the US State is neither monolithic nor static may account in part for the perception of the US (primarily by its own citizens) as Stateless. Since the late nineteenth century, the US State has become increasingly expansive and nationalized if not centralized and coherent.

Relationship with national economic system

The contemporary State does not and probably cannot function independently of its associated economic system. The US State and capitalist economy, for example, are interdependent. Neither controls the other nor is completely free. The 'needs' of capitalism, such as capital accumulation for modernization and profit distribution, influence but do not determine State actions. While potent, capital accumulation needs are not the only influence on the State as evidenced by continuing conflict over State policy and by policy change. Just as neo-Marxist determinism fails to provide a satisfactory account of State action, so too does classical economic theory or pluralist political theory. Neither the US State nor US capitalism is a neutral or free market as the latter theorists contend. Labor and State as well as capitalist groups have become increasingly dependent on the State to further capital accumulation processes — labor to maintain its employment opportunities and the State to maintain its resource base (e.g., taxation). The importance of capital accumulation undermines pluralist theories of the State and politics of education that assume a one-to-one relationship between interest group numbers and State or education system response. It also limits the options of State and educational policymakers. That is, because of the importance of capital accumulation to several large and/or influential groups, the State cannot afford to act very often in ways contrary to capital accumulation even if a majority of voters appears to favor such action in a particular case. Given the value attached to representative political democracy in the US and near universal suffrage, popular consent to State policies tends to be rather carefully managed by and through the mass media.[21]

Given these considerations of the nature of the State, its key actors and organizational features, I turn to the relation of the State to the education system and to questions of curriculum control.

System-State Relations: Questions of Control

Whereas most liberal and conservative observers seem to assume that education in the US is an independent social institution, most radicals see it as a State agency or apparatus. The view taken here is that the US education system is neither an autonomous entity nor a creature of the national State. The education system and the State are interdependent as are the State and the economy. Constitutionally, education in the US is an arena reserved to the fifty states. Traditionally, considerable discretion has remained with local school districts and boards. The several layers of the US State (national, state, local) both constrain and provide leeway to — but do not determine — the education system. The US education system responds to its own internal dynamic and constituencies as well as to changing State coalitions and policies and the State bureaucracy. And, both the system and the State are bound by their own traditions at the same time that they are vulnerable to social movements and changing domestic and international conditions.

Before examining State policy instruments and bureaucracy as major sources of State control of the education system, I briefly expand on my rejection of the view of the US education system as a state apparatus and examine the construct of State interests. Both excursions, I believe, can strengthen efforts to account for as well as describe State and education system action.

Multiple Determinations

With respect to the location of the education system *vis-à-vis* the State in the US, I take as a starting point Archer's definition of a State education as a differentiated and interrelated collection of education-providing organizations whose overall control and supervision is at least partly governmental.[22] 'At least partly governmental' control, however, does not make an education system a State apparatus any more than government licensure of physicians and regulation of medical practice makes medicine a State apparatus. In the US and probably elsewhere, most individuals and groups, organizations and systems, are subject to some State regulation and receive some State support. To reduce them all to arms of the State neither describes nor explains their operation or change.[23]

In addition to this reductionist, all-or-nothing, assumption, two other over-simplifications are employed in support of the education system-as-State apparatus interpretation. One is that changes in the State necessarily and automatically cause parallel changes in the education system. That both the education system and the State are subject to and may respond similarly to changing conditions or external influences does not necessarily mean that the State acts first and then carries the education system along. For example, professionalization and bureaucratization of the US education system and State occurred at about the same time, and largely from the bottom up, during the late nineteenth and early twentieth centuries. The evidence does not support a claim that professionalization and bureaucratization of the State led to, caused, or directed parallel changes in the education system.

Second, that the education system can be seen to serve State functions or interests does not necessarily mean that it is a State apparatus. For example, as noted earlier (Chapter 2), education systems have been a means of nation-building, of defining and providing socialization for national citizenship and incorporating diverse populations (or, maintaining the hegemony of dominant groups), of preparing workers for the economy (or, supporting existing relations of production), and of conferring credentials that allocate individuals to different positions in society (or, rationalizing social and economic inequities). These purposes or effects serve social, economic and individual as well as State interests.

That the US State does exert some direct control over the education system, most notably through the courts with respect to matters of equity, does not mean that the State controls the education system *in toto*. The US education system is state-related, partially subject to and dependent on the State, and partially autonomous (or beholden to other interests). The education system's 'multiple integration' or interdependence with other societal institutions both increases the complexity of its operation and change and decreases its control by any one.[24]

Although the US case may be atypical, it ought not to be dismissed as irrelevant. Even in nations where the education system-State relationship is demonstrably close (e.g., France, Korea), there are good reasons for rejecting the education system-as-State apparatus interpretation. When education systems are treated simply as agencies of their respective States, at least three, usually unacknowledged implications follow. The little or no autonomy assumption denies local variation within an education system; it also denies internally initiated change and change stemming from external transactions with some segment of the education system. No education system is totally State determined if for no other reason than the impossibility of controlling every aspect of educational acitivity. Secondly, the preoccupation with State control minimizes recognition of transnational influences on or within education systems and obscures potentially important variations in system-State relations across national boundaries. Finally, if the education system is simply a State apparatus, there are few if any grounds for examining education as a separate sector or considering educational and curricular policy and planning apart from other State policy and planning (or, for planning any change when the State, in turn, is viewed as determined by the economy). In contrast, when education systems are viewed as State-related and multiply determined, multiple sources and means of change become possible.

The assumption of multiple determination also is relevant to consideration of State interests or purposes. Here, I focus on State interests in relation to the education system and curriculum practice and change. Examination begins with Green's formulation of a 'structure of interests'. Green locates control of the US education system in a structure of interests composed of State, parental, societal and incumbent (people occupying positions in the education system) interests.[25] State interests are of two kinds, compelling and derived. The State's compelling interests are that '(1) each individual attain economic independence, and (2) that each grant minimum obedience to civil law'.[26] Derived or secondary State interests, like constitutionally implied powers, arise from the State's efforts to secure its compelling interests in survival. They include

> determination of who can teach, who will be educated for how long, what will be taught under what conditions, and what will constitute an acceptable level of attention to these problems on the part of the family and the local community. Thus, the derived interests of the state can extend to the control of finance (both capital and operating), the licensing of teachers, the specification of curriculum, and standards of attendance.[27]

Green's concept of a 'structure of interests' is appealing insofar as it (a) recognizes multiple sources of education system control as interests are translated into political action and policy, (b) specifies particular State interests and (c) acknowledges conflicting and changing interests that might affect curriculum. However, I would elaborate his formulation to include additional State interests and special interests such as those of capital, labor, women and people of color, and to consider how the State attempts to operationalize its priority interests. As suggested previously, the State also has compelling interests in sustaining capital accumulation and mediating social conflict. In addition to State, parental, societal and incumbent interests, the 'structure of interests' that controls the education system includes organized special interest groups. Parental and societal interests, for example, are crosscut by class, gender and racial-ethnic interests stemming from economic, social and political differences.

Based on her comparative, historical study of the English and French education systems, Archer identified the State, organized non-governmental elites and professional groups as sources of control. The State exerts control by means of political action or manipulation, organized elites by external transactions with the education system (directly or through the State) and professional groups by internal initiation (directly or through the State). Which of these forms of 'assertion' will be undertaken or successful depends on the nature of the system, the State, and their relation and on the societal distribution of resources (e.g., wealth, power, expertise).

A related argument is offered by Bacchus, based largely on his historical study of curriculum in the former British West Indies from the 1830s to the 1940s.[29] Concerned with the subject matter content of the primary education program, he shows that economic reproduction arguments do not explain curriculum practice and that technocratic approaches do not change it. Instead, he argues that curriculum policy and practice result from the conflicting interests of different groups whose interests and relative resources change over time; curriculum is shaped by a 'multiplicity of factors and dialectical processes'.[30] Among these factors is the nature of the State, which he defines primarily in governmental terms, and its changing role. With respect to the former, Bacchus points to differences in the approaches of two of the largest curriculum development institutes — The Republic of Korea's KEDI (Korean Educational Development Institute) and India's NCERT (National Council for Educational Research and Training) — which he relates to the nature of their respective States. In South Korea,

> the State tends to be politically more autocratic and this is reflected in
> the directive and interventionist mode used by KEDI in its

curriculum development activities. On the other hand in India
... the State ... has a greater commitment to political democracy.
This, along with the fact that education is more of a joint rather than
a central government responsibility alone, affects the operational
mode of NCERT, which tends to be more collaborative and
cooperative with the lower levels of government and with
educational institutions. NCERT seeks to exert its influence on
curriculum changes less by direction and more by persuasion and
demonstration through curriculum research activities.[31]

The changing role of the State and implications for the education system and
curriculum are well illustrated in the West Indies after the abolition of slavery.
Rather than repression, the State's interest now was in 'developing among the
masses of a new moral infrastructure to underpin the plantation society which
succeeded slave society',[32] which meant, among other things, providing
primary education. According to Bacchus,

the responsibility of the State for the 'proper socialization' of the
West Indian masses was considered so important that the Secretary of
State for the Colonies in 1835 strongly urged all West Indian
legislatures to introduce compulsory education locally, almost
thirty-five years before such a step was taken by the British Government at home.[33]

Later, the State

began to direct its activities at incorporating previously unenfran-
chised groups into the body politic and subsequently on preparing a
'comprador elite' class to take over the reins of government just prior
to the withdrawal of colonial rule.[34]

The State's role and education policies changed as its interests, or means of
attaining them, changed.

A further and perhaps overriding State interest is what has come to be
characterized as legitimacy or legitimation. In order to survive without
resorting to physical coercion, the State needs to be seen by its citizens as a
credible normative and political authority. However, both the authority of the
State and its policymaking processes have been targets of increasing criticism
and loss of public confidence in the last decades of the twentieth century.
Recent attention to the erosion of State legitimacy or the 'legitimation crisis'[35]

faced by modern States has generated various interpretations and purported remedies. Following Weiler's analysis,

> [c]ommon to most conceptions of the legitimacy issue is the notion that, as the range and scope of the state's activities increase, there is a corresponding but disproportionate increase in the need for legitimation — a need that the state in turn seeks to satisfy by even further expanding its activities, thus perpetuating the spiral of increasing legitimacy needs that are forever harder to satisfy.[36]

Whether the State's legitimacy problem is of crisis proportions and whether its sources are seen to lie in an overload of demands, inadequate modes of citizen representation, the class structure of capitalist society, or inherent tensions between capitalism and democracy is less important here than the State's interest in legitimacy and how this interest influences its relation with the education system and, consequently, curriculum practice and change.

Compared to other social sectors, education appears to be particularly vulnerable to its own legitimation problems and a favored target of State actions intended to enhance the State's legitimacy. In contemporary western societies,

> education has a key role in allocating statuses and in socializing different groups in society into accepting and sustaining existing structures of wealth, status and power. In this role, education is particularly exposed to conflicting norms and thus in need of especially high levels of legitimation. At the same time, however, educational systems in many modern societies face an unprecedented crisis of confidence of their own which seems both to reflect and to compound the general legitimacy problem of the state.[37]

State education policies, following this interpretation, can be seen as 'strategies of compensatory legitimation'.[38] Education system initiatives also can be interpreted from a legitimation perspective. Compensatory legitimation strategies are examined in the next section on State policy instruments.

Within education, curriculum practice and change are especially susceptible to legitimacy problems and likely to be the target of State and education system legitimation strategies. Widespread educator and public acceptance of 'new' responses to the continually contested questions of curriculum knowledge requires compelling justification or legitimation.

Curriculum and exams represent the knowledge and cultural traditions that 'society' wishes to transmit to the next generation through its education system. Following Weiler, curriculum

> represent[s] the most tangible and detailed expression of an educational system's objectives; plans for developing or changing curricula, therefore, tend to reach rather deeply into the normative fabric of society and thus become a political phenomenon of considerable salience. The making of curricular decisions is thus inherently conflictual and is influenced by a variety of different and not necessarily convergent considerations: the individual's interest in the optimal development of one's talents; the society's actual or anticipated needs for certain kinds of skills and qualifications; the needs, based on the existing structures of power, to socialize people into certain attitudes and dispositions toward authority, performance, cooperation, and the like; and the formative weight of the pattern of social relations that prevails in the educational process itself. Given this complexity of the very nature of decisions on curriculum, and given that these decisions tend to be the prerogative of public authority in state-sponsored educational systems, the basis on which the state makes these decisions — that is, the legitimacy of the state's authority in curriculum matters — becomes a matter of considerable significance . . . a good deal of European (especially German) writing on curriculum reform in recent years seems absolutely consumed with the question of how curriculum decisions acquire legitimacy — mirroring the high salience of a number of political controversies over curriculum-reform projects.[39]

Curriculum's legitimacy problems stem not only from the normative aspects of curriculum practice and change but also from the increasingly problematic nature of knowledge and what counts as academic knowledge for curriculum purposes as well as the so-called knowledge explosion.[40] As long as established academic disciplines were or were seen as uncontested and were considered the basis for school curriculum, selecting and organizing curriculum knowledge was less complex and controversial than it has become with more disciplines to select from and more knowledge and competing paradigms within each. The academic disciplines no longer provide consensus and sufficient legitimacy for decisions regarding the selection, organization and treatment of curriculum knowledge. Cultural and academic heterogeneity exacerbates problems of curricular legitimacy and increases the likelihood of States and education systems employing compensatory legitimation strategies with respect to curriculum.

With this expanded conception of a structure of interests including state interests influencing education systems and curriculum, and the assumption of education systems as state-related rather than State agencies as background, I turn to examination of specific means by which States attempt to exert control over education systems, namely policy instruments or strategies and bureaucracy. As indicated earlier, State influence or control can be direct (e.g., authoritative mandate) or indirect (e.g., exhortation). Further, other influences or sources of control of education systems such as tradition, social movements and domestic and international conditions and trends may be mediated by the State through its policies and bureaucracy.

State Policy Instruments

The State can attempt to initiate, negate, or modify education system action. The qualifying language of 'attempt to' is necessary at least in the case of the US given the limits of liberal-democratic State power, the difficulty of controlling a large, decentralized (or fragmented) education system, and the holding power of socially shared understandings of education. Initiating, negating, and modifying can be accomplished by several means including court decision, legislative action, administrative regulation, voluntary programs made attractive by federal or state technical assistance and/or funding, and what in the 1980s came to be known as the 'bully pulpit' whereby State representatives exhort others to support and carry out their desired changes in the education system.[41] The turbulent history of Title I of the Elementary and Secondary Education Act first funded in 1965 (now incorporated into Chapter I of the 1982 Education Consolidation and Improvement Act, the Reagan administration's 'block grant' program) provides illustration of several of these processes in an effort to 'enhance the education of disadvantaged children, improve their achievement, and hence redistribute economic and social opportunities in society'.[42]

Of the various ways of categorizing State policy instruments, a modification of McDonnell and Elmore's typology of four generic categories of 'alternative policy instruments' is adopted here.[43] McDonnell and Elmore define alternative policy instruments as 'mechanisms to translate substantive policy goals (e.g., improved student achievement, higher quality entering teachers) into concrete actions'.[44] Their four categories of policy instruments are described as follows:

1 *Mandates:* rules governing individual and organizational action, requiring enforcement and intended to effect compliance; include court decisions, legislation, administrative regulations; examples include bilingual education requirements, secondary school graduation standards.

2 *Inducements:* conditional transfers of money or technical assistance to individuals or organizations in return for provision of desired products or services, usually involving regulations regarding how funds or assistance can be used; include voluntary grant programs to states, school districts, or individual schools; examples include compensatory education programs, science curriculum materials development.

3 *Capacity-building:* transfers of money or technical assistance to individuals or organizations as investments in material, knowledge, or human resources for anticipated future benefits; examples include basic research in 'higher order thinking' and problem-solving, establishment of curriculum and R and D centers.

4 *System-changing:* transfers of authority among individuals and existing or new organizations intended to alter the structure of provision or delivery of educational products or services and perhaps the nature of those products or services in order to increase efficiency or effectiveness or alter the distribution of power; examples include school choice or voucher programs, school-based curriculum development.

To these four categories I would add a fifth that is more prominent at the national than sub-national (e.g., state, provincial) level in the US and elsewhere and less tangible but seemingly no less potent.

5 *Exhortation:* rhetoric directed toward a mass audience intended to mobilize support for action to be undertaken by others; includes the bully pulpit of the Reagan administration in the US and the speeches of national leaders such as Castro on literacy in Cuba and Nyere on Education for Self Reliance in Tanzania.

Whereas mandates and inducements are intended to effect change within the education system, capacity-building and especially system-changing (which may invoke mandates or inducements) are intended to change the structure of the education system. System-changing explicitly alters the distribution of authority to provide a product or service supported or subsidized by the State. Exhortation can be directed towards either change within the education system or systemic change.

Mandates are based on the assumption that all affected individuals and agencies can and should do whatever is mandated, that is, on the possibility and desirability of standardization. Inducements, in contrast, are based on the assumption of variability in capacity and willingness to undertake the change in question. They can be seen as more sensitive to differences in local conditions. Capacity-building appears more likely to involve inducements and to foster differentiation while system-changing appears more likely to involve mandates and to result in re-standardization.

Whether State policymakers adopt one or another policy instrument or some combination appears to be influenced by several factors. McDonnell and Elmore hypothesize that, once the decision to act has been made and the actors (State agency and level) have been determined, the definition of the policy problem and the resources and constraints facing policymakers are the most influential factors shaping choice of policy instruments.[45] Problem definition, as noted earlier (in Chapter 2), directs problem solution. In other words, how a problem is defined (e.g., low student achievement, inadequate supply of curriculum materials) also defines the nature of the desired change and policy response (e.g., raise school graduation standards, provide more curriculum materials). Resources and constraints identified by McDonnell and Elmore are of six types: institutional context; governmental capacity; available fiscal resources; political support or opposition; availability of credible, relevant information; and past policy choices that establish precedents and encumber funds. Given the present focus on system-state relations and questions of the education system and curriculum control, what McDonnell and Elmore call institutional context, governmental capacity and political support or opposition are of particular interest.

Institutional context is similar to what I have called structure — established roles and relationships (among individuals and organizations or agencies), including operating procedures, shared beliefs, and norms (i.e., tradition, culture) — and refers to the State, the education system and relations between them. Where local control of schooling is the norm, State (national or sub-national) mandates are less likely than where there is a tradition of strong central authority.

Governmental capacity, for McDonnell and Elmore, refers to availability and ability of personnel to implement a policy and varies across local settings. Lack of State and/or education system capacity (e.g., to enforce compliance, to meet policy targets) makes mandates and exhortation less viable options than other policy instruments.

State policymaking typically occurs in an arena of multiple actors and competing interests where, from the State actors' perspective, political support needs to be mobilized and opposition minimized. State policymakers probably have more access than non-State actors to resources that enable them to shape elite and mass opinion in support of their preferences. Faced with strong internal or external opposition, State policymakers are more likely to pursue inducements such as small grants than mandates.

The means as well as the extent of State control of the education system, then, is shaped by institutional or structural context, capacity and political support or opposition among other factors — all of which can be expected to vary from one situation (time, place, issue) to another. A different configuration of factors can be expected to influence state action *vis-à-vis* the education system with respect to issues of universal primary education, science education and teacher preparation curriculum, for example.

A further influence on State action that merits extended consideration is the State's interest in maintaining or enhancing its perceived legitimacy. Here, Weiler's analysis of compensatory legitimation strategies employed by advanced capitalist or western States is most helpful.[46] Weiler posits three specific compensatory legitimation strategies — legalization, participation, and expertise — and a fourth, more general strategy that I characterize as symbolic reform. These strategies are viewed as means of fostering the State's normative and political credibility at least as much as attempts at resolving identified educational problems.

Legalization invokes constitutional or legal norms; it is policymaking by the courts and duly elected representative bodies (e.g., legislatures, school boards) rather than administrative or bureaucratic decision. Legalization confers legitimacy by linking educational policy with democratic values and procedures. Examples include the US Supreme Court's 1954 Brown decision for school desegregation and subsequent Congressional and federal court action, and a series of decisions by the West German Federal Constitutional Court directing that a range of education policy decisions be subject to formal legislative action rather than administrative decree in the interests of equality and due process. Legalization, which typically results in judicial or legislative mandates, can either increase the State's control of the education system or shift control from one agency of the State (executive) to another (judicial, legislative).[47] A legitimation perspective suggests that executive, administrative, or bureaucractic initiatives are more likely to take the form of inducements, capacity-building, or exhortation than mandates or system-changing.

Participation as a compensatory legitimation strategy also draws on the democratic values and procedures of citizen representation. In the US, provision for client (e.g., student, parent, community) participation in designing and implementing a variety of educational programs has 'become almost a standard ingredient in federal and state legislation'.[48] Examples include parent involvement in special education program development and community involvement in Teacher Corps programs. In Europe, according to Weiler, investigations of interest group or citizens' initiatives view their emergence

> as an indication of the erosion of the legitimacy of conventional mechanisms and structures of interest aggregation. At the same time, the toleration and, indeed, encouragement of the phenomenon by the state is seen as a way of coping with the very crisis that the emergence of citizens' initiatives reveals.[49]

The compensatory legitimation potential of direct participation by those affected is employed not only by the State but also by the education system through local advisory councils, site-based management schemes that devolve decision-making authority to local school personnel, and provisions for school-based curriculum development. Participation can be an adjunct to all four of McDonnell and Elmore's policy instruments and a topic of exhortation.[50]

Expertise refers to various ways of using knowledge to justify the process and substance of policymaking. This strategy draws on assumptions and traditions of scientific research that are highly esteemed in Western cultures. Research, evaluation and planning are the primary manifestations of expert knowledge use for legitimation explored by Weiler.[51] His analysis and illustrations focus on mainstream models of research, evaluation and planning in the 1960s and 1970s. Scientific (in the mainstream, technocratic sense) research, especially experimentation and the evaluation of experimental programs, has become a prominent feature of educational policymaking and change efforts worldwide since World War II.

> The notion of 'reforms as experiments' — applying the classical paradigm of scientific methodology to the realities of public policy — held the prospect of being able to say, with scientific conviction and credibility, that one social program was 'better' than another, that advocates of a given policy were 'right' and its opponents 'wrong'.[52]

Examples of state sponsored, experimental educational program evaluations in the US include Head Start, Follow Through and National Science Foundation curriculum materials development projects. The introduction of comprehensive secondary schooling in Sweden in the 1950s and early 1960s was accompanied by experimental studies of several elements of the new system that 'played a rather significant role in reinforcing the arguments of the advocates of the reform, even though some of the findings were later challenged'.[53]

Experimentation and evaluation also are employed by non-State organizations and the education system as legitimation strategies and/or practical means of attempting to bring about change. Examples here include teacher education and curriculum materials development projects sponsored by US private foundations and professional organizations in the 1960s and 1970s (e.g., the Ford Foundation's Master of Arts in Teaching programs, the American Sociological Association's *Sociological Resources for Secondary Schools*) and educational development projects sponsored by international agencies such as the World Bank and USAID.

Research and evaluation, until recently primarily in a technocratic mode, contributes to the States's legitimacy in at least two ways.

> First, given its prominent standing as the most genuinely scientific of all methodological constructs in research, the experiment commands an exceptionally high level of prestige and credibility. The notion of experimentally 'exploring' the strengths and weaknesses of alternative policy propositions thus exemplifies — in the eyes of the public as well as those of policymakers — a particularly powerful source of 'organizational rationality' and thus a particularly rich and compelling source of added legitimacy for the policy process. Indeed, it seems that it is the legitimacy of the *process*, rather than that of its

results, that stands to gain the most from the scientific connotation of the experiment.[54]

Experimental research and evaluation not only lend credibility to policymaking and planning processes but also serve as means of conflict management. In situations where there is strong disagreement about the nature, severity, or resolution of an educational problem, experiments have the

> advantage of temporizing or defusing a potentially explosive political situation; 'trying out' something new can satisfy both the advocates of the status quo and the advocates of change . . . . Experimentation as a device to manage and defuse conflict responds precisely to one of the most acute legitimacy dilemmas of the modern state, namely, how to deal with conflict without either resorting to coercion or risking disintegration — either of which would be potentially fatal for the continued functioning of the state.[55]

Planning, like experimentation and experimental program evaluation, can serve to link the credibility of science with State policymaking and policies. Curriculum planning that appears to embody scientific rationality, particularly its procedural elements, connotes comprehensiveness, orderliness and objectivity.[56] Technocratic planning is seen as both an indicator and source of legitimacy of the resulting plans.

Experimentation, evaluation and planning — legitimation by expertise — might be associated with any of McDonnell and Elmore's alternative policy instruments and become topics of exhortation. They might precede, accompany, or follow State policymaking. For example, evaluation of an experimental program might precede a wider mandate. Presumably, planning would precede and accompany a system-changing policy, and evaluation would follow. In considering expertise as a legitimation strategy, research, evaluation and planning need not be limited to technocratic models. As expanded and alternative conceptions of science and rationality gain currency, so too do alternative models of curriculum practice and change.

The fourth compensatory legitimation strategy, symbolic reform, which is treated only briefly by Weiler, has been elaborated by others.[57] By symbolic reform, I refer to the rhetoric of reform and 'going through the motions' of educational change whether or not that activity holds any promise of improvement. Symbolic reform as a legitimation strategy overlaps considerably with rhetoric as a policy instrument. It also may be associated with (or be the major effect of) the alternative policy instruments identified by McDonnell and Elmore. As suggested in the presentation of the other three compensatory legitimation strategies — legalization, participation, expertise — any one or a combination could be or become more symbolic than substantive.

The appeal of symbolic reform lies in the 'illusion of progress' it engenders.[58] Given the widespread expectation that a rapidly changing world necessitates compatible educational changes, even the appearance of State (or education system) action toward educational modernization usually is perceived positively. The legitimating ritual of symbolic reform is to establish consensus and maintain institutional viability by creating an image of a State and education system that are responsive to perceived needs and a feeling that things are getting better. Reform then becomes the symbolic orchestration of ritual, and motion is taken as change.[59] The 'effect' is to sustain both the State and the educational *status quo*.

Examples of symbolic reform that appear largely rhetorical, insofar as there does not appear to be much happening beyond the rhetoric, include the 'excellence' movement of the 1980s in the US and, to date, George Bush as the 'education president'. With repetition, the labels come to be taken as real. Ironically, the myriad of commission reports *calling for* US educational and teacher education reform, 1983–86, often were taken as evidence of reform and referred to as reforms. Experimental programs also can be seen as symbolic reforms in that they 'provide a symbolic tribute to the expectation that the modern state should be genuinely committed to reform'.[60] In this view, experimental programs provide their State or education system proponents with the opportunity to demonstrate interest in reform, shield the system and/or the State from other attempts at similar reforms for the duration of the experiment and postpone possibly contentious policymaking (and justify postponement on 'scientific' grounds).[61] Experimental school choice and voucher plans in the US are examples.

The curriculum reform movement of the early 1970s in the Federal Republic of Germany, set in the larger context of conflict laden movement toward comprehensive secondary schooling, provides one illustration of these compensatory legitimation strategies.[62] Legalization was evident, as previously noted, in a series of decisions by the Federal Constitutional Court mandating that a range of curricular decisions (e.g., subjects to be taught at each grade level, general curricular objectives) be made by formal legislative bodies rather than administrative decree in the interests of equality and due process. Expertise in the form of planning and evaluation was evident in the educational and curricular reform discourse of the period. According to Weiler:

> In a country where, not unlike the U.S., the notion of planning used to connote dangerously *dirigiste* and socialist patterns of statism, planning had seen a remarkable surge in currency across a number of policy fields, notably including education, in the 1960s. The discourse through which it was introduced, and its importance argued, leaned heavily towards the importance of rationality in the political decision process. For educational policy, a major planning effort accompanied the reform phase of the late 1960s and early 1970s, with the objective of producing a 'comprehensive educational plan'.[63]

The emphasis on planning curriculum reform communicated 'both the comprehensiveness and orderliness of the approach and the transparency and rationality of the process . . . planning was seen as both a symbol and a source of procedural rationality, and hence as another presumptive source of legitimacy'.[64] A symbolic reform strategy was evident in the argument that existing curricula were out of date and should be updated to reflect contemporary scientific, technological and economic knowledge and needs.

In Weiler's analysis, participation was the most salient legitimation strategy of this curriculum reform period.

> In historical perspective, a more participatory conception of curriculum development is obviously a reaction to a tradition in which — especially in a country like Germany — curricula were developed and decreed by administrative authority and bureaucratic fiat, moderated at most by the involvement of academic subject matter specialists as authoritative experts . . . . In deliberate contrast to this tradition, and in recognition of its loss of legitimacy, stands the conception of an 'integrated' planning and decision process in which those who are affected by the outcome of the process — teacher, students, parents — play an important role alongside the intra-administrative or extra-administrative experts. When the *Bildungsrat*, the government-appointed commission for designing the educational reform of the 1970s, addressed the question of the governance of the future educational system, it devoted a key section

of its recommendation to 'the legitimation of curricular decisions' .... The core idea was the 'autonomous and participatory school', which was to be tied to the general curricular framework set by the authority of the state through parliamentary decisions, but which would have within this framework the latitude and autonomy of actively involving teachers, students, and parents in concrete and specific curriculum development work.[65]

Although the Bildungsrat's recommendations were not fully implemented, considerable participation in curriculum projects occurred in the various West German states, regions and schools. The idea and the practice of broad participation in curriculum development was one of 'the very tangible consequences of the intensive debate over the legitimation of curricular decisions'.[66] Weiler also has suggested that, in the case of West Germany,

> with its rather centralized administrative traditions, this argument
> [that curricular decisions derive further legitimacy from the
> participation of those affected] is complemented by the need for
> decentralising the decision-making process; participation at the 'base'
> of the system makes sense only when the base has something to say.
> The ideal, from the point of view of maximizing legitimacy, is the
> 'autonomous and participatory school'.[67]

The transnational movement toward school-based curriculum development, which is examined in Chapter 7, can be seen as a further embodiment of a participatory legitimation strategy.

In sum, there are at least five types of State policy instruments by which the State attempts to control the education system: mandates, inducements, capacity-building, system-changing and rhetoric. Given a perceived educational problem, selection of a policy instrument is influenced by how the problem is defined, the resources and constraints facing State policymakers, and perhaps overriding concerns with maintaining or restoring the State's legitimacy. Strategies of compensatory legitimation — legalization, participation, expertise and symbolic reform — crosscut alternative policy instruments. That these strategies may not have the desired legitimating effects does not seem to have diminished their appeal as evidenced by their continued practice.

Bureaucracy

Beyond the policy instruments just examined, the State exerts control over the education system through the State bureaucracy that is charged with carrying out its policies. Bureaucracy is treated only briefly here since bureaucratic controls have been well analyzed and documented by others.[68] Further, consideration of the State bureaucracy appears to parallel the education system bureaucracy examined in Chapters 2 and 5.

Following my interpretation of State interests, policy instruments and legitimation strategies, it appears that State bureaucracies lose one form of power (e.g., policy decision-making) as a result of the State's interest in maintaining or enhancing its legitimacy and gain another (e.g., regulatory oversight) as a result of increasing State activity in pursuit of legitimacy and/or public problem resolution. As executive or administrative decree is seen as less democratic and therefore less legitimate than judicial decision or legislative action, the latter expands in part at the expense of the former. Consequently, State bureaucracies are left with fewer policy decisions to make and more to monitor and enforce.

This trend is apt to continue without substantial bureaucratic resistance given its compatibility with bureaucracies' penchant for orderliness, the State's continuing legitimation needs and the always remaining areas of bureaucratic discretion. While it limits some bureaucratic activity, it also provides continuity in the regulatory role and expansion of the regulated field. Thus, bureaucratic roles and activities are modified but not eliminated; if anything, bureaucracies will continue to expand.

Among the aspects of 'bureaucratic consciousness' identified by Berger, Berger and Kellner,[69] three are especially pertinent here: orderliness, predictability and non-separability of means and ends. Orderliness, refers to sets of jurisdictional categories and procedures that are employed so that most everything and everyone has a proper place. Predictability follows from orderliness. With established categories and procedures, there is reasonable certainty about what to do or what will be done. Non-separability refers to attaching more importance to means (i.e., procedures) than ends or effects. It serves to justify procedures. Clearly, these aspects of bureaucratic consciousness both describe and serve to sustain bureaucracy.[70] They also tend to foster conservatism or at least a strong suspicion of change that might obstruct education system and curriculum reform efforts unless they could be shown to further specific bureaucratic interests or to be a political imperative.

It also should be noted that, despite bureaucracies' claims to specialized knowledge, objectivity and impersonality, they may in practice provide 'generous services and little regulation for some whose power is widely feared, and small services and major controls over larger numbers perceived as wielding little power'.[71] This bureaucratic discretion carries the potential to substantially alter State policies.

Consistent with my conceptualization of the State and system-State relations is the observation that the State bureaucracy is not monolithic in its interests or actions. Different individuals and agencies have different purposes and priorities that can reshape the intended process, substance, or effects of decisions made at 'higher' levels of the State. Individuals and agencies may be competitive or work at cross purposes in pursuing their priorities or simply seeking to extend their domain. In addition, individual bureaucrats and agencies have different and changing degrees of power. Consequently, to treat the State bureaucracy as a whole or as static is to misrepresent its operation and actual or potential influence on the education system and curriculum. Also, despite bureaucratic similarities across national boundaries, there are important structural, especially cultural, variations. Instead of being taken for granted, a given State bureaucracy ought to be investigated for the ways in which individual bureaucrats and agencies might facilitate or impede desired curriculum practice and change.

Change over Time

Variability and change over time in the composition and functioning of the State and the nature of system-State relations have been noted throughout this examination of the system and the States. Here, I note changes in State actors and actions and in system-State relations using the US in the 1980s as an example. The 1980s witnessed the emergence of new configurations of State influence on the education system accompanied by patterns of governance different from those of the preceding decades. One aspect of the new configuration is what can be characterized as a shift from educational to general governance of the education system, particularly at the state level.[72] Previously, state education policy was created primarily by education specialists, i.e., elected and/or appointed state officials and their advisors, including the state education bureaucracy and representatives of professional education interest groups such as teacher, administrator and school board associations. In the 1980s, and especially since publication of *A Nation at Risk* in 1983, more individuals and groups in and out of government have taken an interest in educational reform and become involved in educational policymaking. State governors, legislators and prominent businessmen, for example, have taken an active and visible role in educational policymaking. In some states such as Texas, these new players appear to have pushed the traditional educational policymakers to the sidelines, at least for the time being.[73] At the federal level during the Reagan administration, according to Clark and Astuto, except for the Secretary Terrell Bell,

> leaders in ED were non-educationists — appointed without reference
> to or consultation with the educational community. The [Reagan]
> administration went out of its way to snub the largest lobby of all,
> the National Education Association. Consultation with the education
> community about planned changes in education was replaced by press
> conferences to announce the changes.[74]

Expert advisers were involved in federal educational policymaking but they were drawn from business and politics more than academia (either education or social science). This shift appears to have been a result of the explicitly ideological, conservative bent of the Reagan administration and its discrediting of usually more liberal academics by association with the policies that preceded the educational 'crisis' of the 1980s.

A second and related aspect of the new configuration is the substantial initiative taken by philanthropic foundations, such as the Carnegie and Casey foundations, to shape and finance educational reform. For the most part, these initiatives have been directed to (a) the public (e.g., the well publicized Carnegie sponsored report, *A Nation Prepared: Teachers for the Twenty-first Century*), (b) to education professionals (e.g., the multi-million dollar Carnegie grants to its own National Board of Professional Teaching Standards and to Lee Shulman at Stanford University to develop teacher proficiency test protocols), and (c) to the schools (e.g., the multi-million dollar Casey grants to five school districts to create comprehensive academic and support service programs for at-risk students). Relatively few have been routed through state or federal government agencies. As Popkewitz has noted, the merging of national and multinational corporate and foundation interests and activities with those of professional education associations and organizations are viewed typically as laudable, even 'scientific' efforts in the national interest, but rarely as 'new coalitions of control and patterns of governing'.[75]

A third aspect relates to change in the balance of federal and state government control of the education system. The conventional wisdom is that the Reagan administration's educational policy has been one of decentralization that has shifted both control and responsibility to the states and local school districts. Clark and Astuto, for example, have characterized Reagan administration educational policy, 1981–84, in terms of diminution (of federal government financial support of education), deregulation, decentralization, disestablishment (of the Department of Education), and de-emphasis — and given it the highest mark for decentralization, citing the 1982 Education Consolidation and Improvement Act and increases in state level educational policy activity. They also identified devolution (i.e., transfer of control of the education system to state and local levels) as a key educational policy preference of the 1985–88 Reagan administration.[76]

There are at least two problems with the claims of decentralization and devolution. One is that while state governments are increasing their control of those parts of the education system under their jurisdiction, local control at the school district and school level is being eroded. Kirst, for example, has noted increasing centralization of control (a) over school districts via regulation at the state government level and (b) over schools via regulation and specialization at the school district level.[77] Decentralization has not reached the local levels of the education system. Also worth noting is that increased state level activity in the name of educational reform differs from earlier (pre-1980) federal programmatic inducements. For the most part, it reflects expansion of the traditional regulatory function of the states. What the states have been doing differs substantially from what the federal government has given up.

A second and more important problem with the decentralization and devolution claims is that they naively accept Reagan administration rhetoric as reality and mistakenly equate the State with the federal government. Although the federal government has given up operational responsibility for a number of educational programs and initiated few new ones, it has retained and probably expanded its role in shaping State and local educational policy and practice via the 'bully pulpit' with exhortation and the Secretary of Education's 'report cards' on State educational performance. There is seemingly powerful central direction of the education system, albeit without commensurate support.

Taking the Reagan administration at its word and focusing on formal government activity such as legislation obscures other powerful State influences on the education system such as the already mentioned commission reports, foundation activities and organized interest groups. Instead of decentralization, I suggest that there has been and continues to be a reconfiguration and *re-centralization* of control of the education system by the State in which the federal government has played a key but not exclusive role.[78]

This examination of ways in which the State directly and indirectly influences curriculum practice and change through its relationship to the education system has highlighted State actors, policy instruments including legitimation strategies, and bureaucracy. It also has noted heterogeneity, issue and situational contingency and change over time. While brief examples have been provided, critical empirical studies of system-State relations and curriculum practice that would offer extended illustration of how controls operate and change occurs are yet to appear. The present analysis might serve as a framework for such studies or for reinterpreting and extending existing accounts of curriculum practice and change. The case of school-based curriculum development, considered in the next chapter, provides one such opportunity.

Notes

1 This chapter draws heavily from D. Adams and C. Cornbleth, *Planning Educational Change*, Chapter 6, 'The System and the State' (manuscript in progress).

2 H. N. Weiler, 'Legalization, Expertise, and Participation: Strategies of Compensatory Legitimation in Educational Policy', *Comparative Education Review* 27, 1 (1983): p. 259.

3 T. Skocpol, 'A Society without a "State"?' paper presented at the American Council of Learned Societies Institute, 'Foreign Perspectives on the U.S. Constitution', Wingspread-Racine, Wisconsin, September 1987, p. 1.

4 T.S. Popkewitz, 'Teaching and Teacher Education Reforms: Reconstituting a State Bureaucratic Apparatus and Forming a Political Discourse', unpublished paper, University of Wisconsin-Madison, January 1988, p. 24.

5 S. Skowronek, *Building a New American State: The Expansion of National Administrative Capacities, 1877–1920* (Cambridge and New York: Cambridge University Press, 1982), p. 19 (cited in T. Skocpol, 1987, *op cit.*, p. 17).

6   On the role of the intellectual *vis à vis* the State, see, for example, A.W. Gouldner, *The Future of Intellectuals and the Rise of the New Class* (New York: Seabury, 1979).

7   P.B. Evans, D. Rueschemeyer, and T. Skocpol, 'States and the Patterning of Social Conflicts' (introduction to Part III), in *Bringing the State Back In*, ed. P.B. Evans, D. Rueschemeyer, and T. Skocpol (Cambridge: Cambridge University Press, 1985), p. 253.

8   Ibid.

9   J.W. Meyer and B. Rowan, 'The Structure of Educational Organizations', in *Organizational Environments*, ed. J.W. Meyer and W.R. Scott (Beverly Hills, CA: Sage, 1983), p. 84; see Chapter 2.

10 For a critical analysis, see I. Westbury, 'A Nation at Risk', *Journal of Curriculum Studies* 16, 4 (1984): 431–445.

11 For a readable account of the US federal budget process, see A. Stoll, *The Budget Game: How the Federal Budget Process Works Against (Education and Educational Research) Small Players in the Big Leagues* (Washington, DC: American Educational Research Association, Organization of Institutional Affiliates Info Memo, February 1989, 13 pp.).

12 N. McGinn, E. Schiefelbein, and D.P. Warwick, 'Educational Planning as Political Process: Two Case Studies from Latin America', *Comparative Education Review* 23, 2 (1979): 218–239.

13 *Ibid.*, p. 222.

14 M. Carnoy and H.L. Levin, 1985, *op cit.*

15 *Ibid.*, p. 46.

16 *Ibid.*, p. 24.

17 T. Skocpol, 1987, *op cit.*

18 *Ibid.* For an historical account of the US state, see S. Skowronek, 1982, *op cit.*

19 T. Skocpol, 1987, *op cit.*, pp. 30–31. In addition, one could argue that, even in the absence of ideological and programmatic coherence, the democratic State obtains unity from the perceived legitimacy of its claim to authority and its monopoly of coercion.

20 Explanations of State expansion are beyond the scope of this paper. Expansion may be a function of the needs, conflicts and crises (e.g., legitimation, fiscal) of advanced corporate capitalism and the liberal-democratic State as argued, for example, by C. Offe, 'Social Policy and the Theory of the State,' in *Policy-making in Education*, ed. I. McNay and J. Ozga (Oxford: Pergamon, 1985), pp. 85–100. Also, see R. Dale, G. Esland, R. Fergusson and M. MacDonald (eds.), *Education and the State. Vol. 1, Schooling and the National Interest* (London: Falmer Press, 1981) and M. Carnoy, *The State and Political Theory* (Princeton, NJ: Princeton University Press, 1984). Alternatively, State expansion may be the outcome of social conflict as suggested by M. Carnoy and H.L. Levin, *Schooling and Work in the Democratic*

State (Stanford, CA: Stanford University Press, 1985), or it may represent secularization of 'pastoral power' as suggested by M. Foucault, 'The Subject and Power' in *Art after Modernism: Rethinking Representation*, ed. B. Wallis (New York: The New Museum of Contemporary Art/Boston: Godine, 1984), pp. 417–432.

21 For an alternative critique of the over-economistic interpretation of the emergence and expansion of the modern State, see J.W. Meyer, 'The World Polity and the Authority of the Nation-State', in G.M. Thomas *et al.*, *Institutional Structure* (Newbury Park, CA: Sage, 1987), pp. 41–70.

22 M.S. Archer, *Social Origins of Educational Systems* (London and Beverly Hills, CA: Sage, 1984), p. 19.

23 Thus, I take issue with Carnoy and Levin, among others, who claim that 'Education is, of course, part of the State apparatus'. *Op cit.*, p. 49. Interestingly, they do not deal explicitly with questions of control of the education system.

24 M.S. Archer, 1984, *op. cit.*

25 T.F. Green, *Predicting the Behavior of the Educational System* (Syracuse, NY: Syracuse University Press, 1980), p. 20.

26 *Ibid.*, p. 22.

27 *Ibid.*, pp. 23–24.

28 M.S. Archer, 1984, *op. cit.* These ideas were elaborated in Chapter 5.

29 M.K. Bacchus, *The Myth and Reality of Curriculum Planning* (London: University of London, Institute of Education, 1986).

30 *Ibid.*, p. 10.

31 *Ibid.*, p. 10.

32 *Ibid.*, p. 11.

33 *Ibid.*, p. 11.

34 *Ibid.*, p. 11.

35 J. Habermas, *Legitimation Crisis* (Boston: Beacon, 1975).

36 H. Weiler, 1983, *op. cit.*, p. 259.

37 *Ibid.*, p. 261.

38 *Ibid.*

39 Weiler, 1983, *op. cit.*, p. 273.

40 See, for example, M.F.D. Young, 'An Approach to the Study of Curricula as Socially Organized Knowledge', in *Knowledge and Control*, ed. M.F.D. Young (London: Collier Macmillan, 1971); T.S. Popkewitz, 'The Latent Values of the Discipline-Centered Curriculum', *Theory and Research in Social Education* 5, 1 (1977): 41–60; K.J. Gergen, *Toward Transformation in Social Knowledge* (New York: Springer-Verlag, 1982); C. Cornbleth, 'Knowledge in Curriculum and Teacher Education', *Social Education* 51, 7 (1987): 513–516; Weiler, 1989, *op. cit.*

41 On the 'bully pulpit see W.H. Boyd, 'Rhetoric and Symbolic Policies: President Reagan's School-Reform Agenda, *Education Week,* March 18, 1987, p. 28.

42 R.F. Elmore and M.W. McLaughlin, *Steady Work: Policy, Practice, and the Reform of American Education* (Santa Monica, CA: RAND, 1988), p. 25.

43 L.M. McDonnell and R.F. Elmore, 'Getting the Job Done: Alternative Policy Instruments'. *Educational Evaluation and Policy Analysis* 9, 2 (1987): 133–152. It should be noted that my interests are broader than McDonnell and Elmore's focus on state level educational policymaking in the US and that I do not share their implicitly top-down perspective on educational change.

44 *Ibid.,* p. 134.

45. *Ibid.*

46 H. Weiler, 1983, *op. cit.*; H. Weiler, 'Curriculum Reform and the Legitimation of Educational Objectives: The Case of the Federal Republic of Germany' (paper presented at the annual meeting of the Comparative and International Education Society, Cambridge, MA, 1989a).

47 On legalization, also see D.L. Kirp and D.N. Jensen (Eds.), *School Days, Rule Days: The Legalization and Regulation of Education* (London and Philadelphia: Falmer Press, 1986).

48 H. Weiler, 1983, *op. cit.,* p. 272.

49 *Ibid.,* p. 273.

50 Participation, of course, may be more symbolic than 'real'. See, for example, M. Edelman, *'Political Language: Words that Succeed and Policies that Fail* (New York: Academic Press, 1977); T.S. Popkewitz, 'Schools and the Symbolic Users of Community Participation', in *Community Participation in Education,* ed. C. Grant (Boston: Allyn and Bacon, 1979).

51 H. Weiler, 1983, *op. cit.*; H. Weiler, 1989a, *op. cit.*

52 H. Weiler, 1983, *op. cit.,* p. 269.

53 *Ibid.,* p. 269.

54 *Ibid.,* p. 270.

55 *Ibid.*

56 See Chapter 2.

57 See, e.g., M. Edelman, 1977, *op. cit.*; J.W. Meyer and B. Rowan, 'Institutionalized Organizations: Formal Structure as Myth and Ceremony, *American Journal of Sociology* 83, 2 (1977): 340–363; J. W. Meyer and W.R. Scott, 1983, *op.cit.* T.S. Popkewitz, 'Educational Reform: Rhetoric, Ritual, and Social Interest', *Educational Theory* 38, 1 (1988): 77–93.

58 T.S. Popkewitz, 1988, *op. cit.,* p. 81.

59 T.S. Popkewitz, 'Educational Reform as the Organization of Ritual: Stability as Change', *Journal of Education* 164, 1 (1982): 5–29. This argument is elaborated and

illustrated with respect to 1980s US teacher education reform in C. Cornbleth, 'Ritual and Rationality in Teacher Education Reform', *Educational Researcher* 15, 4 (1986):5–14.

60 H. Weiler, 1983, *op. cit.*, p. 271.

61 *Ibid.*

62 H. Weiler, 1983, 1989a, *op. cit.*; H. Weiler, 'Why Reforms Fail: The Politics of Education in France and the Federal Republic of Germany', *Journal of Curriculum Studies* 21, 4 (1989b): 291–305.

63 H. Weiler, 1989a, *op. cit.*, p. 13.

64 *Ibid.*, p. 14.

65 *Ibid.*, pp. 15–16.

66 *Ibid.*, p. 16.

67 H. Weiler, 1983, *op. cit.*, p. 274.

68 E.g., P.M. Blau, *The Dynamics of Bureaucracy* (Chicago: University of Chicago Press, 1954); G.M. Britan, *Bureaucracy and Innovation* (Beverly Hills, CA: Sage, 1981); R.K. Merton *et al.*, *Reader in Bureaucracy* (Glencoe, IL: Free Press, 1952); M. Weber, *The Theory of Social and Economic Organization* (London: Oxford University Press, 1947).

69 P. Berger, B. Berger and H. Kellner, *The Homeless Mind: Modernization and Consciousness* (New York: Vintage, 1973).

70 Parallels between aspects of bureaucratic consciousness and decontextualized or technocratic approaches to curriculum construction and change are noteworthy, e.g., their procedural emphasis.

71 M. Edelman, 1977, *op. cit.*, p. 78.

72 L. Miller, personal communication, April 1988. This shift could be interpreted as a participatory legitimation strategy.

73 D. Adams, C. Cornbleth and D. Plank, 'Between Exhortation and Reform: Recent U.S. Experience with Educational Change', *Interchange* 19, 3/4 (1988): 121–134.

74 D.L. Clark and T.A. Astuto, *The Significance and Permanence of Changes in Federal Educational Policy 1980–1988* (Bloomington, IN: University Council on Educational Administration, Policy Studies Center, 1986), p. 13.

75 T.S. Popkewitz, 1988, *op. cit.*, p. 20. This merging of interests and modes of operation tends to be mutually sustaining. Another important element in this mix is the role played by academic experts (Skocpol's 'policy intellectuals') as advisers to policymakers and sometimes as initiators of policy change. See T.S. Popkewitz, *Paradigm and Ideology in Educational Research. The Social Functions of the Intellectual* (London and New York: Falmer Press, 1984), Chapter 5, 'Social Science and Social Amelioration: The Development of the American Academic Expert', pp. 107–127.

76 *Ibid.*, pp. 17–18, 22.

77 M. W. Kirst, *Who Should Control our Schools: Reassessing Current Policies* (Stanford, CA: Center for Educational Research at Stanford, School of Education, Stanford University, 1988).

78 Similar trends have been noted elsewhere. See, e.g., S. Lindblad, 'The Practice of School-Centered Innovation: A Swedish Case', *Journal of Curriculum Studies* 16, 2 (1984): 165–172.

Part III
Curriculum Action and Inquiry

Chapter 7

Curriculum Policy and Planning

If curriculum is taken as a contextualized social process, and its structural and sociocultural contexts are taken seriously, what are the implications for curriculum policy and planning? As indicated in Chapter 2, viewing curriculum practice and change as socio-structurally constructed does not discount planning and product development; it does suggest modification of their purpose and relation to curriculum. It also recognizes that curriculum policymaking and planning occur at several levels or points within (and outside) the education system and that these various curriculum decisions are not always compatible. Further, the educational policymaking and planning affecting curriculum are much broader than that explicitly acknowledged as curricular.

By planning I mean a 'process of intentionally designing and effecting change in the structure, program, and/or impact of education systems and organizations'.[1] Planning is not simply preactive plan-making; it is a dynamic, iterative process. Initial plans are modified in practice, which affects subsequent planning (and practice). Change is planned, and plans are changed. Policy- or decision-making, which also has been variously defined, may or may not involve planning as just described. Often, policymaking involves only determining the goal to be accomplished (e.g., three rather than two years of science for secondary school graduation), not how or by whom it is to be carried out or what its substance is to entail (e.g., what science is to be offered).

In considering implications of context for curriculum relevant policymaking and planning at various levels throughout the education system, from the classroom of the individual teacher to the office of the education secretary or minister, I attempt to illustrate how the various layers of context interact, especially how the education system mediates State and sociocultural pressures in particular cases. Illustrations are drawn from studies in several national settings, including school-based curriculum development (SBCD). After providing an overview of recent national and state level curriculum policymaking in the US, I turn to cross-national experiences with curriculum policymaking and planning and then to the case of SBCD. In a concluding section, I suggest approaches to contextualized curriculum planning.

Professionalization and Politicization of Curriculum Policymaking

In the US and probably elsewhere, curriculum policymaking and planning have become increasingly complex and contentious. With a few notable exceptions, complexity and conflict as well as the nature of education systems and system-State relations appear to have constrained substantive, sustained reform of curriculum policy and practice during the past three decades.[2] Curriculum becomes a particularly salient public as well as professional issue during periods of change or perceived crisis such as the late 1950s and mid-1980s in the US. The attention to curriculum, however, tends not to translate into genuine reform in schools and classrooms. For example, largely in the name of educational excellence and global economic competitiveness, forty-five states have established or raised the number of courses (credits or units) required for secondary school graduation, especially in mathematics and/or science, since 1980. Little attention has been paid to the content of these newly required courses. The available evidence suggests that, while more 'low- and middle-achieving students' are taking more academic courses, the courses are of a remedial, basic, or general nature that does not contribute to a high quality core curriculum as claimed by their proponents following the recommendations of *A Nation at Risk* and other 1980s reform reports.[3]

The complexity and contentiousness of curriculum policymaking appear to have multiple, interrelated sources. Among these are: normative differences between and among advocates of educational equity and special interests; increasing knowledge and specialization; and increasing State involvement at the national, state, and local levels. Value conflicts are evident in the battles for and against comprehensive secondary schooling and core curriculum, the efforts of religious fundamentalists to substitute 'creation science' for evolutionary theory in biology, and the controversy generated by the NSF sponsored MACOS (Man A Course of Study) curriculum project. Increasing knowledge and specialization within and outside education systems have been accompanied by the professionalization of curriculum and other reform efforts and questioning of the nature and relevance of the traditional academic disciplines as the appropriate basis for curricular content. Increasing State involvement has altered the structure of curriculum policymaking authority. Brief explorations of each of these sources of complexity and controversy, and their interrelations, follow.[4]

Normative Differences, Value Conflicts

Questions of curriculum knowledge — its selection, organization, treatment and distribution — are political as well as epistemological and normative ones. As indicated in Chapter 5, their importance stems from their relation to power, to cultural transmission or transformation and to social reproduction or mobility. Questions of curriculum knowledge and the responses that are offered are politically sensitive because the actors involved or affected have diverse interests, and the stakes are high. The elaborated concept of the 'structure of interests' that controls the US education system (see Chapter 6) points to key actors and conflicting interests in heterogeneous or pluralistic democracies with one or another form of capitalist economy. Endemic social and technological change both extends and exacerbates the arena of value conflict affecting curriculum policymaking.

The contentiousness of curriculum policymaking is intensified also by compulsory school attendance laws in most nations. The compelling interests of States in educating their citizens have been operationalized not only in the provision of national systems of public schooling but also in regulation of independent (private or parochial) schools and so-called home schooling. If schooling were not compulsory, parents who found the school curriculum objectionable could freely educate their children at home or not at all. In a sense, the school curriculum constitutes the 'public orthodoxy', and as such its control is fiercely contested.[5] According to this interpretation, the schools have become an arena of bitter conflict because of their crucial role in the socialization of children, particularly the inculcation of values and the formation of consciousness. Given the role of school socialization in shaping present and future, individual and collective, beliefs and behavior, questions of curriculum control and/or choice are of critical importance to the State and its citizens.[6]

Increasing Knowledge and Specialization

The growth of knowledge and knowledge specialization has vastly increased the range of choices of curriculum knowledge and the number and variety of specialists-experts who claim the right, by virtue of their specialized knowledge, to influence those choices. This growth has occurred within the field of education as well as in the academic disciplines. It has been accompanied by what Moynihan has dubbed the 'professionalization of reform'[7] and by disagreements regarding the nature and relevance of the traditional academic disciplines as sources of curriculum knowledge. With respect to the latter, in the US there have been critiques of the mainstream presumptions of new social studies curriculum materials,[8] and religious fundamentalist challenges to evolutionary biology, as well as continuing debates about disciplinary versus multidisciplinary programs and about child, society, or academic discipline-centered programs.

The professionalization of reform is of particular interest as a relatively new and powerful ingredient in curriculum policymaking. Its treatment here draws primarily on the analyses of Moynihan and Boyd.[9] Professionalization of reform refers both to the institutionalization of reform as a 'shared social understanding' and a way of life, and to the emergence of groups of experts, i.e., professionals, whose role is to initiate and guide the various reform efforts. Institutionalization of reform — the public expectation of continuing improvement efforts in education and other social sectors and the continuing activity of the education system and the State in the name of reform — is consistent with 'rising expectations' on the part of various groups and societies as a whole, the State's (and education system's) legitimacy needs, and the assumptions of progress that are integral to modern western history and culture.

The emergence of professional reformers, especially since the mid-century in the US, reflects growing acceptance of State responsibility for economic and social well-being, the 'knowledge explosion' and the expansion of higher education, the professionalization of the middle-classes and the increasing involvement of private foundations in social amelioration.[10] The curriculum relevant professional reformers include social scientists and academicians of all disciplines as well as curriculum developers (co-ordinators, supervisors), so-called change agents, staff developers and evaluators.

According to Moynihan:

> In times past the impulse to reform and efforts in that direction had, generally speaking, risen among those groups most oppressed by existing conditions, or most likely to benefit from equitable change, or from members of the public regarding middle and upper classes who, from an enlightened and generous understanding, were able to identify their own interests with causes that benefitted others in the first instance but redounded ultimately to the welfare and stability of the society as a whole... pressures for change arise outside the institutions that are to be changed.... Increasingly efforts to change the American social system for the better arose from initiatives undertaken by persons whose profession was to do just that.[11]

Moynihan cites the Kennedy-Johnson administration's war on poverty as a prime example. It 'was not declared at the behest of the poor: it was declared in their interest by persons confident of their own judgment in such matters'.[12] Additional, curriculum examples include the introduction of sex education and the 'new' math and social studies programs of the 1950s and 1960s.[13]

The establishment of federally funded and usually university based regional educational laboratories and R and D centers in the mid-1960s can be seen as contributing to the institutionalization of the professionalization of reform. Although the specific missions, locations, and funding of the laboratories and centers have changed with changing political circumstances, they are still in existence.

Ironically, the professionalization of curriculum reform can serve to deprofessionalize teachers. When reforms are designed by experts, teachers are expected to carry out the experts' directions with, at most, minor modifications to accommodate local settings. Witness the development of presumably teacher-proof curriculum materials in the 1960s. This situation is reminiscent of Harold Rugg's lament more than sixty years ago that, while teachers should be the major designers of the curriculum in their classrooms, they are not able to do so and therefore need the assistance of curriculum specialists (see Chapter 2). However, contemporary curriculum specialists do not seem to share Rugg's wish that teachers be more than managers or competent technicians.

While professional reformers can contribute positively to curriculum practice and change, their individual and collective self-interests ought not to be discounted. Curriculum reformers, like other people, are concerned with career advancement and the maintenance if not enhancement of their organizations.[14] These interests require a continuing supply of 'problems' to be 'solved', symbolically or otherwise. In Boyd's analysis,

> the professionalization of reform has introduced an extraordinary, dynamic, and controversial new force into the social and educational policy-making process. Convinced of their expertise and its prerogatives, armed with 'solutions looking for problems' . . . assisted by an 'educational research establishment, with its built-in incentive to discover failure which justifies ever more research' . . . supported by federal and foundation funding, and stimulated by the discovery, as a result of the civil rights movement, of whole new classes of disadvantaged students and forms of discrimination (e.g., non-English speaking students, handicapped students, sex discrimination), the professional reformers energetically pursue their visions of equal educational opportunity and a better and more just society.[15]

A decade or two later, the vision has been altered to emphasize excellence and economic competitiveness but its energetic pursuit by professional reformers continues.[16]

The re-emergence of interest and activity in action research and the attraction of SBCD in the 1980s can be seen, in part, as reactions to the professionalization of curriculum reform. Action research and SBCD, as collaborative projects that involve people (especially teachers) affected by curriculum reform efforts, could return 'power to the people', manipulate their consent and commitment to change, or co-opt them. There appear to be contradictory movements in curriculum policy and policymaking, toward regulation and technical control and toward teacher empowerment and professionalization. How these movements play out, and their impact on curriculum practice and change, remains to be seen and studied.

Increasing State involvement in curriculum and change over time in key State actors have altered the structure of curriculum policymaking authority. Greater State involvement and change in the configuration of control in the US have been described in Chapter 6.[17] An expanded and reconfigured State presence has had several effects on curriculum policymaking. In Boyd's late 1970s analysis, curriculum policymaking in the US has become 'more complex, legalized, centralized and bureaucratized and includes more veto points'.[18] In support of his conclusions, he cited the greater role played by federal and state courts, teacher unions, special interest groups and professionals. While there were more players than before, some previously important curriculum players had been sidelined, primarily at the local level (e.g., school boards, school personnel, parents).

Ten years later, despite the Reagan administration rhetoric, recentralization of educational and curriculum policymaking appears to be widespread; however, the mix of preferred State policy instruments has changed, and programmatic funding has been cut. Particularly noteworthy with respect to curriculum has been the substantial increase in state level and nationwide assessments of student achievement exemplified by expansion of the federally funded NAEP (National Assessment of Educational Progress) testing of students to enable state-by-state comparisons. At the state level, New York, which has administered Regents Examinations in academic subjects for college bound, secondary school students for decades, now also administers Regents Competency Tests for secondary school students in general classes and Program Evaluation Tests for sixth and eighth graders. Extensive testing of student achievement, and widespread publication of results, may be more effective than mandates in shaping curriculum practice. A new phrase in curriculum discourse, curriculum alignment, suggests that assessment is influencing what is taught and how, as teachers modify their practice in order to boost students' test performance and their own reputations. Evidence from field studies, such as the Critical Thinking Project described in Chapter 4, support this interpretation.

The federal and state courts remain an important factor in curriculum policymaking, and the national teacher unions appear to have increased their role; governors, state legislators and corporate officials have been quite visible. Although Reagan administration education spokesmen (they were, for the most part, men) railed against professionals–experts in favor of common sense (their own), professionalization and bureaucratization continued; the federal bureaucracy, like the national debt, increased 1981–89. Recognized educational leaders may not have been as involved in educational decision-making during the Reagan years as they had been previously, but professional advisers were abundant.

While complexity and legalization are likely to persist, counter-movements such as site-based management, i.e., school level decision-making, and teacher empowerment-professionalization may challenge if not overturn centralizing and bureaucratizing trends. These countermovements appear to have strong support from the two national teacher unions, especially the AFT which has been more willing to risk reform. A major theme of the contemporary efforts toward teacher empowerment-professionalization is teacher involvement in decision-making at the school as well as the classroom level; involvement at school district, state and national levels of the education system presumably is to be left to union leaders and political action committees. The decisions of interest to teachers and their unions encompass those that are curriculum relevant, as well as directly curricular ones: text and other curriculum materials selection; student tracking, assignment, and grading policies; course and class scheduling; budgeting; academic freedom for teachers and students; teacher selection and collaboration such as in team teaching and staff development. In the late 1970s, Boyd observed, somewhat uneasily, that it is

> abundantly clear that unions have the necessary political muscle to influence how and what curriculum will be implemented in the schools, to influence how school boards use the authority they have over the curriculum, and even to cause boards to delegate portions of that authority to the unions.... Beyond their power through collective bargaining in the local school district, the burgeoning teachers unions appear to have remarkable influence at the state and federal levels, and most signs indicate that this influence is likely to increase.[19]

Ten years later, the situation is somewhat different. There are more players in the curriculum policymaking game, and local school districts and boards have lost curriculum and other educational policymaking authority, primarily to the states, leaving less for unions to bargain for locally. However, in the name of reform, several union locals have been successful in negotiating agreements for experimental projects intended to foster student achievement by means of teacher empowerment. To date in the US, changes in teacher and administrator roles and relationships (i.e., structural changes in the education system) are being attempted locally in various school districts (e.g., Akron, Ohio; Dade County, Florida) following more or less detailed and far-reaching collective bargaining agreements.[20] Only a few states have enacted or are considering incentives for such reform.[21] Curricular impact remains to be seen. It is a reasonable speculation, however, that, without a different view on curricular questions and processes, empowered teachers are unlikely to proceed much differently than their administrative or curriculum specialist predecessors.

Another ingredient in the changing structure of curriculum policymaking authority is global in nature. It is the global communication network composed of mass media and professional organizations as well as international agencies and governments that fosters transnational transfer of curriculum and other knowledge and international educational comparisons and competition.[22] Increasingly, State and education system actions are influenced by a global culture or 'world polity' as well as by domestic conditions. From this perspective, the world polity defines State jurisdiction and form, as well as ultimate goals of justice and progress, and provides legitimacy within those boundaries.

> The world polity has evolved out of the peculiar rationalization of Western society [following Weber] and is the cultural or institutional environment of the state. Within this environment, the state emerges as an externally chartered 'project' with progress and justice as overriding purposes. As the institutional environment has increased in rationalization, the project has become more centralized and bureaucratized. Moreover, conflict increasingly is politicized, being centered on the state and formulating claims around different visions of the charter for progress and justice.[23]

Examples of world polity influences on state action and system-State relations, including curriculum policymaking, are: the establishment of national, State or State-related systems of mass public education in both developed and developing countries; increased State intervention in education system operation, such as core (or common) curriculum mandates and testing; and renewed attention in the form of exhortation, mandate, assessment, and/or funding to mathematics and science programs. The important point here is that increasing State involvement in educational and curriculum policymaking is not independent of the actions of other States and the transnational world polity that provides both direction and legitimacy to State actions.

Interrelations and Implications

The sources of complexity and contentiousness of curriculum policymaking examined here — normative differences, professionalization of reform, changing structure of authority — are interrelated in ways that increase complexity and conflict. The professionalization of reform, for example, has highlighted different and sometimes contradictory interests and approaches as each group of specialists promotes its own expertise and approach, often with little understanding or tolerance for others'. These differences are evident within and among specialized fields. Conflicts between proponents of top-down (or, center-periphery) and bottom-up (or, problem-solving) curriculum change, between technocratic and critical curricularists, between advocates of bi-lingual and language immersion programs, and between behavioral and cognitive learning psychologists illustrate the problem. Among specializations, witness the clashing interests of curriculum designers and evaluators, or of 'gifted and talented', mainstream and special educators.

The professionalization of reform also can be seen as crystallizing differences and widening the gulf between experts and the public (i.e., lay or citizen groups), thus distancing educational and curriculum reform efforts from the publics they presumably serve. The introduction of professional reformers into the structure of curriculum policymaking authority clearly has altered local balances of power over curriculum practice and change within the education system. At broader State and societal levels, the influence of professional educational reformers appears to vary with the political climate.

Another contributor to the complexity of curriculum policymaking and the difficulty if not contentiousness of carrying out intended change, is the legacy of prior reform efforts. The legacy is one of form and substance. Boyd, for example, points to the Progressive Era reforms of the early twentieth century in the US, particularly the bureaucratization of education, as impeding subsequent reform that would make education bureaucracies 'more responsive to the public and, especially, to the needs of minority groups heretofore poorly served by them'.[24] More recent legacies include the entrance of professionals, teacher unions and politicized special interest groups into the curriculum policymaking process.

Substantively, currently sought curriculum reforms may be at odds with previous ones. The cycles of attention to and design of academic programs for high and low achieving students in the US are one example.[25] According to Elmore and McLaughlin's analysis:

> When the next shift in policy occurs, the 'problems' that reforms are designed to solve are not just problems with the performance of the educational system, but also those resulting from the incompatibility of earlier policies with the current reforms. With each successive wave of reform, then, the problems of framing and implementing policies become more complex.[26]

For example, emerging policies that promote teacher empowerment or SBCD would seem to contradict and be constrained in practice by recently established teacher and curriculum regulations and by student assessment programs. In the US, the fragmentation of the education system and the State (i.e., one hand not knowing, not caring, or not supporting what the other is doing) increases the likelihood of such contradictions and the stalemating of widespread curriculum change.

Against this background, several observations about curriculum policymaking in the US are offered. First, systemwide, State influenced if not controlled curriculum policymaking is a fact of curriculum life even in the absence of a mandated national curriculum or federal funding for curriculum materials development and dissemination. It occurs directly and indirectly as has been shown by means of State policy instruments such as inducements, capacity-building, system-changing and exhortation. State involvement in curriculum policymaking takes several forms. Atkin and House distinguish: generic curriculum materials development, usually by means of inducement, such as the NSF supported Biological Sciences Curriculum Study (BSCS); categorical program development and provision, usually by means of inducement, such as Right-to-Read; and site-specific development, usually by means of inducement and/or capacity building, such as the Experimental Schools Project.[27] On the basis of their review of federal educational reform efforts, Elmore and McLaughlin distinguish developmental efforts that have attempted to reach directly into the classrooms and change conventional teaching methods from regulatory efforts that have affected 'the internal structure of schools and the classroom practice of teachers' and redistributive efforts that have altered resource allocations between and among school districts and states.[28] However one prefers to characterize and/or categorize the State presence in curriculum policymaking, it cannot be discounted.

This State presence, however, is mediated by several layers of the education system. The call for educational excellence in the US, for example, has been translated into higher standards for secondary school graduation. Many states have increased the number of mathematics and/or science courses required for graduation. Schools, in turn, have provided more mathematics and science courses for their students. Yet, as noted earlier, these courses are often of a remedial or watered down nature. Their contribution to excellence is highly doubtful. Mandating higher standards, based on the assumption that more is better, is simpler than defining and directly pursuing excellence in teaching and learning. Providing remedial mathematics and science courses for students who would not otherwise take additional mathematics or science is easier than helping those students succeed in regularly offered courses.

Within a reform cycle, movement from agenda setting to policy formulation often is characterized by increasing conservatism, or pragmatism, as structural context factors gain ascendancy over sociocultural ones. Thus

> proposed solutions to identified problems are evaluated in terms of what is deemed to be feasible as well as what is desirable. Attention is apt to be given to such factors as the policymakers' jurisdiction, traditional practice, and the legacy of prior changes as well as the immediate considerations of incentives and disincentives for particular changes, available or obtainable resources to support change, and the degree of consensus behind one or another proposal. In the course of these evaluations, previously identified problems may be redefined to make them more manageable. As one kind of problem is translated into another, usually more manageable form, both problems and solutions tend to become routinized.[29]

A second observation is that there is no single, unified or coherent, explicit State curriculum policy or policymaking process. Instead we find overlapping or simultaneous policymaking and sometimes contradictory policies. This seeming chaos or incoherence, as has been suggested, is an historical product of separation and division of governmental powers, decentralization or fragmentation of the education system, and a heterogeneous, politically democratic society. At one level, the absence of explicit and coherent State curriculum policy may be seen as serving to limit State influence, stalemate far-reaching curriculum reform, and/or enable relative local or professional autonomy and initiative. At another level, the absence condones and sustains existing curriculum practice.

A third, related observation concerns what Kirst and Walker have called teachers' 'pocket veto' of others' curriculum policy and reform efforts.[30] Curriculum policy that 'survives emasculation by the administrative hierarchies of federal agencies and state and local officials . . . still faces a pocket-veto by 2,000,000 [now, upwards of 2.2 million] classroom teachers'.[31] In other words, the tradition of relative teacher autonomy 'behind the classroom door' means that teachers can choose to substantially modify or ignore others' curriculum policies simply by doing little or nothing about them. Over the past twenty years, there appears to be increasing if grudging recognition that teachers, individually and collectively, are the 'key' to what does or does not happen in classroom curriculum practice. In this regard, Elmore and McLaughlin note that:

> Policy, regardless of which level of government initiates it, ultimately affects schooling to the degree that it affects [school and classroom] organization and practice. Problems of variability, adaptation, lags in implementation and performance, and the seeming unresponsiveness of the 'system' to shifts in policy all find their roots in what happens in the school and classroom.[32]

Teachers' pocket veto, along with the factors just suggested as accounting for the absence of explicit, coherent national curriculum policy in the US, may explain an important distinction between State control of formal organizational or managerial matters on the one hand and curriculum knowledge and practice on the other. Increasing the number of courses or credits in science required for secondary school graduation is an example of the former; what science is taught and how is an example of the latter. Historically, organizational control of the US education system has become increasingly rationalized and, to some extent, centralized while control of classroom curriculum practice has remained relatively weak and diffuse. Consequently, State efforts to reform the education system have tended to focus on equity and organizational matters and to be largely technical or procedural in nature (e.g., testing, credentialling, accountability reporting).[33] Sustained, substantive curriculum change in schools is less likely to be mandated effectively by the State, although State exhortation and monetary inducements can be an impetus to at least short term, surface change. It follows that State educational and curriculum reform efforts are likely to be technical, at least in part because that is the kind of change over which the State has the most control. The recent and dramatic increase in calls for accountability and in testing of student achievement in the name of educational and curriculum reform can be seen as an effort to change classroom curriculum practice by means of technical controls that measure output rather than mandate input or process.

In sum, events of the past decade have borne out Boyd's observation that curriculum policymaking in the US has become increasingly legalized, centralized and bureaucratized. It also has become more complex and contentious. As a consequence, curriculum policymaking in the US is even more difficult now, and far-reaching curriculum reform is even less likely to result from conventional State policy instruments.

Cross-National Cases

Other nations' experiences with curriculum policymaking and planning can enhance understanding of one's own situation by highlighting aspects unseen at home as well as by illuminating commonalities and differences. Here, I draw primarily on McGinn, Schiefelbein, and Warwick's case studies of policymaking and planning in Chile and El Salvador and on Saunders and Vulliamy's comparative study of the implementation of curriculum reform policy in Tanzania and Papua New Guinea.

Chile and El Salvador

In McGinn *et al.*'s account of successful if not long term, comprehensive educational reform in Chile and El Salvador in the 1960s and 1970s, policymaking and planning at the national level were successful in large part because they did not follow technocratic models.[34] In both cases, State policymaking and planning were largely personalized, political processes. In Chile, the reforms included extension of compulsory education from six years to eight, major revision of the primary school program, and revision of the secondary school program 'to eliminate a class-based separation between academic and vocational tracks'.[35] In El Salvador, the reforms included redesigning the primary and upper secondary school programs, the latter to include numerous separate tracks, and upgrading of teacher preparation programs. According to McGinn *et al.*,

> a strong, charismatic leader directed the Ministry of Education, received unconditional backing from an energetic president, and had more than ordinary amounts of fiscal and human resources available through international technical assistance. In both cases, the leader of the reform effort came from outside the educational system, had personal but not partisan political allegiances to the president, and made most of his proposals before the end of the first half of the presidential term. In both cases the ministers directing the reform were characterized as decisive men of action rather than as thinkers. Both men depended on trusted lieutenants skilled in management and from outside the system . . . to implement the changes proposed.[36]

The Chilean education minister appointed by President Eduardo Frei (1963–1970) and his advisors considered whether a reform proposal

> could gain approval from a sufficient number of interest groups, whether it was possible to implement with the resources available, and whether implementation would result in stimulating further changes throughout the educational system. The reform proceeded on the basis of informed judgment but without careful research or the elaboration of a plan document that specified objectives and procedures.[37]

Instead, in both countries, planning shaped the identification and choice of alternative courses of action, the implementation of decisions, and the institutionalization of the implemented reforms.

The importance of political, contextual factors was especially visible in the process of creating (i.e., planning) a new Chilean primary curriculum. While the curriculum framework was designed by a small committee appointed by the education minister, 'careful attention' was given 'to concerns of, among others, professional bureaucrats within the ministry, two teachers' unions, political parties, the association of private schools, and parents' associations'.[38] According to one interviewee, 'Planning meant doing'.[39]

Concern with opposition from the primary teachers' union, educational publishers, parents, and traditionally oriented interest groups translated into efforts to gain support for the curriculum reform. These included two previously considered legitimation strategies, participation and expertise (see Chapter 6). The national curriculum committee was expanded to include representatives from each of the affected and possibly antagonistic interest groups and State agencies. School personnel were involved in creating new curriculum materials. The new programs and materials were then used in several hundred schools as 'experiments'. Implementation support was provided by a new Teacher Training Center and publications for teachers suggesting how to carry out the program. In addition, the ministry issued numerous press releases noting 'that what was being proposed for Chile were the latest ideas of educators all around the world'.[40]

In both the Chilean and El Salvadoran cases, educational reform was seen as integral to societal reform. The pressures for reform emerging from the sociocultural context were mediated by the State and the education system in ways that made them politically palatable and practically manageable. Curriculum planning in these cases was less plan-making or document development than it was creating the conditions that would enable and encourage desired changes in curriculum practice. While the educational reforms of the period were institutionalized in El Salvador, they were not in Chile where they flourished during the three-year Allende government and then were undermined by the military junta that followed. What is not clear from the McGinn *et al.* account of curriculum reform efforts in Chile and El Salvador is what happened at the classroom level and what was or was not done there to support desired curriculum practice.

Tanzania and Papua New Guinea

The focus of Saunders and Vulliamy's study of Tanzania and Papua New Guinea is on the school level implementation of curriculum reform once policy decisions had been made.[41] In both cases, the purpose was to integrate 'practical action' and academic study in secondary curricula in order to overcome elitist notions of academic schooling and provide education appropriate to rural society (e.g., to encourage favorable attitudes toward agricultural work), to discourage rural to urban migration, to make schools more self-reliant and integrate them with their communities. As post-colonial, agricultural, developing nations, both Tanzania and Papua New Guinea inherited competitive education systems with academic or 'literary' national examinations that limited access to education beyond the early grades. Concern with increasing numbers of 'unemployed secondary-school leavers, whose prior academic schooling made them both unmotivated and ill equipped for self-employment in villages',[42] appears to have been a major impetus for the curriculum reform efforts. The Tanzanian reform policy, introduced by President Nyerere in 1967, was called ESR, Education for Self-Reliance; the Papua New Guinea reform, introduced by the department of education in 1977, was known as SSCEP, the Secondary Schools Community Extension Project. Both ESR and SSCEP called for substantial changes in pedagogy as well as subject matter content and organization, e.g., from didactic to inquiry-oriented teaching. Not only did teachers in both nations have little experience with the intended approaches to subject matter and teaching, but they challenged teachers' competence and beliefs. Both ESR and SSCEP were top-down, State-directed reform efforts. Their contexts and implementation strategies, however, were very different.

Context

In retrospect, it seems clear that interrelated structural and sociocultural context factors played key roles in shaping the curriculum reform experience. Structural factors included the source and manner of introducing the reforms, national examinations, and teacher and student values. Sociocultural factors included timing and societal attitudes regarding agriculture.

In Tanzania, peasant farming and manual labor increasingly were disdained by students in favor of better paying occupations that require educational qualification. Teachers also linked their status to academically oriented education. In contrast, by the late 1970s, Papua New Guinea secondary schools had 'a strong tradition of self-reliance activities'.[43] Agricultural and manual skills training were compulsory subjects in most schools, and manual work was accepted by students and teachers. The stronger and more attractive agricultural, rural village culture in Papua New Guinea rendered the proposed curriculum reforms more congruent with existing values and practice there than in Tanzania.

Another source of conflict in Tanzania was exclusion of Ministry of Education officials from the policymaking process. They were not consulted during the formulation of ESR and were surprised by its publication. 'The policy was dropped upon the national education system with little warning, with the expectation that schools would immediately begin to take up the proposals'.[44] The SSCEP, in contrast, was a Department of Education initiative that was accepted and funded by the national government as a five-year pilot project involving only five schools. Whereas ESR had strong endorsement from State leaders and was highly politicized, SSCEP moved more slowly and at a much lower key.

Two other contextual factors also are noteworthy. In relation to the academic examination system (which remained important to many students, parents, and teachers), ESR was seen as tangential at best whereas SSCEP was seen as compatible and appropriate. Early evidence indicated that SSCEP students performed as well or better than others on the competitive tenth grade examinations that determined access to upper secondary and higher education.[45] Second, the SSCEP was introduced a decade after the initiation of ESR. Much may have been learned from others' experiences with similar reform efforts during this time.

Implementation.

ESR proponents followed a nationwide implementation strategy characterized primarily by mandate and exhortation. Implementation of SSCEP was gradual, characterized by capacity-building with strong elements of expertise and participation. Overall, more attention was given to implementation in Papua New Guinea than Tanzania, and there was more accommodation of context factors that would affect local implementation of the intended curriculum reforms.

The five diverse secondary schools selected as SSCEP pilot sites were provided with intensive, teacher in-service and on-site technical assistance. Teachers at each site created, tried out and revised curriculum plans within central guidelines. Implementation, then, was a centrally guided and assisted local process. The complexity of the curriculum reform was made manageable by means of explicit guidelines and assistance,[46] but this is not to suggest that the pilot was problem free. The extra time and work required were a burden for most teachers, as were shortages of materials. Implementation also was hindered by staff turnover (both local and central), by continuing teacher skepticism regarding SSCEP's effects on academic achievement, and by questionable long-term political commitment to the reform effort at the national level.

In Tanzania, scarce resources to support ESR were stretched very thin. The focus was on preservice rather than inservice teacher education, and little technical assistance was provided initially to local schools. By the late 1970s, when most schools had initiated practical projects (usually agricultural ones), the national ministry decided that each school should have a designated focus — agriculture, commerce, home economics, or technical subjects — and provided further resources and workshops for schools and teachers. However, the ministry's focus designations were not always compatible with local situations, e.g., schools in urban or arid locations designated as agricultural.

Differences in contexts as well as implementation strategies, including attention to context during implementation, can be seen to account for the differential outcomes of these curriculum reform efforts. By the early 1980s, practical projects were in existence at the pilot sites in Papua New Guinea and most of the secondary schools in Tanzania. The Papua New Guinea projects were more locally relevant and better integrated with the schools' academic programs. However, Papua New Guinea had not yet confronted the resource and political as well as practical problems of nationwide implementation.[47]

Concluding Observations

Among other things, these cross-national cases illustrate the advantages and limitations of centrally directed curriculum reform efforts. The centralized education system and/or State can mobilize and deploy political support and resources for intended changes but cannot bring them about. Implementation must occur locally, in various schools and classrooms often far removed from the center, culturally as well as geographically. Efficiencies that might accrue

173

from centralized policymaking and planning are likely to be mitigated by local circumstances.

The importance of context is well illustrated in these cases. Ignoring political and other contextual factors that can facilitate or impede curriculum reform does not negate them. Also illustrated, especially in the case of Tanzania, is the importance of State political support for intended changes and its insufficiency for actually bringing about that change. With respect to classroom curriculum change, the State is not omnipotent.

School Based Curriculum Development

In this section, SBCD is considered as a form of curriculum policymaking and planning, with particular attention to questions of curriculum control and to curriculum practice and its contexts.[48] Current interest and activity in SBCD dates to the early 1970s. It is, in part, a reaction to the centralized curriculum policymaking and planning of the previous decade. Curriculum making during this earlier decade consisted largely of materials development and dissemination from national centers that were either government based (e.g., Australia's Curriculum Development Centre), government funded (e.g., the BSCS [Biological Sciences Curriculum Study] funded by NSF in the US), or funded by private foundations or professional organizations (e.g., *Sociological Resources for Secondary Schools* funded by the American Sociological Association).

Decentralization of curriculum making and related in-service teacher education to the school or school district level, i.e., SBCD, is intended to (a) foster greater teacher involvement and commitment, and (b) encourage curriculum adaptation to local conditions, thereby (c) increasing the likelihood of use and effectiveness of the new curricula. SBCD also can be seen as an education system and/or State legitimation strategy incorporating participation and symbolic reform. It can be initiated by means of inducements, capacity-building, or system-changing policy instruments.[49]

Much of the literature on SBCD, and presumbaly the activity in the name of SBCD, has come from the UK and Australia and also from Sweden, Israel and Canada. As a movement, SBCD has been less prominent in the US, most likely because of the US traditions of local control of curriculum within very broad State guidelines and of teacher reliance on textbooks. Even in New York

State, which has a history of producing syllabi for each school subject area and of statewide examinations in the academic subject areas, teachers are encouraged to use the state syllabus as a guide to their own curriculum planning. For example, in the introduction to the grades seven to twelve social studies syllabi, teachers are advised that the syllabus

> is meant to be used by teachers in developing their social studies program. It is not meant to be a prescription for day-to-day lesson plans. It is, instead, a guide to the objectives of the State social studies program. It should be used by the school district and the teacher as a guide to the selection of materials and strategies to achieve these objectives . . . . It is assumed that changing times, changing information and changing emphases will lead to updating of this suggested content. Since the syllabus cannot be in a constant state of revision, it will be the responsibility of the school district and the individual teacher to accomplish this updating.[50]

Despite a sizeable literature on SBCD, there are relatively few published accounts of systematic investigation of the SBCD experience. One such account is Lindblad's study of participation and communication patterns in SBCD in a Swedish municipality.[51] Since the particulars of SBCD are intended to and probably do vary from site to site, this Swedish case should be viewed as more illustrative than representative.

In Sweden, SBCD was initiated within the context of broader structural change, namely decentralization of education system policymaking and administration. In the 1970s, SBCD occurred under the umbrella of 'local multi-project development schemes'[52] located in municipal districts for five-year periods and co-funded by national and local authorities. State authorities determined the 'general theme' of each scheme which could then encompass several innovative projects. Wide teacher participation was sought in order to foster situation specific problem-solving and 'a climate more conducive to innovation in the schools'.[53]

Data in Lindblad's study were obtained from documents and a survey of school staff including participants and non-participants in the development scheme. Among his findings are the following; SBCD projects more often are initiated by the Swedish National Board of Education (eighteen/twenty-eight) and local education departments (8) than local schools or teachers (2). Approximately 10 per cent of the school staff actually participated in the projects, most because they were asked to do so. Participants were more likely to be head teachers or principals and department chairs than classroom teachers.

Lindblad concluded that

> decentralized innovative work [is] adjusted to the hierarchy of the school. The work is initiated from above. It is performed to a great extent by individuals holding higher positions in the local school system's hierarchy . . . . In sum: decentralized innovative work is — in the present case — run by and for the establishment of the school . . . innovative work of the present kind has less to do with the struggle for change than with the maintenance of the *status quo* and the promise of improvement within current frames.[54]

Further, according to Lindblad, 'similar tendencies predominated in other local multi-project development schemes in Sweden'.[55]

A second illustrative case of SBCD is provided by Orpwood's participant-observation study of 'a curriculum committee deliberating over a new science programme for their Ontario (Canada) school board' in the late 1970s.[56] By this time, Ontario school boards had been given 'significant responsibility for curriculum reform by the Ministry of Education'.[57] Ministry guidelines and the County Board of Education's science co-ordinator specified the curriculum product that was to be produced by a two-tier, appointed committee of teachers: science 'units' for grades seven-to-ten, with especially detailed instructional materials for the seventh and eighth grade units, incorporating 'the 15 different aims prescribed by the ministry'.[58] The committees, chaired by the science co-ordinator, determined the units to be taught at each grade level so that writing teams could develop specific instructional materials. Two years later, the county board of education approved the science program developed by the committees.

In both the Swedish and Canadian cases, SBCD was initiated and guided if not directed by education system and/or State actors outside and 'above' individual schools. In important ways, control remained at higher levels while locals were expected to do the work, i.e., to create as well as implement new curriculum plans. Parallels between SBCD and the Reagan administration's decentralization policy are noteworthy in this regard.[59] Especially clear in the Canadian case, curriculum was viewed as a document or plan, and curriculum change as document revision. Curriculum practice appears not to have been a major or immediate concern of either the SBCD projects or the studies. Although attention appears to have been given to context in terms of local conditions, few specifics were provided in the studies.

Teacher involvement or participation and teacher influence or control in these cases was much less than that advocated or claimed by SBCD proponents, providing grounds for a legitimation interpretation. In other words, with its promise of wide teacher (and other school staff) participation, SBCD creates an image of democratic curriculum making that lends credibility to the process and thus to its education system and/or State sponsors. Since the studies did not provide data about the substance, use, or effects of the new curriculum plans, we cannot tell the extent to which the SBCD reforms were symbolic or substantive. In these two cases, the potential of SBCD seems not to have been realized.[60]

In the early 1980s, Hargreaves[61] cautioned that the optimism and enthusiasm of SBCD advocates appeared to be promising more than could be delivered and obscuring ways in which SBCD goals (e.g., democratization, diversity, reform) were obstructed by the structure of the education system. Thus, SBCD proponents could be undermining the movement from within. Reviewing the SBCD literature at that time, he noted that it

> encapsulates the highest ideals of liberal democracy as worthy and readily attainable goals in the management of schools. In effect, it promises no less than the realization of liberty (individual diversity), equality (participation and grass-roots democracy), and fraternity (collaboration).[62]

Locating SBCD firmly 'within the cherished tenets of social democratic thought and practice',[63] while increasing its appeal, does not necessarily mean that it will be carried out as intended with the desired effects. Arguing for systematic and contextualized research on SBCD in practice, Hargreaves questioned 'whether teacher participation leads them at present to being *in control* of the curriculum, or to their remaining *in service* to ends formulated by others'.[64] The paternalistic potential of SBCD ought not to be ignored.[65]

In addition to questions of participation and control, one also might question the knowledge and vision of reform that teachers bring to the task of SBCD. Teacher created curriculum plans are not inherently more intellectually sound or more reformist than those created by others.[66]

In sum, the promised benefits of SBCD as a form of curriculum policymaking and planning have not yet been widely realized. Given available knowledge about SBCD experiences and the structural/education system context of curriculum, it would be naively idealistic at best to expect widespread and successful SBCD. Even if SBCD were to become widespread and successful on its own terms, we are not likely to see desired changes in curriculum practice in many classrooms or schools as long as curriculum is conceived as a document or plan rather than as a contextualized social process.[67] Changing curriculum practice, as argued and illustrated in earlier chapters, requires compatible contextual change. To the previously raised reservations about the SBCD movement is added a further reservation about the adequacy of its conception of curriculum to bringing about substantive reform of curriculum practice.

Contextualized Curriculum Planning

One of the implications of the foregoing analysis and illustrations of curriculum policy and planning is that policymakers ought to consider the contexts of curriculum practice as well as desired outcomes in formulating curriculum policy. Considering the contexts of curriculum practice means recognizing what it will take by way of contextual, especially structural, changes to bring about the desired changes in curriculum practice and effects. Those who would influence curriculum policy also need to consider and reckon with the contexts of policymaking.

Recognition of contextual influences on curriculum practice and that curriculum change requires compatible contextual change would alter the mix of policy instruments employed. There would be fewer mandates and more inducement and capacity-building policies and perhaps even more system-changing efforts — depending on the condition of the education system, system-State relations and the nature of the desired change.[68] Contextual awareness also would increase recognition of education system and State legitimation needs and strategies and decrease the likelihood of mistaking legitimation strategies for curriculum policy reform.

Curriculum planning would be a recursive process, overlapping policymaking and implementation. Planning would not mean planning curriculum change *per se*, as if a curriculum plan (e.g., new curriculum document) constituted the desired reform. Instead, planning would be planning *for* curriculum change, that is, identifying or creating the conditions necessary to support the desired curriculum practice and the means of bringing about those conditions. Designing the desired curriculum practice (i.e., the preferred selection, organization, treatment and distribution of knowledge) is only one aspect of contextualized curriculum planning. A second and more important aspect is creating the necessary supporting conditions or context — usually a much more complex and difficult undertaking. However, without complementary contextual change, plans for reformed curriculum practice are likely to remain unrealized. Curriculum planning and product development thus play a supporting rather than a leading role in efforts to reform curriculum practice.

Notes

1 D. Adams and C. Cornbleth, *Planning Educational Change* (manuscript in progress).
2 See, e.g., H. Weiler, 'Why Reforms Fail: The Politics of Education in France and the Federal Republic of Germany', *Journal of Curriculum Studies* 21, 4 (1989): 291–305.
3 W. H. Clune, *The Implementation and Effects of High School Graduation Requirements: First Steps Toward Curriculum Reform* (New Brunswick, NJ: Center for Policy Research in Education, Rutgers University, 1989).
4 Interestingly, there have been few systematic studies or analyses of curriculum politics and policymaking in the US, maybe because of the widespread presumption, until recently, that curriculum decision-making is a nonpolitical, technical matter and maybe because of the tradition of local control. See W. L. Boyd, 'The Changing Politics of Curriculum Policy-Making for American Schools', *Review of Educational Research* 48, 4 (1978): 577–628. In contrast, there is a substantial literature in the UK. See, for example, G. Whitty and M. Young (eds.), *Explorations in the Politics of School Knowledge* (Nafferton, Driffield: Nafferton Books, 1976); D. Lawton, *The Politics of the School Curriculum* (London: Routledge & Kegan Paul, 1980); G. Whitty, *Sociology and School Knowledge: Curriculum Theory, Research, and Politics* (London: Methuen, 1985).
5 S. Arons' *Compelling Belief* (Amherst: University of Massachusetts Press, 1986).
6 For a review of Arons' book and critique of his call for the separation of school and state, see C. Cornbleth, 'Compelling Belief — Nagging Questions', *Journal of Curriculum Theorizing* 7, 3 (1987): 93–100.

7 D. P. Moynihan, *Maximum Feasible Misunderstanding* (New York: Free Press, 1969).

8 See, for example, T.S. Popkewitz, 'The Latent Values of the Discipline-Centered Curriculum', *Theory and Research in Social Education* 5, 1 (1977): 41–60.

9 D. P. Moynihan, 1969, *op. cit.*; W. L. Boyd, 1978, *op. cit.*

10 D. P. Moynihan, 1969, *op. cit.*; also, see T. S. Popkewitz, *Paradigm and Ideology in Educational Research* (London and New York: Falmer Press, 1984), Chapter 5, 'Social Science and Social Amelioration: The Development of the American Academic Expert', pp. 107–127.

11. *Ibid.*, pp. 22–24.

12. *Ibid.*, p. 25.

13. See W. L. Boyd, 1978, *op. cit.*, pp. 591–593.

14. In the US, the professional educational organization with the largest membership is ASCD, the Association for Supervision and Curriculum Development.

15 W. L. Boyd, 1978, *op. cit.*, p. 593.

16 Interestingly, Atkin and House suggest that the authority of professional reformers may be usurped by their own technical rationality, i.e., that the authority of the technique may be replacing the authority of the person. This possibility could be undermined by the disappointment of technical rationality and the growing appeal of alternative rationalities. See J.M. Atkin and E.R. House, 'The Federal Role in Curriculum Development, 1950–1980'. *Educational Evaluation and Policy Analysis* 3, 5 (1981): 5–36.

17 Also, see J.M. Atkin and E.R. House, 1981, *Ibid.*

18 *Ibid.*, p. 611.

19 *Ibid.*, pp. 616–617.

20 See L.M. McDonnell and A. Pascal, *Teacher Unions and Educational Reform* (Santa Monica, CA: Rand Center for the Study of the Teaching Profession, 1988).

21 The state of Wisconsin, for example, has sponsored experimental projects to create career ladder and incentive programs for teachers. However, 'the restructuring prompted by reform efforts in fact reduces teacher responsibility through standardization of conduct, increased bureaucracy, and greater monitoring'. These outcomes can be seen as illustrating education system mediation of external reform proposals as well as 'a reform discourse that ignores the value and power relations engrained in schooling experiences'. T. S. Popkewitz and K. Lind, 'Teacher Incentives as Reforms: Teachers' Work and the Changing Control Mechanism in Education', *Teachers College Record* 90, 4 (1989): 575–594, pp. 575–576.

22 See, for example, J. G. Lee, D. Adams and C.Cornbleth, 'Transnational Transfer of Curriculum Knowledge: A Korean Case Study', *Journal of Curriculum Studies* 20, 3 (1988): 233–246.

23 G. M. Thomas, J. W. Meyer, F.O. Ramirez and J. Boli, *Institutional Structure*

(Newbury Park, CA: Sage, 1987), p. 40. This argument is elaborated in J. Meyer's Chapter 3, 'The World Polity and the Authority of the Nation-State', pp. 41–70, and directed to education system-state relations in F. O. Ramirez and J. Boli's Chapter 8, 'On the Union of States and Schools', pp. 173–197.

24 W. L. Boyd, 1978, *op. cit.*, p. 620. Also, see M. Edelman, *Political Language: Words that Succeed and Policies that Fail* (New York: Academic Press, 1977), Chapter 5, 'The Language of Bureaucracy', pp. 77–102.

25 See, for example, P. W. Jackson, 'The Reform of Science Education: A Cautionary Tale', *Daedalus* 112, 2 (1983):143–166.

26 R. F. Elmore and M. W. McLaughlin, *Steady Work: Policy, Practice, and the Reform of American Education* (Santa Monica, CA: The Rand Corporation, 1988), p. 8.

27 J.M. Atkin and E.R. House, 1981, *op. cit.*

28 R. F. Elmore and M. W. McLoughlin, 1988, *op. cit.*, p. 33.

29 C. Cornbleth and D. Adams, 'The Drunkard's Streetlamp? Contexts of Policy Change in U.S. Teacher Education', in *Governments and Higher Education, The Legitimacy of Intervention*, ed. Higher Education Group (Toronto: Ontario Institute for Studies in Education, 1987), p. 339.

30 M. W. Kirst and D.F. Walker, 'An Analysis of Curriculum Policy-Making', *Review of Educational Research* 41, 5 (1971):479–505.

31 *Ibid.*, p. 505.

32 R. F. Elmore and M. W. McLaughlin, 1988, *op. cit.*, p. 37.

33 J. W. Meyer, 'Innovation and Knowledge Use in American Public Education', in *Organizational Environments*, ed. J. W. Meyer and W. R. Scott (Beverly Hills, CA: Sage, 1983), pp. 236–260.

34 N. McGinn, E. Schiefelbein and D. P. Warwick, 'Educational Planning as Political Process: Two Case Studies from Latin America', *Comparative Education Review*, 23, 2 (1979): 218–239.

35 *Ibid.*, p. 221.

36 *Ibid.*, p. 222.

37 *Ibid.*, p. 223.

38 *Ibid.*, p. 228.

39 *Ibid.*, p. 229.

40 *Ibid.*, p. 230.

41 M. Saunders and G. Vulliamy, 'The Implementation of Curriculum Reform: Tanzania and Papua New Guinea', *Comparative Education Review* 27, 3 (1983): 351–373.

42 *Ibid.*, p. 355.

43 *Ibid.*, p. 357.

44 *Ibid.*, p. 356.

45 The tenth grade examinations emphasized skills over content and used multiple-

choice questions to minimize bias favoring students with better English language facility. Changes introduced in 1982 increased the proportion of content questions on these examinations.

46 The SSCEP pilot is an example of SBCD, which is considered further in the next section.

47 A 1985 report of the Educational Research Unit of the University of Papua New Guinea indicates that, in a second phase, SSCEP was extended to five more high schools. The earlier plan to add five schools every two years was superceded by a 1985 proposal to integrate 'the SSCEP approach' into all Papua New Guinea high schools. Integration is to be accomplished by 'maintaining the present ten SSCEP schools as models; distribution of core-project packages [developed at the pilot schools] to all schools; [and local school-level planning] . . . for outstations and/or community extension'. Further, 'on-the-job in-service training' is to be expanded through a diploma program at the University of Papua New Guinea. S. G. Weeks, Ed., *Papua New Guinea National Inventory of Educational Innovations* (Port Moresby: University of Papua New Guinea, Educational Research Unit Report No. 52, 1985), p. 49.

48 The treatment of SBCD here is necessarily selective. For fuller accounts, see, for example, J. Walton and T. Morgan (Eds.), *Some Perspectives on School Based Curriculum Development* (Australia: University of New England, 1978); J. Eggleston, *School-based Curriculum Development in Britain* (London: Routledge & Kegan Paul, 1980); M. Skilbeck, *School-based Curriculum Development* (London: Harper & Row, 1984); P. Knight, 'The Practice of School-based Curriculum Development', *Journal of Curriculum Studies* 17, 1 (1985): 37–48.

49 Alternative policy instruments and compensatory legitimation strategies are described and illustrated in Chapter 6.

50 Bureau of Curriculum Development, *Social Studies 11: United States History and Government*, Field Test Edition (Albany, NY: State Education Department, 1986), p. ix.

51 S. Lindblad, 'The Practice of School-Centered Innovation: A Swedish Case', *Journal of Curriculum Studies* 16, 2 (1984): 165–172.

52 *Ibid.*, p. 166.

53 *Ibid.*, p. 167.

54 *Ibid.*, pp. 171–172.

55 *Ibid.*, p. 171.

56 G. W. F. Orpwood, 'The Reflective Deliberator: A Case of Curriculum Policymaking', *Journal of Curriculum Studies* 17, 3 (1985): 293–304.

57 *Ibid.*, p. 293.

58 *Ibid.*, p. 294.

59 See Chapter 6. Decentralization as a largely symbolic reform and compensatory

legitimation strategy is well argued and illustrated by: N. McGinn and S. Street, 'Educational Decentralization: Weak State or Strong State?' *Comparative Education Review* 30, 4 (1986): 471–490; H. N. Weiler, 'Education and Power: The Politics of Educational Decentralization in Comparative Perspective', (Stanford, CA: Center for Educational Research at Stanford, 1989). On problems associated with decentralization, see H. Tangerud and E. Wallin, 'Values and Contextual Factors in School Improvement', *Journal of Curriculum Studies* 18, 1 (1986): 45–61, especially pp. 54–57.

60 At least in its pilot stage, the SSCEP project in Papua New Guinea can be seen as a successful case of SBCD. See M. Crossley, 'Strategies for Curriculum Change and the Question of International Transfer', *Journal of Curriculum Studies* 16, 1 (1984): 75–88.

61 A. Hargreaves, 'The Rhetoric of School-Centered Innovation', *Journal of Curriculum Studies* 14, 3 (1982): 251–266. Hargreaves uses the SCI (school-centered innovation) label to refer to school-based or school-focused curriculum development and to school-based or school-focused INSET (in-service education and training).

62 *Ibid.*, p. 258.

63 *Ibid.*, p. 254.

64 *Ibid.*, p. 255.

65 On pp. 257–258, Hargreaves further describes 'an ideology' of SBCD. Also, see D. Kirk, 'Ideology and School-centered Innovation: A Case Study and a Critique', *Journal of Curriculum Studies* 20, 5 (1988): 449–464.

66 See, e.g., N. Sabar, 'School-Based Curriculum Development: Reflections from an International Seminar', *Journal of Curriculum Studies* 17, 4 (1985): 452–454. Similar questions could be raised of so-called deliberative approaches to curriculum policymaking and planning.

67 A partial exception to the prevailing documentary conception of curriculum in SBCD is found in Kirk's study of SBCD at an upper secondary school in Australia. Here the study, if not the SBCD effort, acknowledged contextual influences as 'immediate structural influences on teachers' innovative actions'. D. Kirk, 1988, *op. cit.*, p. 461. These included the time frame, teachers' biographies, school management structures (particularly administrative mandates) and the nature and perceived needs of the student population.

68 See, e.g., D. Adams, C. Cornbleth and D. Plank, 'Between Exhortation and Reform — Recent U.S. Experience with Educational Change', *Interchange* 19, 3/4 (1988): 121–134.

Chapter 8

Curriculum Knowledge and Knowledge about Curriculum

In this concluding essay, I return to questions of curriculum knowledge, the differing knowledge that becomes part of school curricula in various contexts, and to the nature and role of knowledge about curriculum in research and reform efforts. By redirecting questions about curriculum conceptions, practice and change to curriculum studies, my purpose is to encourage analysis and constructive critique. Just as the social values and assumptions that become routinized in curriculum and schooling become invisible, so too do those social values and assumptions that become routinized in curriculum studies. Analysis and critique of technocratic values and interests in curriculum and curriculum studies have been amply documented earlier in this volume and elsewhere. Consequently, my intent here is to focus on alternative, purportedly critical, approaches to curriculum and curriculum studies.

Curriculum Knowledge

Overall, the studies presented earlier, especially in Chapter 4, 'Curriculum Practice', and other studies that might be cited, show the selection, organization and treatment of curriculum knowledge to be largely fragmented, fixed, public or distant from students, and presumably reproducible or applicable and transmittable to students. Knowledge has been reified as an object or product to be revealed to students over the course of their schooling. Further, curriculum knowledge is largely mainstream or consensus knowledge, the knowledge deemed important by dominant groups if not agreed upon by most people. Excluded groups (e.g., women, racial and ethnic minorities, working classes) have had to battle, not without some successes, for inclusion of their histories, cultures and perspectives as legitimate curriculum knowledge.

Whether this conception of curriculum knowledge is purposeful, i.e., intentional on the part of those who convey it, is of less concern than whose purposes it seems to serve and what changes its illumination might engender. After elaborating this characterization of the prevailing pattern of curriculum knowledge, exceptions are explored to suggest conditions that might support alternative patterns of curriculum knowledge and alternative curriculum practices.

Typical Curriculum Knowledge

Fragmentation of curriculum knowledge is evident in the persistence of separate school subjects and in the subdivision of these subjects into presumably discrete segments (e.g., facts, concepts, skills; topics, subtopics). These segments typically are arranged sequentially or hierarchically and presumed to add up eventually to a coherent body of knowledge within the subject or to the subject itself. In contrast, an integrated view of curriculum knowledge assumes that what others see as discrete segments within subjects cannot be understood adequately in isolation and that the 'whole' is something more or different than the sum of its parts. An integrated view might be extended beyond subjects to the integration of subjects in multidisciplinary or interdisciplinary (or possibly nondisciplinary) studies.[1]

The fixed nature of curriculum knowledge refers to its presumed certainty. Knowledge is treated as secure and unchanging; it is to be accepted as given by teachers, texts, or other authoritative sources. In contrast is a view of knowledge as tentative, accepted for the time being but subject to revision given new information or reinterpretation. Closely related to the fixed nature of curriculum knowledge is its presumd public character and thus its distance from students' day-to-day lives. Curriculum knowledge is assumed to be different from and best studied apart from everyday experience and general world knowledge; it is external to and independent of individuals. The assumed externality of knowledge stems from the further assumption that knowledge is a pre-existing truth or reality 'out there' to be discovered and verified by experts. It is not created by ordinary people, certainly not by students. The pedagogical practice of relating unfamiliar public knowledge to what students already know is intended to make the public knowledge accessible and acceptable to students, not to transform it.[2] In contrast is a view of curriculum knowledge as becoming personal or personalized through relations with everyday experience and general world knowledge and students' individual or collective interpretation. This alternative view also invites students' participation in the construction and critique of knowledge.

Curriculum knowledge as reproducible or applicable and as transmittable to students refers to the interrelated assumptions that knowledge can be communicated or given to students who can then reproduce it (e.g., on examinations) or apply it outside school (e.g., determine whether the large or giant size box of popcorn is the better buy, identify the symbolism in a play or novel). In contrast is a view of curriculum knowledge as constructed by students in interaction with each other, teachers, materials and milieu. Knowledge is seen as useful in interpretive and generative as well as instrumental ways. That is, new knowledge helps us to make sense of or reinterpret experience and to create further knowledge. Science, for example, can be valued primarily for its utility or as a way of knowing and creating knowledge — or both. Dichotomies have been sketched here to illustrate the range of variation of curriculum knowledge, not to suggest that curriculum knowledge does, must, or should represent one or another extreme.

In sum, the selection, organization and treatment of knowledge in curriculum tends to portray knowledge as a product to be revealed to students over the course of their schooling. Typically, curriculum knowledge is a thing or object to be possessed more than a way of knowing or coming to know. Correct answers to teacher questions, demonstrating possession of the given knowledge, are emphasized at the expense of reasoning or knowledge creation. This characterization of prevailing curriculum knowledge is clearly evident in the studies presented in Chapter 4, particularly in Popkewitz, Tabachnick and Wehlage's account of technical schooling[3] and McNeil's account of defensive teaching in the schools she studied.[4] In the US elementary schools that Popkewitz *et al.* described as technical, curriculum knowledge consisted of presumably discrete skills and pieces of information. Knowledge was standardized, and learning tasks tended to be mechanistic and unrelated to students' experiences. Students were offered a preplanned series of activities intended to produce measurable 'competencies'.

In the US secondary schools where administrators emphasized controlling students more than educating them, McNeil found defensive teaching to be the norm. Defensive teaching aims to control students by controlling curriculum knowledge, particularly simplifying subject matter content and reducing demands on students in exchange for order and compliance. Curriculum knowledge is fragmented and reduced to lists, and complex or controversial topics are treated superficially if at all. Knowledge is given, to be accepted by students and reproduced on exams in order to obtain passing grades.[5]

The purposes that seem to be served by this selection, organization and treatment of curriculum knowledge are three-fold, reflecting the interests of US society as a whole, currently dominant socioeconomic groups and teachers. Very briefly, curriculum knowledge that communicates information and skills deemed necessary for civic and economic participation as well as 'important truths' that sustain the national image contributes to cultural transmission and societal maintenance if not reproduction.

It also serves the particular interests of dominant socioeconomic groups (e.g., corporate and political leaders, managers, professionals) by providing a minimally literate citizenry and competent workforce that is ill prepared to seriously challenge the political, economic, or social *status quo*. As suggested in Chapter 5, 'Curriculum and Structural Change', power increasingly operates through historically shaped and socially shared conceptions and understandings (e.g., democracy, curriculum knowledge) and through definition of appropriate patterns of communication including rules of reason and rationality. Knowledge of these conceptions, patterns and rules provides access to power, i.e., knowledge can be empowering. Self-conscious knowledge enables their redefinition and possibly the redistribution of political and economic power. By self-conscious knowledge, I mean knowing what one knows, for example: knowing that one is constructing a 'logical' argument by means of agreed upon (rather than natural or intrinsic) rules of logic, not merely constructing the argument; not merely following the Tyler rationale in developing a curriculum plan, but knowing that one is adopting a particular kind of approach to curriculum. When curriculum knowledge excludes these conceptions, patterns, and rules — or treats them only superficially — students are denied access to power. Curriculum that unreflectively employs the prevailing discourse becomes an element of social regulation.

Thirdly, the typical selection, organization and treatment of curriculum knowledge serves the interests of most classroom teachers by enabling them to meet their obligations in the absence of preparation and support for alternative curriculum practice. The conditions of classroom teaching in most US schools, as described with reference to the Critical Thinking Project in Chapter 4, would not foster incorporating 'minority' histories, cultures and perspectives as legitimate curriculum knowledge or treating curriculum knowledge as integrated, tentative, personalized, constructed, or interpretive and generative even if teachers were so disposed. To do so would be impractical under the circumstances and entail considerable ambiguity and risk for teachers.

Curriculum Knowledge Alternatives

The undesirably restricted and rather dismal pattern of curriculum knowledge just portrayed is not without exceptions. Exceptions were noted in the studies cited earlier in this volume and have been noted by others.[6] Too often, however, atypical schools and teachers are merely noted, and attention is centered on general features and tendencies. In re-examining the curriculum knowledge of atypical schools, I focus on the contextual conditions that appear to support alternative patterns of curriculum knowledge and alternative curriculum practices.[7]

What Popkewitz *et al.* described as constructive schooling provides one example.[8] At Kennedy elementary school, curriculum knowledge was treated as tentative and permeable, and attention was given to multiple ways of knowing and creating knowledge. Subject matter content often was integrated across subject boundaries and linked to students' experiences. Students had opportunities to examine a broad range of knowledge and engage in a variety of learning activities. Importantly, with respect to knowledge-power relations, curriculum knowledge and learning activities were designed to foster students' interpersonal and communicative fluency, and students were expected to demonstrate initiative and independence as well as responsibility to others. In short, curriculum knowledge at Kennedy school was empowering and potentially transformative.

Among the contextual conditions of constructive schooling presented by the authors were a pedagogical context (just described), within an occupational context of teaching with its own ideologies and legitimation strategies, nested in a social/cultural context consisting of local community norms, expectations and demands reflecting local concerns and larger social issues. At Kennedy school as well as the other schools studied, teachers' and administrators' perceptions of community lifestyles, occupations, values and expectations of students and the school influenced their curriculum practice. As previously noted, the selection, organization and treatment of curriculum knowledge at Kennedy school responded to the social and cultural orientations of a professional community.

During the course of the Popkewitz *et al.* study, however, the school district's curriculum policy changed in ways that undermined the just described curriculum practice at Kennedy school. In the name of curriculum consistency, common behavioral objectives were specified for several grade levels, a districtwide reading program was adopted (and a reading enrichment program at Kennedy was dropped), common spelling textbooks were adopted, and teachers were directed not to provide handwriting instruction prior to the second grade. These districtwide curriculum policies were instituted despite the opposition of the Kennedy principal and teachers who defended their alternative curriculum practice and argued for professional autonomy. According to Popkewitz *et al.*, while the teachers at Kennedy 'felt that they could get around the district requirements and retain most, if not all, of their professional prerogatives',[9] their enthusiasm was dampened as they saw their efforts undermined.

The experience of Kennedy school illustrates both the intrusion of structural context on curriculum practice and the difficulties involved in remaining atypical. It suggests that the press for standardization is strong but not unassailable. Popkewitz *et al.* refer to 'the complex of competing interests' and 'the conflicting ideologies of consistency and constructivism'[10] being played out at Kennedy school. While Kennedy's situation may have been more turbulent than that of most schools, it reminds us that curriculum practice is not context free; it is continually if not continuously contested and rarely secure.

Another account of an atypical school is provided by McNeil.[11] While not absent, defensive teaching was less common at Nelson High School where there was more administrative support for teaching and incentive for instructional quality than at the other three schools she studied, and where 'teachers responded by demanding more of themselves in the preparation and presentation of lessons'.[12] Personal and public knowledge were not rigidly separated, fewer lists and more extended descriptions were provided, dependence on textbooks as authoritative sources of knowledge was less common than use of a variety of materials, and student discussion was more common.

McNeil accounts for the more authentic and empowering selection, organization and treatment of curriculum knowledge at Nelson in terms of its more supportive school structural context, particularly the school organization and culture and the priorities set by school administrators. Except for its size (940 compared to 1050–2280 students), Nelson was not outwardly different from the other three schools. The background of the social studies teaching staffs, composition of student populations, union contracts, resource bases and per pupil expenditures, and absence of special interventions or innovative programs were similar. Nelson served two working-middle-class suburban communities and a rural area. Less than 2 per cent of Nelson's students were classified as minority, and more than one-third intended to go to a four-year college.

What made Nelson different was a history of community support and sense of responsibility for the school since its establishment in the 1950s. Student discipline problems at Nelson were similar to those at the other schools, but 'administrative attention to discipline did not noticeably intrude into teachers' time'.[13] Nelson was known as a school with 'academic' principals who had not lost touch with the classroom or curriculum concerns. Teachers and administrators worked together in a collegial atmosphere toward meaningful curriculum knowledge and high quality teaching.

Beginning in the mid-1960s, at the principal's suggestion and with his guidance, teachers collaboratively developed a 'unified' curriculum. Curriculum knowledge was selected and organized in terms of interdisciplinary themes within and across broad subject areas such as social studies and science. Teachers exchanged some classroom autonomy (i.e., determining what to teach) for tangible support for their unified curriculum (e.g., departmental offices, resource center, secretary and aide, services of the school print shop, summer money for curriculum work). The social studies department chair, who enjoyed a positive rapport with his teachers, served as a resource person, representative to the administration, schedule co-ordinator and program overseer. When economic decline threatened Nelson's community in the 1970s, a 'Concerned Coalition' of teachers and administrators was formed to address broad issues and set non-binding policy outside the formal administrative and collective bargaining channels.

Key aspects of Nelson's context that appear to support alternative conceptions of curriculum knowledge and alternative curriculum practices are its collegial rather than rigidly hierarchical organization and its widely shared culture that sets education as a priority. A sense of community and common purpose was created and maintained within the school and between the school and its 'clients'. Individuals, especially Nelson's principal during most of its history, played important roles within this setting. However, it is unlikely that these individuals would have had such positive impact under other, less favourable circumstances. As indicated in the case of both Kennedy and Nelson schools, multiple contextual conditions interact over time to shape curriculum.

The multiplicity and interaction of context influences on curriculum merits emphasis. No doubt, the persistence of single factor theories such as great man and social class explanations of curriculum and other phenomena have appeal beyond their simplicity. However, they permit too many exceptions. For example, a social class explanation of the selection, organization and treatment of curriculum knowledge would locate the typical pattern described earlier in schools serving working and lower middle-class communities, with more constructivist patterns in schools serving more affluent communities, as in Anyon's study.[14] However, the apparent correspondence is not immune to other influences. While Kennedy school served a relatively affluent professional community, Nelson High School did not. In the IGE study, technical schooling was found in an affluent, religiously-oriented, business community as well as in a working-middle-class suburb and a poor rural community. As already noted (in Chapter 4), religion, geographic location and community stability also appear to be influential aspects of sociocultural context shaping curriculum.

The alternative patterns of curriculum knowledge and alternative curriculum practices evident at Kennedy and Nelson schools, while atypical, are not oppositional. They make meaningful and high status knowledge available to students but do not explicitly challenge the political, economic, social or intellectual *status quo*. There was no evidence of sustained inclusion of minority histories, cultures, or perspectives or of radical/critical concepts or critique.[15]

Critical patterns of curriculum knowledge would draw on a critical as opposed to a technocratic rationality and a constructivist conception of knowledge. By constructivist, I mean a conception of knowledge as socially created, albeit historically and culturally bound, rather than given or revealed (divinely or scientistically), tentative rather than fixed or certain, personal as well as public or formalized, and integrated rather than fragmented. An important implication of this view is that knowledge can be reinterpreted or reconstructed.[16] Critical rationality, as noted earlier, is characterized by wide-ranging questioning as well as grounding in logical argument and empirical data. It entails probing beneath surface appearances and questioning claims, evidence, and proposals — including assumptions and assertions about what constitutes rationality. What technocratic rationality probably would take for granted (e.g., operational definitions, standards of verification), critical rationality might well make problematic.

Combining critical rationality with a constructivist conception of knowledge could generate a reconstruction of curriculum knowledge along the following lines. The selection of curriculum knowledge would include diverse points of view (e.g., minority as well as dominant culture, conflict oriented or generating as well as consensual) and concepts such as domination and alienation as well as functionalism and individualism.[17] Curriculum knowledge would be organized by teachers and students, not into lists, but in patterns and relationships including links to students' experience and personal knowledge. It would be recognized as partial and tentative, subject to scrutiny, and made available to all students. Curriculum knowledge would be used for purposes of understanding, interrogation, and informed action. Thus, its use would be interpretive and potentially emancipatory as well as instrumental. And, its particular features or aspects would vary from one setting to another; they could not be planned or prescribed in advance, even locally. Broad outlines or directions, however, can be suggested. In science, social studies and literature, for example, attention might be given to various instances of (a) conflict, conflict resolution efforts, and consequences, (b) domination, resistance or rebellion, and liberation or repression, and (c) tradition and social/cultural change.

Importantly, curriculum knowledge as the knowledge made available to students means the opportunity to construct, reconstruct, or critique knowledge, not the giving of knowledge as some kind of commodity. Curriculum knowledge is not a consumer product displayed for sale or a tangible gift to be given by society through its teachers to students. Critical patterns of curriculum knowledge are not constructed simply by substituting one knowledge object for another or by reorganizing and redistributing knowledge objects. The treatment of knowledge as socially constructed, largely in/through/by discourse and prevailing discursive practices, is played out in classroom practice. For example, opportunities might be provided for students to (re-)construct knowledge about recent history or plant growth, to critique knowledge about art or literature, and to examine where, when, and how various number systems were created. Students might have opportunities to learn established knowledge of conceptions, patterns and rules, and to learn that they have been established rather than given. Curriculum knowledge, as knowledge out of school, remains problematic and partial.

A critically constructivist conception of curriculum knowledge and compatible curriculum practice requires recognition of underlying political and cultural assumptions about the relation of individuals and groups to society and its institutions and about the values that give moral direction to personal and social life (i.e., critical consciousness). It also requires a new mode of curriculum discourse. The old language and conventions cannot help but sustain the old ways.[18]

Knowledge about Curriculum

To redirect questions about curriculum conceptions, practice and change to curriculum studies — and to question the social values and assumptions that are embedded and have become routinized in curriculum studies — is to take a critical stance. Such questioning is difficult on at least two counts. One is that it requires, in a sense, stepping outside oneself in order to look back in. The second is that what one finds may be discomforting. Recognizing these difficulties or limitations of reflexivity, I presume only to sketch some possibilities that seem to merit further exploration.

Paradigmatic Considerations

The nature and role of knowledge in research and reform efforts varies with the paradigmatic preference and affiliation of the researcher or reformer.[19] By paradigm I mean a worldview or framework through which one 'sees' and makes sense of the world or some part of it, that is, one's background assumptions about the world and how it works. In research, including educational and curriculum research, paradigmatic conceptions shape how researchers perceive, think and talk about, study and act on the world. Paradigms thus sustain and are sustained by assumptions about appropriate concepts and values as well as research questions and procedures. Paradigms can be considered as windows to the world that enables us to see what is 'out there'. Just as windows have boundaries or frames that limit our view, so too do paradigms. Their conceptual, normative and procedural frames limit what can be seen and how it is to be interpreted and interrogated.

Various categories or typologies for distinguishing among paradigms have been offered. For present purposes, I adopt Habermas's distinctions among three types of science or 'knowledge constitutive interests' as elaborated with reference to educational research by Popkewitz.[20] These are the empirical-analytic, the interpretive and the critical. Each takes a different stance toward the nature and role of knowledge and gives emphasis to different knowledge. More specifically, within each paradigm, different assumptions are adopted about curriculum knowledge and knowledge about curriculum; different knowledge is sought, and that knowledge is differentially used.[21] The following brief overview of three paradigms is intended to map the theoretical terrain of curriculum studies more broadly than in previous chapters, foster clarification of differences among positions or approaches and suggest apparent contradictions within critical curriculum studies that could become points of departure for future work in the field. Brief treatment necessarily highlights paradigmatic differences and downplays internal variations. The empirical-analytic paradigm includes functionalist and what I have characterized as technocratic approaches. The interpretive paradigm includes symbolic and hermeneutic approaches, and the critical paradigm includes radical humanist and radical structuralist/Marxist approaches.

Within an empirical-analytic paradigm, knowledge is taken to be impersonal or disinterested and discoverable. Particularly valued is knowledge that can be formalized and/or quantified, which assumes the existence of discrete, measurable variables and regular, generalizable relationships among them. The role of knowledge, and thus the purpose of much empirical-analytic research, is prediction and control that can enhance effectiveness. In other words, the knowledge constitutive interest or use of knowledge within an empirical-analytic paradigm is technical, the instrumental application of knowledge in order to attain given objectives as efficiently as possible.

Technocratic approaches to curriculum construction and change — what

I have characterized as curriculum out of context — are located within this paradigm. When curriculum is conceived as a document to guide classroom practice, valued knowledge about curriculum is knowledge which can be used to increase the effectiveness of curriculum documents in shaping practice. Curriculum knowledge is studied via the document as in systematic, usually quantitative, content analyses of syllabi or textbooks. Classroom studies from an empirical-analytic perspective typically focus on teacher and/or student behavior, not curriculum knowledge. Questions about curriculum knowledge-in-use (i.e., the selection, organization, treatment and distribution of knowledge actually made available to students) are much less likely to be raised by researchers adopting an empircal-analytic than an interpretive or critical stance. Empirical-analytic studies about curriculum practice tend to rely on self-report data obtained from questionnaires and interviews rather than direct observation.

Curriculum questions that have been raised by empirical-analytic researchers include: What kinds of curriculum documents are most understandable and acceptable to teachers? What are the levels of use of new curriculum documents? To what extent have the new curriculum documents been used or implemented as intended by their developers? The first question seeks knowledge about curriculum that might be used to improve the construction of curriculum documents.[22] The second and third questions seek knowledge about the course of document use and perhaps also about obstacles to intended use.[23] Assumptions about curriculum as document and about disinterested, generalizable knowledge to be instrumentally applied remain largely unquestioned.

Within an interpretive paradigm, knowledge is taken to be created in the course of human interaction. Of particular interest is knowledge of the negotiated interpersonal rules that underlie social life. The role of knowledge, and thus the purpose of interpretive research, is understanding social interactions and everyday patterns of communication that create and sustain (or modify) social rules and meanings. The knowledge constitutive interest or use of knowledge within an interpretive paradigm is practical in the sense of comprehending social interaction.

Conceptions of curriculum associated with an interpretive paradigm are partially contextualized. Curriculum is conceived of as a social process, and valued knowledge about curriculum is knowledge of the social rules underlying curriculum practice. Both curriculum knowledge and knowledge about curriculum are assumed to be socially constructed — by students, teachers and other school personnel, authors and publishers of curriculum materials and researchers, among others. Curriculum questions that have been raised by interpretive researchers include: What academic and social knowledge is constructed in the discourse of classroom interaction? How is it constructed?[24] These questions seek knowledge that will enhance understanding of curriculum practice. Typically, in interpretive accounts of curriculum, little or no attention is given to curriculum context beyond the classroom or school, to the moral acceptability of the values reflected in curriculum practice, or to curriculum change. Interpretive curriculum researchers tend to be present oriented and attempt to remain disinterested. While adherents to an interpretive paradigm might study curriculum change, as researchers they rarely are interested in bringing about such change. Knowledge is to inform observers of classroom life, not to reform curriculum. Assumptions about the primacy of the immediate situation and about distinterested knowledge remain largely unquestioned.

Within a critical paradigm, knowledge is taken to be created in the course of human interaction over time in specific organizational and social structures. Knowledge is neither contemporaneous nor solely the result of human interaction, as in the interpretive paradigm, but historically shaped and socially located. Of particular interest is knowledge that illuminates aspects of domination (of some individuals or groups by others) in ways that can inform efforts to enhance human possibility and social justice. The role of knowledge, and thus the purpose of critical research, is normative and liberating. The knowledge constitutive interest or use of knowledge within a critical paradigm is emancipatory, that is, for enlightenment and empowerment.

Approaches to curriculum construction and change as contextualized social processes — what I have characterized as curriculum in context — are located within a critical paradigm. Both curriculum knowledge and knowledge about curriculum are assumed to be socially constructed over time, in particular organizational and cultural settings. Valued knowledge about curriculum is knowledge that illuminates how curriculum contributes to social/cultural, political, and economic domination or emancipation and the conditions that support one or another selection, organization, treatment and distribution of curriculum knowledge.

Curriculum knowledge and schooling more generally are seen to have both constraining and liberating potential.[25]

Curriculum questions that have been raised by critical researchers extend the 'what's happening?' question of interpretive researchers to include questions such as: Whose knowledge is given preference? Who has access to which knowledge? Who benefits or is disadvantaged? What conditions beyond the immediate situation shape the selection, organization, treatment and distribution of curriculum knowledge?[26] These questions seek knowledge that will not only enhance understanding of curriculum practice but also inform reform efforts. In contrast to the empirical-analytic and interpretive paradigms, a critical paradigm is explicitly normative, broadly contextualized, and reformist. Whereas adherents to an empirical-analytic paradigm seek increased efficiency within an existing system, adherents to a critical paradigm seek to change the system, that is, to foster structural reform not only of the education system but within society at large.

The assumption that curriculum practice reflects and acts back upon its context means that curriculum reform entails compatible structural and sociocultural change. Reform is assumed to be enabled by knowledge of practice and context, particularly their disjunctures or points of conflict which are seen as sites for the initiation of change. The contradiction between equity ideals and discrimination against women, for example, continues to be exploited, within and beyond curriculum, so as to interrupt male domination. Further, reform is assumed to require collective political and practical action. The individual acting alone is not given much chance of success. Assumptions about the primacy of sociostructural conditioning and about the possibility and desirability of universal human enlightenment and empowerment remain largely unquestioned.

Critique of the Critical

In person and in print, educators who affiliate with a critical paradigm have been critical of empirical-analytic and interpretive curriculum studies. Shortcomings have been noted, and critical approaches have been offered as desirable alternatives. The present volume is but one example. However, we have not turned as searching or critical a light on ourselves. My purpose is not to disparage the groundbreaking work that has been accomplished in the past decade or two,[27] but to suggest several ways in which work in the field of curriculum studies that has been self-identified or identified by others with a critical paradigm denies its own tenets or embodies contradictions that have yet to be resolved. I am assuming that critical approaches are not beyond critique and, more importantly, that they merit attention and refinement given their potential for illuminating curriculum practice and enabling substantive curriculum reform.

Four seeming contradictions within critical curriculum studies are examined here. They are (1) inadequate attention to curriculum practice, (2) predilection for single factor explanations of curriculum practice, (3) neglect of structural context and (4) distancing from teachers and other school people. The first three are related to the major themes of this volume — that curriculum be conceptualized and treated as a contextualized social process and that context is multidimensional. They also refer to explanations of curriculum experience. The last is of a different order, referring to the discourse of critical curriculum studies. All four contradictions can be seen as reflecting a curious gulf between macro theorizing on the one hand and micro research studies and classroom practice on the other.[28]

Inadequate attention to curriculum practice.

Critical empirical studies of curriculum and efforts to reform curriculum consistent with values of human possibility and social justice have tended to focus on curriculum documents such as syllabi and textbooks rather than curriculum practice. More attention has been given to curriculum intention than to its realization, for example, in content analyses of textbooks and proposals for curriculum revision.[29] As previously argued, curriculum plans and textbooks do influence practice, more so in some situations than others, but they are neither synonymous with practice nor sufficient to bring about substantive change in curriculum practice, specially the kinds of change envisaged by critical curricularists. A curriculum plan is like an architect's blueprint. A blueprint outlines how a not yet constructed building will look. Further, the creation of a blueprint does not mean that the building will be constructed as originally planned or that it will be constructed at all, especially if the architect proposes a radical design. Nor does it mean that the building, even if constructed in accordance with the blueprint, will function as intended. While it would be foolish to attempt to construct a viable building without a blueprint or some sort of plan, it would be absurd to mistake the blueprint for the building.

To focus attention on curriculum documents is, in effect, to adopt a key element of a technocratic position. This adoption is counterproductive as well as contradictory. It is counterproductive insofar as it helps to sustain technocratic approaches to curriculum and is likely to have relatively little impact on the curriculum knowledge made available to students. The contradiction lies primarily in employing instrumental, prescriptive means in what is to be an emancipatory process. Further, it is curious that those who would foster systemic or structural change would adopt an approach intended to increase efficiency within existing systems — and a weak method at that. It is time for critical curriculum studies to move beyond document analysis and design to examination of practice in context and contextualized approaches to curriculum change.[30]

Goodman's work on critical curriculum design can be seen as a point of departure from preoccupation with planning toward focus on enabling conditions of desired practice.[31] Although the five phases of what he calls 'a critical approach to curriculum design' (developing curriculum themes, exploring resources, developing learning activities, pupil evaluation and unit evaluation) sound conventional, their elaboration is not. In developing curriculum themes (selecting and organizing knowledge), for example, teachers are asked to consider 'what topics would enrich the children's lives and broaden their horizons'[32] and the social and political implications of their content selections. They also are asked to organize themes (i.e., concepts, issues) in web diagrams to demonstrate 'the holistic nature of knowledge'[33] According to Goodman:

> Perhaps the most essential characteristic of knowledge is its ambiguity and constant change. Rather than focusing upon predetermined objectives (e.g., facts, skills and 'right answers'), themes contain questions, theories, and mysteries, as well as specific information.[34]

In describing the use of this approach in a preservice teacher education methods/curriculum course with prospective elementary and middle school teachers in the US, Goodman acknowledged that not all of the prospective teachers had the opportunity to try out their units in school field placements because they were expected to 'teach the regular curriculum' or 'follow the school's curriculum guide'.[35] He briefly described efforts to inform prospective teachers of the 'politics of teaching' and help them become 'change agents in the schools'.[36]

> They consider the problems of initiating substantive change within a given set of constraints in ways that do not needlessly alienate administrators, other staff, and/or parents. Planning for short-term and long-term changes, developing a support system among other progressive individuals within the school and community, writing proposals for curriculum change, and presenting ideas at local and state conferences are some of the strategies examined.[37]

Following my earlier arguments, further attention to these kinds of 'strategies' probably is helpful but not sufficient to bring about substantial, critically oriented changes in curriculum practice. Also needed is direct attention by teachers and others to ways of modifying the conditions of teaching and learning to support critical curriculum practice. Critical work within existing education systems is extremely difficult and limited by structural arrangements.

Single factor explanations

When curriculum practice is the focus of critical curriculum studies, explanations of observed practice too often are reduced to a single factor such as social class. For example, Anyon accounts for differences in the selection, organization, treatment and distribution of curriculum knowledge in the five US elementary schools that she studied in terms of the socioeconomic status of the communities served by the schools.[38] Alternatively, McNeil accounts for differences in curriculum knowledge across the four US secondary schools that she studied in terms of the schools' structure, particularly their administrative organization and culture.[39]

Given the premises of a critical perspective, one would expect more richly textured explanations of curriculum practice drawing on the multidimensional contexts of curriculum — structural, sociocultural, and biographical within an historical perspective. Here, the contradiction lies in the disjuncture between the theoretical promise of broad and deep contextualization enabling comprehension and empowerment and the much more limited practice. This observation is not to discount the work that has been done, for it is a significant step beyond document analysis, but to call for broader and deeper accounts of curriculum practice. Without such accounts, possibilities for both enlightenment and empowerment will remain limited.

Neglect of structural context.

More richly textured accounts of curriculum practice from a critical perspective cannot neglect the structural context of curriculum, i.e., the various layers of the education system and their relations to the State. It is contradictory that even critical curriculum studies tend either to remain local (at the level of the classroom or the school) and thus relatively decontextualized or to at least implicitly assume that larger sociocultural dynamics such as race and gender enter directly into curriculum practice, escaping mediation by intervening layers of the education system.

McNeil's study, with its attention to the structural context of the schools, is an important exception despite its reliance on a single factor explanation.[40] However, it remains localized, ignoring the broader education system in which the schools are situated. The apparent decentralization (or fragmentation) of the education system and the State in the US ought not to mislead us into assuming that they make little or no difference. Nor should the difficulties of tracing structural context influences on curriculum preclude the effort to do so.

Distancing from teachers.

Even with resolution of the three contradictions just sketched, critical curriculum studies would have little impact on curriculum practice and change without resolution of this fourth contradiction between detachment from and involvement in curriculum practice and change. The detachment of concern here differs from the disinterest of empirical-analytical and interpretive researchers and the presumed neutrality of technocratic curricularists. Critical curricularists have made their social values and interest in curriculum reform explicit if not specific. Yet, as a group, we have distanced ourselves from teachers and other school people by the abstractness of our theorizing and the unfamiliarity of our discourse to outsiders. These discursive practices, while providing a sense of community and protection from indifferent if not hostile publics, tend to mystify and exclude rather than illuminate and include those most directly involved in curriculum practice. Occasionally getting one's hands dirty by engaging in classroom research or teaching is far different from joining hands with others who, collectively, could make a difference. Detachment and distance leave the curriculum field to empirical-analytic and interpretive educators and researchers, thus diminishing the possibilities for substantive curriculum reform.[41] Perhaps the enlightenment and empowerment that are called for are our own as well as others'. What are appropriate roles for critical curriculum researchers, practitioners and theorists?

In one sense, these contradictions within critical curriculum studies can be seen as discrepancies between macro theoretical and micro empirical work, that is, research and practice that lag behind their presumably guiding theory, or theory that is too far removed from the phenomena of concern to be relevant. In another sense, these contradictions can be seen as effects of reductionism carrying over from mainstream, technocratic approaches to curriculum. Critically oriented studies of curriculum that adopt mainstream concepts and assumptions (such as distinctions between overt/intended, hidden, and in-use curriculum) are bound to be contradictory. We ought to be interrelating rather than fragmenting aspects of curriculum and examining them in context rather than isolation.

Concluding Note

In attempting to sketch and interweave aspects of a critical approach to curriculum construction and change — curriculum as a contextualized social process — I have tried to argue, in effect, for a different mode of curriculum discourse. It is a critical discourse whose focus is on curriculum practice and context, including the education system and the State. It also is a discourse that is accessible, structurally as well as linguistically, to those within and outside schools and universities who are interested or involved in curriculum and who care about realizing human possibility and social justice. Further, it is a discourse that can challenge the basis as well as the particulars of the well established mainstream curriculum discourse (see Chapter 2). Such a discourse cannot be proclaimed or discovered and then conveyed to others by prescription or exhortation. It must be created by its speakers in relation to one another and their historically shaped circumstances.

Notes

1 My distinction between fragmented and integrated curriculum knowledge is similar to Bernstein's distinction between collection and integrated codes. See B. Bernstein, *Class, Codes and Control* (New York: Schocken, 1975), Chapter 11, 'On the Classification and Framing of Educational Knowledge', pp. 202–230.

2 A vivid example, dealing with the sociological concept of family, is provided in N. Keddie, 'Classroom Knowledge', in *Knowledge and Control*, ed. M. F. D. Young (London: Collier Macmillan, 1971), pp. 133–160.

3 T. S. Popkewitz, B. R. Tabachnick and G. Wehlage, *The Myth of Educational Reform* (Madison: University of Wisconsin Press, 1982).

4 L. M. McNeil, *Contradictions of Control: School Structure and School Knowledge* (New York: Routledge & Kegan Paul, 1986).

5 Further illustration of this kind of selection, organization and treatment of curriculum knowledge can be found in the working and middle-class schools described in J. Anyon, 'Social Class and School Knowledge', *Curriculum Inquiry* 11, 1 (1981): 3–42.

6 See, e.g., B. R. Tabachnick, 'Intern-Teacher Roles: Illusion, Disillusion, and Reality', *Journal of Education* 162 (1980): 122–137.

7 Within school differences in the selection, organization, treatment, and distribution of curriculum knowledge, including the bases and effects of tracking practices, also could be explored. See J. Oakes, *Keeping Track: How Schools Structure Inequality* (New Haven, CN: Yale University Press, 1985); R. Page and L. Valli, (Eds.), *Curriculum Differentiation* (Albany: State University of New York Press, forthcoming).

8 T. S. Popkewitz *et al.* (1982) *op. cit.*

9 *Ibid.*, p. 113.

10 *Ibid.*, p. 119.

11 L. M. McNeil (1986) *op. cit.*

12 *Ibid.*, p. 177.

13 *Ibid.*, p. 59.

14 J. Anyon (1981) *op.cit.*

15 For examples of the latter, see R.J. Gilbert, 'Social Knowledge, Action and the Curriculum', *Social Education* 45 (1985): 380–383; H.A. Giroux, *Schooling and the Struggle for Public Life: Critical Pedagogy in the Modern Age* (Minneapolis: University of Minnesota Press, 1988).

16 This version of constructivism differs from currently popular views of constructivism in cognitive psychology in at least two important ways. First, the latter treats knowledge and its construction as asocial and ahistorical. Second, it assumes individual construction of predetermined knowledge. Thus, knowledge is

decontextualized and reified, and its construction becomes a reproductive process. See E. E. Sampson 'Cognitive Psychology as Ideology', *American Psychologist* 36 (1981): 730–748.

17 See F. J. Gilbert (1985) *op. cit.*

18 C. Cornbleth and E. E. Gottlieb, 'Reform Discourse and Curriculum Reform', *Educational Foundations* 3, 3 (1989): 63–78; E. E. Gottlieb, 'The Discursive Construction of Knowledge: The Case of Radical Education Discourse', *Qualitive Studies in Education* 2, 2 (1989): 131–144.

19 Research as used here refers to both theoretical and empirical inquiry.

20 T. S. Popkewitz, *Paradigm and Ideology in Eductional Research* (London and New York: Falmer Press, 1984), Chapter 2. For a more philosophical treatment of these three interests or paradigms and their interpretation in relation to curriculum, see S. Grundy, *Curriculum: Product or Praxis* (London: Falmer Press, 1987).

21 Paradigmatic differences in the conceptualization and study of context are examined in C. Cornbleth, 'Research on Context, Research in Context', in *Handbook of Research on Social Studies Teaching and Learning*, ed. J. P. Shaver (New York: Macmillan, forthcoming).

22 See, for example, I. Westbury, D. C. Anderson, J. K. Olson, I. B. Harris and W. A. Reid, 'Symposium: How Can Written Curriculum Guides Guide Teaching?' *Journal of Curriculum Studies* 15, 1 (1983): 1–46.

23 See, for example, R. D. Kimpston, 'Curriculum Fidelity and the Implementation Tasks Employed by Teachers: A Research Study', *Journal of Curriculum Studies* 17, 2 (1985): 185–195; H. Thompson and C. E. Deer, 'The Institutionalization of a Senior Secondary Curriculum in New South Wales High Schools', *Journal of Curriculum Studies* 21, 2 (1989): 169–184.

24 See, for example, M. LeCompte, 'The Civilizing of Children: How Young Children Learn to be Students', *Journal of Thought* 15, 3 (1980): 105–127; J. J. White, 'An Ethnographic Approach', in *An Invitation to Research in Social Education*, ed. C. Cornbleth (Washington, DC: National Council for the Social Studies, 1986), pp. 51–77.

25 These points were elaborated in Chapter 2, 'Beyond Hidden Curriculum?'.

26 See, for example, J. Anyon (1981) *op. cit.*; T. S. Popkewitz *et al* (1982) *op. cit.*,; J. Oakes (1985) *op. cit.*.

27 E.g., G. Whitty and M. Young (Eds.), *Explorations in the Politics of School Knowledge* (Nafferton, Driffield: Nafferton Books, 1976); M. W. Apple, *Ideology and Curriculum* (London: Routledge & Kegan Paul, 1979); J. Anyon (1981) *op. cit.*

28 On similar developments in British sociology of education, curriculum and knowledge, see G. Whitty, *Sociology and School Knowledge* (London: Methuen, 1985).

29 J. Anyon, 'Ideology and United States History Textbooks', *Harvard Educational Review* 49, 3 (1979): 361–386; T. S. Popkewitz, 'The Latent Values of the

Discipline Centered Curriculum', *Theory and Research in Social Education* 5, 1 (1977): 41–60.

30 Focusing on and even celebrating practice, interpretive researchers do offer rich accounts of the social construction of knowledge at the micro, usually classroom, level. However, they tend not to pay attention to the broader contexts of classroom practice or to question why particular knowledge is constructed in the observed ways.

31 J. Goodman, 'Teaching Preservice Teachers a Critical Approach to Curriculum Design: A Descriptive Account', *Curriculum Inquiry* 16, 2 (1986): 179–201.

32 *Ibid.*, p. 185.

33 *Ibid.*, p. 187.

34 *Ibid.*, p. 186.

35 *Ibid.*, p. 196.

36 *Ibid.*

37 *Ibid.*

38 Anyon (1981) *op. cit.*

39 McNeil (1986) *op. cit.*

40 *Ibid.*

41 A parallel argument could be made about critical curricularists' detachment and distance from mainstream curriculum specialists.

Index

abstracted empiricism 54
action research 160
Adler, M.: *Padideia proposal* 120
allocation theories 56
alternative policy instruments 134
Anyon, J. 45, 191
Archer, M. S. 100, 101, 102, 103
Astuto, T. A. 145, 146
Atkin, J. M. 165
at-risk students 110
authority 71, 72
authority of specialized competence (elite)
    56

Bacchus, M. K. 129, 130
bargaining power 104
Bell, Terrell, 145
Bennett: *James Madison curriculum* 120
Berger, B. 20, 21, 108, 143
Berger, P. 20, 108, 143
Biological Sciences Curriculum Study
    (BSCS) 165, 174
block grant program 133
Bobbitt, Franklin 19
    Curriculum, The 20
    How to Make a Curriculum 20
bottom-up model 18
Boyd, W. L. 158, 160, 161, 162, 168
Brown v. Board of Education Supreme
    (1954) 113, 136
BSCS (Biological Sciences Curriculum
    Study) 165, 174

bully pulpit 119, 133
bureaucracy 143–4
bureacratic consciousness 20–2, 143
bureaucratic control 106
bureaucratization 162
Bush, George 140

Canada, school-based curriculum
    development in 176
capacity-building 134, 135, 136
Carnoy, M. 122
Casey Foundation 121, 145
Castro Fidel, 134
Charters, W. W. 19, 20
Chile, curriculum policy in 168–70
Clark, D. L. 145, 146
compensatory legitimation strategies
    136–42
componentiality 21
conceptual decontextualization 13
consciousness, definition of 20
constructive schooling 47, 77
contextual dynamic
    bureaucratization 108–9
    national systems 103–4
    system stability and change 101–9
    within schools 105–8
    within systems 104–5
contextualized curriculum planning 178–9
critical curriculum 24–32, 184–205
    conceptual integration 24–6
    sociocultural context 31–2

structural and sociocultural
  contextualization 26–8
system as structural context 28–31
critical rationality 25, 192
critical thinking and curriculum 80–90
  conditions of classroom teaching 86–7
  curriculum co-optation 89–90
  fragmentation 83
  meanings given to 81–3
  mechanization 83–4
  pre-existing beliefs and practices 85–6
  product orientation 84–5
  school district goals and policies 87–8
  understanding teacher interpretations 85
Critical Thinking Project 80–1, 87, 89,
  108, 161
curriculum and structural change 99–116
  implications 109–14
curriculum knowledge 6, 100, 157,
  184–93
  alternatives 188–93
curriculum planning 139, 155–83
  contextualized 178–9
curriculum policy 155–83
  cross-national cases 168–74
    Chile and El Salvador 168–70
    Tanzania and Papua New Guinea 170–3
  professionalization and politicization
    156–68
    increasing knowledge and
      specialization 158–60
    increasing state involvement 161–4
    interrelations and implications 164–8
    normative differences, value conflicts
      157–8
curriculum practice 9, 62–95

decentralization 146
defensive teaching 74, 76, 187, 189
Densmore, K. 106
Doyle, W. 89
Dreeben, R. 72

Education Consolidation and Improvement
  Act (1982) 133, 146
Education for Self Reliance in Tanzania
  171–3

El Salvador, curriculum policy in 168–70
Elmore, R. F. 133, 135, 136, 137, 139,
  140, 165, 166, 167
empirical-analytic paradigm 194, 195
Evans, P. B. 118
exhortation 134, 165
Experimental Schools Project 165–6
expertise 140, 142

Farrar, E. 90, 92, 110
Ford Foundation 121
  Master of Arts on Teaching programs
    138
Foucault 100
Frankfurt school, 3
Frei, President Eduardo 169
functionalist and structuralist social theory
  52

gender relations 7
Goodman, J. 199
Green, T. F. 128
Grundy, S. 6–7

Habermas, J. 194
Hargreaves, A. 177
hidden curriculum 9–10, 42–61
  contradiction and mediation 49–53
  empirical evidence 44–8
  interpretive claims 43–4
  irony of context in isolation 53–7
home schooling 104, 157
House, E. R. 165
Hunter, Madeline: 'Essential Elements of
  Instruction' 108

illusory schooling 47, 78
implicit curricula of schooling 43–8
  see also hidden curricula
Individually Guided Education (IGE) 33,
  47, 76–7, 89, 90, 108, 191
inducements 134, 135, 165

Kellner, H. 20, 108, 143
Kennedy elementary school 188, 191
Kirst, M. W. 146, 167

knowledge about curriculum 193–202
  critique of the critical 197–8
  distancing from teachers 201–2
  inadequate attention to curriculum
    practice 198–200
  neglect of structural context 201
  paradigmatic considerations 193–7
  single factor explanations 200–1
knowledge and power 100
knowledge constitutive interests 194
knowledge explosion 132, 158

legalization 136, 137, 140, 142
legitimation crisis 130
Levin, H. L. 122
Lindblad, S. 175, 176

McDonnell, L. M. 133, 135, 136, 137,
    139, 140
McGinn, N. 122, 168, 169, 170
McLaughlin, M. W. 165, 166, 167
McLuhan 43
McNeil, L. M. 74, 75, 76, 80, 186, 187,
    189, 190, 200, 201
  Contradictions of Control 73, 76, 108
mandates 134, 135
mediation 49–53
Meyer, J. W. 31, 56, 57
Mills, C. W.: *Sociological Imagination, The*
    3
Moynihan, D. P. 158, 159
Myth of Educational Reform, The 76, 79,
    108

NAEP (National Assessment of
    Educational Progress) 88, 161
Nation at Risk, A 119, 121, 145, 156
*Nation Prepared: Teachers for the Twenty-first
    Century, A* 145
National Assessment of Educational
    Progress (NAEP) 88, 161
National Commission on Excellence in
    Education 119, 120
National Education Association (NEA)
    121, 145
National Science Foundation (NSF) 138,
    157, 174

nationwide assessments of student
    achievement 161
NCERT (National Council for
    Educational Research and
    Training) 129–30
Nelson High School 189, 191
Nyerere, President 134, 171

Orpwod, G. W. F. 176

Papua New Guinea, curriculum policy in
    170–3
participation 137, 140, 142
Popewitz, T. S. 47, 78, 80, 89, 90, 146,
    186, 188, 189, 194
  Myth of Educational Reform, The 76, 79,
    108
professionalization 10, 162
  and politicization of curriculum
    policymaking 156–68
  of reform 158, 159, 164
  teacher 102
Progressive Era reforms 164

rational management model 14–15
Reagan administration 119, 124, 133, 134,
    145, 146, 147, 161, 176
reforming curriculum reform 9, 76–80
'regimes of truth' 100
Rowan, B. 31
Rueschemeyer, D. 118
Rugg, Harold 23, 159, 160

Saunders, M. 168, 170
Schiefelbein, E. 122, 168
school-based curriculum change 90–2
school-based curriculum development
    (SBCD) 134, 142, 156, 160,
    165, 174–8
school-based decision-making 103
'schooling rule' 31, 119
Shulman, Lee 145
Sizer, Theodore: 'Coalition of Essential
    Schools' 105
Skocpol, T. 118, 124
sociocultural contextualization 26–8
sociocultural decontextualization 17–18

SSCEP (Secondary Schools Community Extension Project) 171, 172
state and curriculum controls 9, 117–52
  change over time 144–7
  nature and operation of 118–26
    key actors 120–2
    organization 123–5
      centralization and coupling 123–4
      coherence 124–5
      relationship with national economic system 125
    system-state relations 126–47
      bureaucracy 143–4
      change over time 144–7
      multiple determination 126–33
      state policy instruments 133–42
state policy instruments 133–42
structural context of curriculum 9, 99–116
structural contextualization 26–8
structural decontextualization 17–18
structure of interests 128, 157
Sweden, school-based curriculum development in 175
symbolic reform 139, 140, 142
symbolic universe of modernity 20, 21
system-changing 134, 135, 165
system-state relations
  multiple determination 126–33
  questions of control 126–47

Tabachnick, B. R. 47, 76, 106, 168
Tanzania, curriculum policy in 170–3
teacher-administrator relationships 102
teacher de-skilling 33
teacher empowerment 33, 165
teacher professionalization 102
technical control 107, 108
technical schooling 47, 77–8, 186, 191
technocratic curriculum 8, 12, 13–23
  conceptual separation 13–17
  structural and sociocultural isolation 17–18
  technocratic approaches 194–5
  technocratic persistence 18, 19–23
technocratic planning 139
Tyler 19, 20, 187

Vallance, E. 43
Vulliamy, G. 168, 170

Walker, D. F. 167
Waller, W. 52
Warwick, D. P. 122, 168
Weber 163
Wehlage, G. 47, 76, 186
Weiler, H. N. 131, 136, 137, 139, 141
world polity 163

Zeichner, K. M. 106, 107